Gorgeous, Sexy and Rich

Money for Women in Good and Tough Times

NORMA SIT

© 2009 Marshall Cavendish International (Asia) Private Limited

Project Editor: Lee Mei Lin
Design by Rachel Chen /Cover art by Opal Works Co. Limited

Published by Marshall Cavendish Editions
An imprint of Marshall Cavendish International
1 New Industrial Road, Singapore 536196

All rights reserved

No part of this publication may be reproduced, stored in a retrieval system or transmitted, in any form or by any means, electronic, mechanical, photocopying, recording or otherwise, without the prior permission of the copyright owner. Request for permission should be addressed to the Publisher, Marshall Cavendish International (Asia) Private Limited, 1 New Industrial Road, Singapore 536196. Tel: (65) 6213 9300. Fax: (65) 6285 4871. E-mail: genref@sg.marshallcavendish.com. Website: www.marshallcavendish.com/genref

The publisher makes no representation or warranties with respect to the contents of this book, and specifically disclaims any implied warranties or merchantability or fitness for any particular purpose, and shall in no events be liable for any loss of profit or any other commercial damage, including but not limited to special, incidental, consequential, or other damages.

Other Marshall Cavendish Offices
Marshall Cavendish Ltd. 5th Floor 32–38 Saffron Hill, London EC1N 8FH • Marshall Cavendish Corporation. 99 White Plains Road, Tarrytown NY 10591-9001, USA • Marshall Cavendish International (Thailand) Co Ltd. 253 Asoke, 12th Flr, Sukhumvit 21 Road, Klongtoey Nua, Wattana, Bangkok 10110, Thailand • Marshall Cavendish (Malaysia) Sdn Bhd, Times Subang, Lot 46, Subang Hi-Tech Industrial Park, Batu Tiga, 40000 Shah Alam, Selangor Darul Ehsan, Malaysia

Marshall Cavendish is a trademark of Times Publishing Limited

National Library Board Singapore Cataloguing in Publication Data
Sit, Norma.
Gorgeous, sexy and rich : money for women in good and tough times / Norma Sit. – Singapore : Marshall Cavendish Editions, c2009.
p. cm.

ISBN-13 : 978-981-261-495-7
1. Women – Finance, Personal. 2. Investments. I. Title.

HG179

332.0240082 – dc22   OCN311703207

Printed in Singapore by Times Graphics Pte Ltd

Norma

To women,
my great-grandmother, grandmother and mother
who gave me Life and Wisdom,
and my daughter, Elizabeth

Keon

To my mother and my daughter, Sarah

Special Thanks To

Dato Dr Jannie Tay for her support

Lee Mei Lin, Violet Phoon and Saw Puay Lim
from Marshall Cavendish for their unstinting support

Allen Lim, Ann Tan, Anthonia Hui, Celene Lim, David Ong,
Fong Ee-Lyn, Guy Baker, J. Yap, Jennifer Khoo, Karen Tan,
Michael Lee, Ophelia Cheung, Perlita Tiro and Tan Su Shan
for their contributions on their life experiences

Hi Jaolyn Pok Pok,

I read this book half way (actually) and I thought is quite interesting. Would like to share with you. Have fun reading.

Xylia 2009

Contents

Foreword By Dato Dr Jannie Tay 6

Introduction 8

Part One: Being A Woman
1. What Do Women Want? 12
2. Two Sexy Words 21
3. Breaking Through Self-Barriers 32
4. A New Self 46

Part Two: Money Fundamentals
5. A Budget To Spend Like Crazy 62
6. The 'I Am Rich' Number 73
7. The Disappearing Dollar And The Magic Of Risk 81

Part Three: Personal Financial Products
8. Personal Borrowings And Debt 94
9. Managing Debt 119
10. Love-Hate Insurance 128

Part Four: Investment Products

11 Stocks, Bonds And Unit Trusts **149**
12 Exotic, Intriguing, Complex And Alternative **167**
13 Diversification And The Three Baskets **190**
14 Understanding Yourself As An Investor **202**

Part Five: Life's Passages

15 Single, Footloose And Fancy Free **212**
16 Getting Married And Marrying Again **223**
17 Money And Your New Family **244**
18 Divorce **252**
19 Widowed But Not Unhappy **264**
20 The Other Woman **274**
21 Becoming The Matriarch **283**

Note From Norma **287**

A Man's Point Of View **288**

Foreword

Women today have opportunities beyond the imagination of our fore-mothers. Unlike in the past, we can now become astronauts, jet-setting investment bankers, leading CEOs of multinational companies commanding billions of dollars in resources, prime ministers or presidents of countries, or happy homemakers. With education and a good mind, a woman can go far. We can dream and make our dreams our reality.

We live in an era where one in three or four marriages seem likely to end up in divorce. Yet, we know how women who would often give up good paying jobs in deference to families and husbands. We also know many high-flying women in the corporate world who would set aside their corporate climb to preserve their marriages. Despite their sacrifice, statistics indicate that a larger percentage of women than men are financially broke after divorce or the death of their spouse. Worse, most women, even those with careers, are not financially independent in their own right.

Why do educated women allow themselves to become financially broke? Why do women not protect themselves financially when their lifespan is longer than the man's? What holds women back from being financially intelligent?

In her book, Norma defines being financially independent as a state where a person can maintain their preferred lifestyle without needing to work any further. Being financially independent is good for both men and women. Women must learn how to handle money, how to earn it, keep it and grow it. It is an imperative for women to find financial freedom. Without that freedom, they are not free. Without that freedom, they are subject to the decisions of others in their lives, whoever those others might be.

I am glad that Norma wrote this book. She said she learnt many things from observing me as her mentor. It is good to know that her current freedom to choose her life comes from being financially free. I urge all women to become so.

Dato Dr Jannie Tay
Co-Founder and Vice-Chairman, The Hour Glass Ltd
Founder, Save the Planet Foundation
President, ASEAN Business Forum
President, Commonwealth Business Women Network
Founder President, International Women Forum Singapore
Founder President and President, Women Business Connection

Introduction

Why I Love Super Successful Women

Oprah Winfrey. Martha Stewart. Ellen DeGeneres. Tyra Banks. Super women of our times.

We either love them or hate them. I love them. They are super successful, beautiful and brimming with ideas on how we can make our lives better. I especially love Tyra. "Who?" I hear some of you ask.

Tyra…the world's most famous supermodel according to Forbes magazine, and creator and host of reality television show "America's Next Top Model" and "The Tyra Banks Show". In 2008, Tyra reportedly drew a salary of US$23 million!

"Wow!" Yes, wow. So let me share with you why I love Tyra.

She is undoubtedly super gorgeous, super sexy and super rich. But as importantly, she is full of life and appears real and accessible in spite of being supermodel tall! She hugs, she tears, she empathises, she corrects, and she creates a strong role model for women on her talk show. Even when she sometimes wears an over-expensive outfit that is obviously so wrong for her, I can't help but love her style and confidence. Each time Tyra appears, I am glued to the TV screen watching her laugh and cry with her audience. She is stunningly beautiful, not because she is physically so but because she projects someone who is so complete, so WHOLE.

I truly believe that successful women have a strong starting point of knowing what they want in life and going for it. They set their life goals and work towards it, giving all of themselves. And they determinedly pay the price for success.

Knowing this, if we want success, why can't we all do the same? Why do we not set clear life goals, and with an itemised plan in hand, work steadfastly towards success? After all, we all pay some price anyway, whichever life we live, successful or humdrum. Why not choose success and pay that price instead?

That's what all the positive thinking programmes are about—self-vision, goals, objectives, roadmaps, finding out the price of success and paying it. I'm all for it. I believe that success lies within us. With clarity of purpose, we can strive towards and achieve our goals. Without clarity, our lives can become aimless meanderings, pushed by everyday happenings.

For me as a woman, success means being independent, beautiful, loved and respected.

Role Model

I'm often asked who my role model is. I do not have one but many. I learn life lessons all the time from strangers and friends. Some lessons are bitter pills to swallow. Others are gentle nudges on my consciousness to embrace life.

If, however, I have to name a single role model for my life, it would be the woman described in the Bible under the Book of Proverbs, Chapter 31, verses 10–31. She is my inspiration. She is strong, virtuous, a leader and respected. She has a family. She runs her family well. She rises early every morning and looks after their needs. She considers properties and buys them. She is rich. She is diligent, wise and wholesome. She is well dressed and well spoken of by society and the community. She is married and her husband loves her.

Such a woman is a great woman. Perhaps not a Tyra Banks drop-dead gorgeous and sexy woman. But a great woman with virtue, wealth and love. These things go hand in hand with being beautiful and rich. This is the woman I aspire to be. And this is the vision I work towards daily.

I have attained some of these things I write about. I've been featured in newspapers and magazines, interviewed on television, won scholarships and awards, and invited to speak on various platforms which I delight in doing. Googling 'Norma Sit' returns more than one page of hits and I am seen as someone with reasonable success. Yet, when all is said and done, my real success and buttress in life is my financial independence.

This is why I've written this book. I want to share *Gorgeous, Sexy and Rich* with you. I want you to walk feeling on top of the world, swinging to life's wondrous beat, feeling beautiful, and knowing that whatever life throws at you, you are ready for it. I want you to know the magic of living a financially free life.

At this juncture, I must introduce Keon who is co-author to many of the financial and investment portions of this book. Keon is the author of the best-selling *Make Your Money Work For You*, a financial and investment book by Marshall Cavendish. He is also my husband still, the last time I looked.

Between us, Keon and I have three children and a dog. We had to give our incorrigible cat away because much as I loved it, it was happily chewing away at the electrical wires at home. Sometimes in life, though it hurts, we just have to be practical. Life management and money management hold many parallel lessons. Sometimes we do need to be emotionally tough so we can push on ahead. I miss the cat, but she now has a great home, and I have my electrical wires all intact.

Let's now start our journey together to becoming Gorgeous, Sexy and Rich.

Part One
Being A Woman

1 What Do Women Want?

"Norma, you are a woman. Tell me, what do women want?" The CEO of a highly successful electronics company asked me this question at the plenary session of a well-known conference.

I answered, "Being successful at work of course!"

He shook his head and said, "Love. Women want love more than they want anything else in the world. If you ask my wife to choose between all my money and my love, she will choose my love."

I wasn't sure what he was really trying to say, but I was getting rather uncomfortable with what I felt was the typical male ego response. Not wishing to show my discomfort, however, I replied, "If your wife thinks your love is more important than money to her, what's more important to you?"

He laughed quietly. "Power," he said. "With power, comes everything else—the wife, the women, the love, the money. When you have power, you have everything."

How inequitable, I thought. His poor wife.

We know that men and women want different things. For me, nothing captured the difference as strongly as that whispered conversation with this high ranking CEO. Perhaps not all men want power, and perhaps not all women have love as their top priority. But what men want and what women want are different.

The different priorities that men and women hold cause them to choose differently when it comes to life decisions. For example, more men than women find it more important to work than to spend time with their children. While some men are getting better at achieving balance, this imbalance is historical and frequently causes misunderstandings between married couples.

James Walsh, a UK-based online freelance writer on divorce, wrote that men and women in the UK tend to divorce for different reasons (www.allydirectory.com). Men, he says, divorce their wives for the lack of attention represented by sex. Women divorce their husbands for money reasons, or rather, the lack of security represented by the lack of money. He concludes that both men and women have expectations from marriage, but these expectations are represented differently for men and for women.

This book is not about what men want. It is about what women want. Until we are clear about what we want in life, it is difficult to target getting it.

I grew up paranoid about money. Money was scarce in my family. I wanted many times back then to have been born a boy. The boys seemed to have it all. I was not a tomboy, but I did think that if one were born a boy, one could go so much further in life. After all, all the grown-up women I knew were housewives, and all the grown-up men seemed so much more important than their wives or their secretaries. The men had the 'all-important-money' in their wallets. The men drove bigger cars while their wives ran around in tiny Toyotas that their husbands had bought them.

As a child, I thought that if I wanted to drive a big car, do great things and have important conversations while wives disappeared to kitchens to complain about their husbands, I had to become a tomboy or become as good as the boys were. I remember how, when I realised that boys were better at Mathematics than girls were, I decided to do the subject for my Higher School Certificate (the equivalent of 'A' levels). Becoming as good as a boy was important as I wanted to become independent fast and not have to depend on my parents for up-down, yes-no funds. I did not want to worry if there was enough money for a new pair of school shoes the following year or if I could participate in the next school camp. (I realised later, of course, that girls are and have always been as good as boys, but at different things. I learnt to value the things boys and girls were naturally good at.)

Struggling with these thoughts, I learnt something important when I turned thirteen. My Aunt Catherine, who happened to be visiting from Perth, said to me, "Norma, the most important thing in life is your education. Whatever you know cannot be taken away from you." That was a defining moment. Her words stuck.

From then on, I equated a good education with being independent. I had found a lifelong key to independence and freedom. For most of my life thereafter, education, personal development and career achievement underpinned how I was made up. I pursued success with a passion because I pursued financial independence with a passion.

So while some of my friends saw university as hunting ground for the right husband, I focused on getting good grades. I had a comparatively boring university life as a result. So focused was I.

For women, marriage is sometimes the path towards security and financial success. Career is often the necessary evil which falls further down the priority ladder after the first baby arrives. This was never the case for me. Having my own money was always as important as love and marriage. The dual goals created many hurdles and challenges for me and my marriage. Knowing what I want and how I am made up enabled me to understand my own actions and reactions to life, but it takes a very secure man to accept how I viewed life and personal success.

I'm not saying that getting married was not important to me. But someone back then would really have had to cut off my legs before they could make me stay home as a homemaker. I just always wanted my own money. To me, it was scary enough to depend on someone for love and emotional security. I could not depend on someone for *both* love and money!

The question to you is "What do you want?" What do you want in life? How are you made up with respect to money? Unless you are clear on this, it is difficult for you to chase it down as a goal in life.

Why 'Gorgeous, Sexy And Rich'?

My publisher asked me, "Why *'Gorgeous, Sexy and Rich'*?" I told the wonderful team at Marshall Cavendish that that was what women want. It raised a few eyebrows.

You see what I mean, don't you? There are already many good financial books in the market, and whatever books that are applicable to men are also applicable to women. Money knows no gender, and money management principles are true for men and women. Yet, why aren't women more financially savvy?

The answer? Women must want to read beyond page 10 of the books out there.

In fact, I told Keon that his best-selling book, *Make Your Money Work For You*, was probably read more by men than women although it is good and easy to understand. I explained: "Women want to know what is relevant to their lives on the whole, not just the money part. Women are a lot more complex in that we want to know how to get rich, look great and keep our husbands. We also want to have fun, laugh and live!"

Yes, most women don't want to be rich only. We also want to be gorgeous and sexy. Let me tell you why.

- Women generally spend a lot of money every year to look good. Regardless of our age or culture, we want to be loved for who we are and also to be admired for how we look by the people who matter. The question is always whether we should afford it. Should we buy that bag? Should we purchase that new blouse? We feel we need to use the money for things other than for ourselves. We feel guilty. Our children need the money more. Our parents need it more. The charity needs it more. How we finally spend our money is one thing. How we want to spend it is another.

- Women generally have a secret desire to be sexy. Why else would women's underwear cost so much? What's all the lace and ribbons for when plain, boring underwear would function just as well? Admit it, we want to be the femme fatale to the men in our lives. We want to be adored and pampered. We want our men to see us as more desirable than Cindy Crawford in her heyday. This is why *Sex And The City* draws women viewers. If we can afford it, we want the bags, shoes, hairstyles, cleavages and friendships. We watch the show because we want to be those women, enjoying those friendships, laughing at the stupidities of men and embracing the love of our lives.

- Women want to be rich. When we use the word 'rich' in this book, we refer to the state of being financially independent. We do not want to feel that we need to stay in a job if we hate the way our boss treats us. We do not want to feel that we have to stay in an abusive marriage just because we have no idea how to survive financially without the man.

The question is: Can we become Gorgeous, Sexy and Rich, and stay that way? I feel a woman can be fantastic all her life, from her swinging twenties to her retiring eighties. It's a mindset. We know grandmothers who are full of zest in life, laughing and serving the community. At 70, some of them are more alive than their young friends. Theirs is not a here-today-gone-tomorrow beauty. It's a lasting inner beauty immersed in happy thoughts and a super sense of well-being. I hope that is what you want for your life. It is what I want for mine.

Living A Great Life

Women can and should feel really good about themselves. We should feel attractive whatever our age or however many the lines on our faces. We should be confident enough to be feminine and to redefine the word as 'New Feminine'. We should be happy, laughing and having fun with life, just like Carrie and her friends in *Sex And The City*. Women should live meaningful, self- and financially-empowered lives.

Such a great life, however, can only happen after we have taken responsibility for money issues in our lives. This is regardless of career choice, whether one is a homemaker or a business person. Both are 'career' choices. Both choices carry financial decisions that the woman must make to ensure she can take care of herself financially at all times. Whether her husband abandons her suddenly, or the industry she has invested her worklife in suddenly moves to China to lower production costs and she is forced to retire early, a woman must be prepared financially to meet the challenges life brings. Without that preparedness, it is difficult to sustain being happy or having a sense of well-being.

What complicates things for women is that they tend to have many distinct roles and phases in one lifetime. Each phase carries different responsibilities and needs. Women are caught deep in each phase—finding the right man, marrying the right man, carrying the baby, delivering the baby, nurturing the child until she is old enough to fly away, and then facing the remaining years of her life either with joy or with a sense of emptiness.

For women, our roles and life phases carry many choices and decisions. What are some of the important ones that affect her well-being years later? In this book, we cover those that would impact her financially.

THE CORNERSTONE

The cornerstone is the first stone set in the construction of a masonry foundation. It is a critical stone since all other stones for that building will be set in reference to this stone, thereby determining the outcome of the entire building.

Personal financial independence is the cornerstone of successful lives. Unless we set this right in our lives, all other stones or building blocks in our lives would tend to be without proper reference or anchor, and, therefore, have a tendency to be crookedly placed.

This is not about being mercenary or money-minded. FINANCIAL INDEPENDENCE IS THE CRUX. If you were a farmer and the harvest did not come in that season, you might starve. So you would focus on setting aside some of your yield for the leaner months each season. If you were a hunter, you would ensure that the meat from the game you hunted lasted through the winter. Somehow, as society developed, we lost that sense of having to take care of ourselves financially. What we earn, we often spend. In modern-day living, we have forgotten to strive towards financial independence and what that could mean for us.

How do we set this cornerstone in our lives then? This is what the book is about.

Setting Financial Goals

In the next few chapters, we will discuss Self-Vision and setting life goals. When done holistically, your self-vision, including your financial self-vision, underpins your success in life. The stronger the vision, the greater will be your motivation to make it happen for yourself. Likewise, the clearer your life goals, the higher will be your chances of achieving them. Vagueness leaves too much to chance and causes you to drift along without achievement and milestones.

Working Towards the Goals Daily

Setting goals is not enough. Becoming financially independent is something that people need to work towards. It does not happen by accident, but by choice and determination.

Starting Now

Unless you were born rich or marry rich, becoming financially free may take you years to achieve. For many, you may only achieve it in your forties, thereby having the ability to retire 20 years earlier than your friends if you so wish. For others, you might have had a great streak of luck and you are able to retire in your thirties. For some, you cannot retire even at 65 because your finances do not allow for that.

Your best bet is to start as soon as possible. In fact, START NOW. Becoming rich, or financially independent, does not happen by accident. We women, and especially we mothers, are all too busy to remember to chase it down as a goal. We are so caught up in our everyday life. All the more so then, we must set it aside to be worked on. We must remember to work towards it. No one else will for us.

> Your financial goals are as important as, if not more than, your goal to find romance and love.

Women, More Than Men, Need Financial Literacy

Women, more than men, *must* place financial independence as a top goal. Statistics from the US (www.efmoody.com) show that over 75 per cent of women tend to be widowed at the young age of 56 years, and that about 90 per cent of all women, either through divorce, widowhood or because they have never married, will be solely in charge of their own finances at some point in their lives.

What this says is that at some point in your life, you will be solely responsible for yourself and your financial state or well-being. Your husband will not be there. Your parents might be gone by then. You might have your children, but they are dependent on you for financial support. You have no one but yourself to depend on to bring home the bacon.

If that is not bad enough, other statistics show that:

- Fifty-three per cent of women are not covered by a pension, compared with only 22 per cent of men.
- Almost one in four women is broke within two months of a husband passing away.
- A staggering 87 per cent of the poverty stricken elderly are women.
- Women suffer a 27 per cent drop in standard of living after a divorce. On the other hand, men gain a 10 per cent increase.

These statistics are gloomy. It means more women will be in financial despair than men. It seems so unfair that women have to be the ones to bear the children and look after the family. Now we are also potentially the ones who are left behind to face poverty and loneliness, possibly for the rest of our lives.

Confirming the dominating position of men in financial league tables, the Merrill Lynch and Capgemini Asia-Pacific 2007 Wealth Report found that the majority of high-net-worth individuals (HNWIs) in all markets are men. The highest proportions are in

India, Australia and South Korea at more than 80 per cent. Taiwan, on the other hand, has the highest proportion of female HNWIs at 43 per cent.

Given these statistics, it is our responsibility as women to become financially educated and to manage our money. It is our responsibility and no one else's. Having a good husband now or eventually does not take away the responsibility. It only makes the load lighter. Never fall into the self-deception that it is no longer your responsibility.

Financial Intelligence—A Growing Trend

To some extent, and increasingly a saving grace, there is a movement in the developed world for women to become financially educated. With divorce rates going up, the number of households headed by women has increased over the years and is near equal to the number of households headed by men. Market-driven companies today are selling new financial products to women as a target group and are going out of the way to help women understand money.

The fact that you are holding this book is proof that you are one of the new women eager to find out how to become a financial identity in your own right. Congratulations! What you must now do is really get into the business of becoming financially independent.

> Being financially independent is YOUR responsibility. Never fall into the self-deception that someone will take care of you forever.

2 Two Sexy Words

Two sexy words—financial independence. This has meant different things to me over the years. When I was a young girl, I hated being told what to do and I hated having to ask my parents for money. In my mind, if they gave me money, I had to obey them. Since I was a relatively strong-willed child, I wanted to be financially independent—fast. I looked forward to the day when I need no longer ask my parents for money, as I looked forward to the day that I could be totally independent.

Today, I understand the beauty of interdependence. And I value this as fiercely as I value independence. True interdependence, however, can only come about after one becomes independent. That's how it works.

LEVELS OF FINANCIAL INDEPENDENCE

During my university days in Australia, I waited on tables at a Chinese restaurant three nights a week. My father's business was an up-and-down roller coaster ride, and in the third year of my undergraduate studies, my parents had little money to send me. My part-time job earned me A$30 in wages and A$10 in tips every night that I worked. That's A$120 a week or A$480 a month and it was a princely sum. It paid for food and part of my rent. It gave me a great sense of freedom and was the beginning of my journey towards financial independence.

For over two years after graduation, after I started work full-time, financial independence was about earning enough to pay my own bills without financial help.

When my salary increased and I managed to have 'leftovers' to save every month, a new view of financial independence emerged. Someone told me that financial independence meant that one should have at least six months' salary in the savings account for rainy days. That made sense to me when I was in my twenties. I thought, if I were to lose my job or suffer a medical emergency, the six months of salary would tide me over. My pay then was $1,500 a month. I agonised over how I would save the huge total of $9,000 in as short a time as possible. I was a young woman with a big spending appetite for shoes, clothes, make-up and handbags. The only way I could build my six-month safety net and still shop till I dropped was through budgeting.

Today, some financial gurus advocate a nine-month safety net. Also, some financial advisers say that for every $10,000 in annual pay, you need to have a buffer of a month's salary to look for a new job. So if you are earning $40,000 to $60,000, your buffer should be about four to six months' salary. If you are a high-level person earning $300,000 to $500,000 per annum, your buffer has to be between 30 and 50 months of salary!

This advice might seem ludicrous to some of you. Wouldn't a headhunter come along and snap me up for another job if I was earning $300,000 a year? Yes, possibly, but often the new job would not draw the same amount. Are you willing to settle for less? Furthermore, headhunters tend to 'hunt' for people in jobs and are difficult to locate when you need a job.

In the last ten years, I have come to understand financial independence in two new ways:

- Financial independence is the total number of months or years you can afford to live a lifestyle that you are comfortable with after you have stopped working.

- Financial independence is when the returns from your investments cover your expenses, while still retaining or growing the capital.

One would imagine that someone as financially paranoid (and educated) as I could have thought all these things out when I was growing up. Well, I did not. It took me years to discover these lessons.

Four Levels Of Financial Independence

We now discuss the four levels of financial independence. Let's make these levels your desired financial goals or desired financial states.

- **Level 1:** Financially independent of your parents. This means that your earned income is equal to your expenditure.

- **Level 2:** Financially independent enough to be out of a job for six months. This means that your savings or investments is at least equal to six months' salary in the bank.

- **Level 3:** Financially independent enough to not need to work for the next ten or 20 years, or the rest of your life. This means that your savings or investments is equal to the number of years you do not need to work if you retire today, in this case, ten, 20, or more years of your age.

- **Level 4:** Financially independent and wealthy so that your investments generate enough income for your expenses while keeping or growing the base capital. This means that your investment income is equal to your expenditure, or that your investment income is greater than your expenditure.

Most young women are at Level 1. They are happy thinking that they do not need to ask their parents for money.

Some of you, if you have been working for a few years, are at Level 2, with six months or more of salary in your savings account.

Some of you are fortunate enough to be at Level 3. Congratulations if you are! If you are at Level 3, you are rich. You would be one of the few people who do not need to work for the rest of your life, if you choose not to, and still have enough to support your desired lifestyle. Using this definition, I am, therefore, also considered rich.

If you are at Level 3, please consider that we should be giving back to society through contributing our time and talent to help those less fortunate. That is why I am heavily involved with social enterprise and charity work today. It is giving back time.

If you are at Level 4, that is wonderful. Please contact me. I am working towards this as my financial goal. I want to learn from you.

For all at Level 1 and Level 2, read on.

Start States, End States, And How To Get There

Fortunately, financial issues can be solved logically and systematically for the most part. One can outline steps to change things and to move a person from one financial state to another. With a plan in hand, what it takes is strong will and determination to execute the plan to make the change, whether fast or slow. Isn't that great?

If you are reading this book, there are three financial starting states that you can be in:

- **Broke:** You are broke and need to find a way out.

- **So-so:** You are not doing too badly financially. You want to know how to become financially independent.

- **Doing well:** You already are doing well and want to benchmark how well you are doing.

Let's deal with the first two starting states. You are either broke or doing not too badly. You want to become financially independent. You do not wish to work for the rest of your life and you would like to retire early.

Now, let's identify what you want your desired end state to be. We go back to the four levels of financial independence for that. Choose one of the states. I suggest choosing Level 3. (See Table 2.1 opposite) All you need to do now is to work out what is required to get you from your current start state to your desired end state. You now have a path forward.

Table 2.1. Levels, Targets and Paths Forward to Your Desired Financial End State

Level	Your Financial State and Target	The Path Forward
1	• Your Earned Income = Your Expenditure You want to earn enough to cover your monthly expenses.	Create and stick to a budget. If you are a wage earner, the keys to higher pay are education, leadership, performance and unique competencies.
2	• Your Earned Income > Your Expenditure • Savings or Investments = 6 months' salary in bank You want to save up to six months' salary to stash away.	Focus on the chapter on budget immediately (Chapter 5).
3	• Your Earned Income > Your Expenditure • Savings or Investments = number of years you do not need to work if you retire today You want to be able to retire early and not work for the rest of your life, living instead off your investments and savings.	• Have the discipline to save and budget. • Invest. • Be aware of your risk profile and what you can afford to invest in at the different stages of your life.
4	• Your Earned Income > Your Expenditure • Savings or Investments = number of years you do not need to work if you retire today • Your Investment Income = Your Expenditure • Or better yet, Your Investment Income >> Your Expenditure You want to have so much money that the interest generated by your investments alone covers your monthly expenses for the rest of your life.	For the majority of wage earners, whether you earn $3,000 or $30,000 a month, this is a goal that is presently beyond your reach. One of the ways to become so fabulously rich without inheriting wealth or marrying into wealth is to become a successful entrepreneur.

Budget And Invest: Two Crucial Ways To Get Rich

As you can see from Table 2.1, whether your starting states are broke or so-so, financial independence or becoming rich all starts with BUDGETING. Big emphasis here. If you cannot budget, you will not become rich. After you learn to budget, you need to learn how to invest.

Years ago, my good friend Yaw Nam said to me, "You know, we will never get rich this way."

"Huh?" was my response.

"The money we earn is not sufficient. We need to manage our money to become rich. No one is going to teach us how to do that. We must do it ourselves. We also need to guard the number of hours we work overtime as there is no time left to do the really important things in life like looking after our financial position. Or generate passive income."

Yes, we cannot get rich if we budget like crazy, work like mad, and then forget to manage the money and our lives. You got it? I hope so.

Back to budgeting and why YOU must do it. Too many people I know ignore budgets. Even more people believe that things will be alright somehow. These people are smoking pipe dreams.

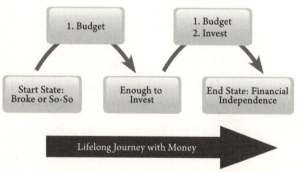

Figure 2.1. In a Nutshell Steps to Financial Independence

Financially Blind and Smoking Pipe Dreams

One of my financial adviser friends, Max, relates how he meets clients every day who say they want to retire and have monthly incomes of $5,000 to retain their current lifestyles. Max says he would ask these prospects how much money they have in their savings. What are the investments in their portfolio? Have they paid up fully for their mortgage? Do they have children? Do they have other dependants? How will they take care of their children's education?

Max tells me that he comes across many people who simply have no idea how much net worth one needs to have to retire at the age of 65 with a monthly income of $5,000 adjusted annually for inflation. He says that financial planning gives him the opportunity to help many of the financially blind to see the steps ahead so they don't end up old, broke and homeless.

OTHER WAYS TO BECOME RICH

If you have read the book till here, let me assume you are a sensible woman who agrees it is important to become financially independent. However, you might refuse to believe that budgeting and investing are critical to achieving your objective. You might even be wondering, "Besides budgeting and investing, how do I get really rich fast?" Here then are some other ways to become rich.

Inherit Wealth

You might already be financially independent if you were a lucky person born into inheritance. Some of us are born into fortunes! If you were, your concerns would be vastly different from the rest of us mere mortals who have to earn our keep to find financial independence across Levels 1, 2 and 3.

I know several women who are born into money. They never have to work for the rest of their lives if they choose not to. They were, however, raised by their families to earn a living and to live within their means by way of their earnings. Their inheritances are not spoken of. I have always marvelled at the self-restraint of my wealthy friends when it comes to shopping. Someone said that the truly rich never look rich. Going by my rich friends, I believe it.

Marry Rich

Yes, you can become rich by marrying rich. Yes, you can make 'marrying rich' a career decision. Ha-ha. Isn't that a contradiction, you ask? Am I not advocating independence? Won't marrying rich tie you down? What independence is that?

No, it is not a contradiction. Whether it is independence depends on whether your rich husband gives you wealth, how much, when he gives it to you, and whether there are strings attached.

If 'marrying rich' is your career choice, please do background work on what it takes to become financially independent this way. In fact, see a good divorce lawyer even before you are married as part of the strategy plan. Get good advice on what it will take to obtain your deserved portion of his money, should there be a divorce. I say the "deserved portion" of his money as the law has much to say about wealth division in divorce cases on what is due to the spouse for his/her contribution. (See Chapter 18 on Divorce.) You do not need to wait till divorce happens to work out a game plan.

Today, with prenuptials, men and women can come to agreement on what would be theirs on divorce. Having a prenuptial or not having one can be important, depending on the personality of your future husband. We cover this in Part 5 of the book.

Win the Lottery

Some of you reading this book may regularly buy lottery tickets in the hope of striking it rich. Then, one fine Sunday, you do. You've won 1st prize! You're one in 15 million!

There are three things wrong with this picture. Firstly, one in 15 million are not great odds for you. Secondly, unless you win 1st prize, the total sum you win may not make you financially independent. Thirdly, research shows that those who get rich quick through lucky windfalls often cannot keep or manage their sudden wealth. So even if you did get wealthy this way, you need to read this book to figure out how to stay wealthy, and better still, get wealthier!

Have Tiny Needs
One way to become financially independent very quickly is to have small needs. Very small needs. The smaller the better.

The Singapore newspapers reported some time back of a 45-year-old gentleman who said that he could live on $1,000 per month for the rest of his life. Therefore, with as little as $400,000, he was already financially independent if he continued to be frugal and if he left his money in a safe, interest-bearing investment instrument such as government bonds. With some luck, inflation would not eat away at his funds.

Create Wealth and Build Wealth
Robert Kiyosaki in his books discusses four types of personal incomes, of which two are wealth created through generating passive income and wealth built through building businesses.

An example of the first are writers, artists and inventors who create something of value, then patent or copyright it, and earn royalties on it. Entrepreneurs and business people create and build businesses as their roads to wealth. They build a business and earn regular income from that to grow rich. Or they build a business to sell off for a large sum of money.

You can be working in a full-time job and be involved in this kind of wealth creation. You would, however, still need to finish reading this book if you do not know how to budget and invest the money you have earned.

Work, Invest, Work … and Invest Again
Some of you reading this may have no idea when you can stop working and start enjoying life and the fruits of your labour. Is such a goal possible? Don't most people expect to work for the rest of their lives into, and perhaps past, retirement?

These questions are important because most of us need to work for a living. Few are born rich; few marry rich. Most of us do not want to have tiny needs. We want to have comfortable needs, not excessive, just comfortable. Since most of us work for our money, we must know how to make our money work for us. Working and investing is, therefore, the hardest, but surest, route to financial freedom.

I'm sure that all I have said so far has triggered thoughts for many of you on how to become rich. I might even have triggered a birth of 'gold-diggers', lottery-happy punters, writers, artists or entrepreneurs. I stress that the last two routes—creating and building wealth, and working and investing—are the most sustainable. The two are not mutually exclusive and, in fact, I don't think you can build wealth unless you can work and invest.

The Bridge Between Thinking Rich And Being Rich

When we surf the Internet today for information on getting rich, we are inundated by websites selling Napoleon Hill's idea of 'thinking rich'. Books such as *The Law of Attraction* are best-sellers. This genre of books emphasises positive thinking and thinking your way to money. Some even promise that money will come in through the door if you believe hard enough.

I am a firm believer in the power of visualisation for the purpose of goal attainment. A lot of what we are is caused by how we think. If we think negative, we become cynical and defeatist; we become naysayers and will not run towards our goals. If we think positive, we become energised towards our goals.

What many positive thinkers forget to say was aptly captured by a *Straits Times* article on Singapore's remisier king, Peter Lim, where he described multibillionaire Robert Kuok. Paraphrased, Peter Lim said that Robert Kuok not only has a vision, he knows step by step what it takes to attain that vision.

If you are one of the many people who read the 'think to get rich' genre of books, my advice to you is that beyond thinking, there is *doing*. Someone said: "Think it, then do it, and really, really do it."

SO WHY IS FINANCIAL INDEPENDENCE SEXY?

Remember the movie *The Stepford Wives* where men decided to turn their smart, high-earning wives into busty robots that obeyed their every whim by remote control?

New research shows that truth is far from that. Men and women are changing their attitudes towards each other as money talks for both men and women today.

According to the article "Men Prefer Sexy, Smart UnStepfords, Yes, Really" by Dr Rosalind Chait Barnett and Caryl Rivers, men are more flexible today. It used to be that men preferred women who weren't too smart. The two researchers found that divorce was today more than twice as likely if the woman did not earn a salary.

Having no income can be risky for a woman, and not just in the stability of her marriage. A wife who drops out of the workforce and stays out for a long time will never make up for that lost economic ground, even if she returns to the workforce. Worse, if her husband's income starts to slip—an all too common event these days—the couple can be in trouble, both financially and emotionally.

Are you financially independent? If you stop working tomorrow, how many years can you continue living the lifestyle of your choice?

3 Breaking Through Self-Barriers

In Chapter 1, I discussed why women must become financially aware and financially independent. We live longer and chances are that we will become single, whether through divorce or the earlier death of a spouse. Furthermore, women suffer more financially in these events than men do as we are generally less prepared.

At this point, we need to ask: Why do so few women plan for their future? Why do women allow themselves to suffer financially? Even though as many as 42 per cent of married women in the US earn more than their spouses, why is it that we don't seem to know better? We raise families and work miracles every day, balancing a hundred and one things. Why is it that we cannot see the criticality of financial independence? What hinders us? Are we born financially dumb?

One possible answer: Men and women value money differently. How do I know? Two big clues: The way women view shopping and the way they view investing.

Women And Shopping

Keon's sister, Ping, was a consultant for shopping malls and was the head honcho behind the success of several malls in the region. In their recent annual family trip to Kuala Lumpur, the family was comparing the success of different shopping malls. Ping posed the question, "Why do you think Mall A is so much busier and more successful than Mall B? After all, Mall B looks more posh than Mall A and has the best names in town."

Keon replied, "Mall B is too masculine."

Ping's eyes nearly popped out of her head. "Wow. You have become smarter!" she said.

Shopping malls do not just happen to be the way they are. Malls pay retail experts top dollar to get the right tenant mix and to understand who the shoppers are. Malls even plan the number of steps the average woman shopper can totter around in high heels before she enters a shop to rest, to buy something, or to have tea.

In every country, the statistics show that women earn less than men do. So, if men are the money bags, why build huge complexes that target women as the primary customer? Isn't it illogical for the malls to target women?

No. Why? The fact: Men and women spend differently. Women see money as the means to facilitate a lifestyle for herself and her loved ones, and her willingness to spend is higher than that of men. She is the primary target of shopping malls, impulse buying, season shopping, closing down sales, and all the tricks that have given rise to consumerism. Women are definitely the alpha when it comes to shopping. They are the gatherers. They shop for themselves, their spouses, their children, and so on.

Lately, some malls have started to cater for the metrosexual male. The primary shopper, however, is still the woman. Prime space in every single department store is always allocated to cosmetics, costume jewellery and women's clothing. I have never walked into any store where prime space is given to men's clothes or shoes, or even children's clothes or shoes. Notice that there are few shops selling *just* men's shoes! This is planned and not by chance.

The fastest moving item with the highest margin per square centimetre of space—that's what gets prime space. It is economics and pure common sense. You will never sell pots and pans on the entrance level floor of a great store. The basic formula is: ATTRACT WOMEN INTO THE STORE! The rest will follow! A woman will always find a reason to buy; you only have to suggest it to her subconscious.

According to Cotton Incorporated's Lifestyle Monitor™ Tracking Research, it was found that 23.6 per cent of the male respondents liked shopping compared with 53.4 per cent of the female respondents. Even as I write this, I know I make up one of the 46.6 per cent female respondents. Meanwhile, Keon makes up one of the 76.4 per cent male respondents except when it comes to certain branded menswear!

It is reported that women spend US$4 trillion annually and account for 83 per cent of US consumer spending, which makes up two-thirds of the nation's gross national product, according to WomenCertified, a women's consumer advocacy and retail training organisation headquartered in Hollywood, Florida (reported 28 November 2007 in Knowledge@Wharton).

In the book, *The Millionaire Next Door—The Surprising Secrets of America's Wealthy*, by Thomas J. Stanley and William D. Danko, the authors remarked quite a few times that the men who were millionaires in the US tended to have frugal wives who saved and cut out discount coupons almost religiously. Their wives were plainly dressed and were also often the financial planner in the family.

The problem with shopping is not the shopping. The problem with shopping is that *excessive* shopping or constant shopping for wants, and not needs, financially disempowers women. How do women get trapped into shopping excessively? Let's examine the traps that retailers lay for us.

> If women stop shopping tomorrow, all the malls would go broke. A woman may not know how to fix up her computer, but she knows how to find that unique designer bag on eBay!

Money Trap #1: Living It Up

It is called by many names: 'Keeping up with the Joneses' or 'Living it up'. Advertisements bombard us with images of what it means to be successful. The woman is decked out with diamonds on her fingers, her earlobes, her clothes. She is carrying glitzy handbags, wearing to-die-for Jimmy Choos and the latest slinky neckline-plunging evening dress. The man stands next to a highly polished sleek looking car, computer, handphone or gizmo. We watch movie stars at award nights, our idols looking all shiny and confident. We want to be there. We want to live that 'shiny new life'.

There is nothing wrong with the desire to want these things. But looking at the diamonds on their fingers, I do wonder how many zeroes, before the decimal place, these people have on their bank accounts. Going downtown on a Saturday night, I wonder how many of the big spenders I see at fine restaurants, the 'cool-cool' hang-outs and the 'hot-hot' clubs are in debt.

No one talks about it. Everyone encourages everyone else to have fun. So in keeping up with others, cool people must somehow have either starved themselves to make it for that night out or they are living from hand to mouth.

Money Trap #2: The Very Expensive 'I Feel Great' Hairdo

Most women love beauty salons and feeling like a million dollars coming out of them with their hair all done up. The best feeling in the world is when your hair looks great. Your face suddenly comes alive, your clothes look brighter, you feel like a prom princess all over again. I have come out of salons, hundreds of dollars poorer in cash, but feeling great. I have been crazy enough to spend $500 on a hairdo. I have tried the best salons in Singapore, Kuala Lumpur and Hong Kong. Those salons were an adventure in themselves. First class decor and service. I was really so young and so foolish.

Now, supposing someone were to ask you to switch to a $50 salon in the neighbourhood estate instead of doing your hair at the downtown glitzy shopping mall salon where rentals alone are three times that of the neighbourhood salon. Would you? What if the stranger said that she would give you $1,000 to change over? Would you? You just might.

How good would you feel if the money you spent at swanky salons were invested into stocks, and that amount showed improvement from year to year? You would be rich! Now substitute Hairdo and Salon for Spa and Beauty Rooms, Facials and Health Bars, and Dinner and Fine Restaurants. You see, you have been having such a great life. No wonder you are broke!

Money Trap #3: Buy A Package To Save Money

Another thing I have now learnt to avoid—package deals. Salons sell hair treatments that cost $200 per treatment. The girls are trained to ask you to buy a package of ten treatments so that the average cost would be about $100 per treatment. You then fork out the $1,000 to pay for the ten treatments. You think you have saved money by doing that, but in reality, you have just bought into the future of the salon and your relationship with it.

Let me tell you about my very expensive hair treatments at a leading middle class hair salon in Singapore where five years ago, I bought about $1,000 worth of O2 hair treatments. Each O2 treatment would have cost me $180. With the package, I would pay $100 per treatment. At the rate that I went to salons, which was once in three months, I had bought three years' worth of treatment. I had locked myself into one service provider for three years. Sheer stupidity.

The first three treatments over a period of a year went well. My hair looked great, but being a woman I was not satisfied. I decided to do a ceramic perm and forked out $350 to get it done. It was a new process then and pictures of ceramic-permed hair just looked so good!

My naturally curly waist-length hair went horribly wild after the perm, and started to break and fall off. I had to cut it into a really short bob. I did not walk into the salon for months. But I still had $700 credit balance in my favour. If it were not for that $700, I probably would have never gone back there. When my hair was finally shoulder length, I asked them to convert a part of the credit value into hair-colour sessions since I did not have much hair left to 'O2'. They agreed. My hair was then killed a second time. I don't know what they did, but my entire head of hair frizzed up. Two weeks later, I had to cut it all off again. I was very angry this time. But what could they do? They blamed it on my hair texture and said, "Please come back. We'll give you a steam treatment for free on your next visit."

Free? Not on your life! In total, I had spent $1,350 for three O2 treatments and one hair-colour session. I should have stuck to the list price of $180 per O2 session without the package deal. It would have been much cheaper. Now, each time I walk past the salon, I freeze up. I toss my hair subconsciously, grateful that it finally grew out. I no longer buy packages from any kind of salon—hair, spa or nails.

If you do buy packages, ensure that you use well-tested services regularly and the salon is reputable. There are savings to be enjoyed. It is, however, not my cup of tea.

Money Trap #4: Upsizing

Upsizing is the fastest way to sell. In sales terminology, it is selling to the same customer twice. It's fast and easy selling. It increases sales with low customer acquisition cost. Executed well, it is powerful. Think of McDonald's and their upsizing deals.

It even works in chic restaurants. Keon and I were lunching once at this very new restaurant and the very persuasive waiter kept trying to 'upsize' our order. "How about this, ma'am?", "Would you like to try that, sir?", "This is our newest addition to the menu. Customers love it, ma'am." I should have hired the waiter to join my sales team.

Upsizing happens a lot at beauty salons. They always tell you that your hair is too dry, too oily, too streaky, too undernourished and, therefore, you need this, and that, and that, and also this. I have concluded that I must look like easy meat. The stylists hover around me, showing me the latest shampoo, conditioner and hair treatment cream. They delight in telling me how damaged and unmanageable my hair is. Panicking, I buy. I now have bottles of pink, purple and orange shampoos in my bathroom. One takes out the frizziness, another puts back the body, another keeps the colour intact and another puts zest in my day with a 'pick-me-up' citrus smell.

Upsizing happens at checkout counters in supermarkets. Consider the attraction of new lady shavers, sweets and gadgets at the checkout counter, and you'll realise that customers are tempted to upsize all the time. Upsizing also happens online. See what the final few boxes of your checkout screen says: "Other people who bought what you did have also bought this item at $10 which has a total value of $50. Would you like to add this to your shopping cart now?" Yes, would you?

Remember, upsizing means more money for them, and less money for you. If you are a regular upsizer, you will end up broke and with a home full of stuff that you don't need. Upsizing always takes away a little bit each time. That is how upsizing is meant to work. Add a little each time just when you are paying. Over time, upsizing leaves nothing in the bank account. And you wonder why you are broke?

Money Trap #5: Averaging Down
Here is a story of how I went out to buy one suitcase and ended taking home THREE! It happened in the 1980s and I was at a large mall known then for bargain goods and cut-throat retailers.

I must have walked through about five shops when I bought a suitcase I liked that cost $100. I paid for it and rolled it out of the shop, walking on to window-shop. I then saw the same suitcase in another shop on a higher floor.

The shopkeeper asked me how much I paid for my suitcase. He then told me that with the $100, he would have sold me that suitcase plus a smaller one. Upset, I returned to the first shop and asked the chap what he meant by selling me the suitcase for $100. He laughed and told me that the second shopkeeper would have never sold me two suitcases for $100. I asked him if he would return my money if I could indeed purchase the other two suitcases for $100. He agreed.

I trudged back to the second shop, climbing the stairs and dragging my big new suitcase all the way up, and bought the other two suitcases for $100. Now armed with three suitcases, I went back down to the first shop and demanded my money back. The first shopkeeper was shocked and said that I was probably sold old stock that was imported at an old exchange rate. He added he could not give me the refund as his 'boss' would not allow him to do so. After a long argument and me threatening to report the shop to the Consumer's Association, he agreed to refund $30 to me since the large suitcase must have cost $70 and the smaller suitcase, $50, totalling $120. What was I to do? I took the $30. How does *anyone* go shopping for one suitcase and return with three? Was I nuts, my husband asked.

But hang on, we women do this all the time! Perhaps not in such a crazy way as I did. Remember when you bought that pair of designer trousers for $200? Immediately after that purchase, you found another pair in the same design selling next door for $50? What would you do? If you were like most women, you would have bought a second pair in a different colour. Together, the two pairs cost $250, but each pair alone cost $125. Averaging down, you felt less stupid.

How totally insensible and illogical! But yes, that's what people do. The next time this happens with clothes, handbags, accessories, pots and pans, curtains and bedsheets, STOP! YOU DO NOT NEED THE SECOND PURCHASE! Save the money!

Does Shopping Make Sense?

So what are we saying? Stop spending and live the life of an ascetic? Shopping is not a bad thing. I shop. In fact, to some of my friends, I don't shop ... I buy. It used to be that when I find the time to go shopping, I would buy several pieces of the same item in different colours. Shop assistants loved me. I did that simply because time was scarce, and looking for the right item with the right design, the right fit and the right price was not enjoyable.

I believe in being groomed for the job. Brian Tracy in his book, *The Psychology of Selling*, says "a whopping 95 per cent of the first impression you make on a customer is determined by your clothes. This is because in most cases, your clothes cover 95 per cent of your body." Tracy goes on to say that when you are well dressed, properly groomed, shoes polished and looking professional, the customer unconsciously assumes that you are working for an excellent company and that you are selling an exceptional product or service. So, dress and shop with purpose. Dress for your job. In fact, dress for the job you want to land or be promoted to. That self-image is important. But please do not blow the bank account or overload your credit card. Here are some smart shopping tips:

- Never buy anything you cannot fit into thinking you will lose the weight to fit into it.

- Never buy something just because it is on sale. Buy something on sale because you already needed it before it went on sale.

- Wait for sales when you can buy staple items at good prices. Most people can't tell the quality of the clothes you are wearing, but most people do know if you are wearing cheap shoes and carrying a really cheap handbag. If your staple work shoes and handbag look cheap, whatever else you have on will also end up looking cheap. Good shoes and handbags are important investments. And so is a good wristwatch!

- Do not ever feel compelled to follow fashion trends and be a slave to the latest craze. Develop your own dress style. Women on a career track should try to dress consistently and create a distinct style that is theirs alone. Developing your own style, however, does not mean being dressed in every single new style from the designers. Not unless you are in the business of fashion and beauty.

These are my five absolutes for wise spending:
- Invest in a good education. This should take TOP priority in your shopping list.

- Invest in language and speech. Hire someone to teach you how to articulate properly, speak well, write accurately.

- Invest in your mind. Spend time and money

> To change the way you spend money, you need to feel that financial products and investing into YOUR FUTURE are as important as, if not more than, that new pair of shoes. To do that in a sustainable manner, you need to have a STRONG VISION of your future self to work towards. You also need to link that vision to clear financial goals.

on this. Read, watch documentaries, engage in conversations that give new knowledge.

- Invest in good teeth to ensure fresh breath. Go for regular check-ups. Please, no foul breath and no crooked teeth.

- Invest in good relationships. Spend time with your family and really get to know them.

WOMEN AND INVESTING

In her research, INSEAD Assistant Professor of Finance Lily Fang reported that 80 per cent of women don't actively engage in financial planning. She also said that career women, even successful ones, tend to leave financial planning to their husbands! Yet because women live longer than men do, going by statistics, women should be more engaged in financial planning and investment.

In surveys about personal preferences for investments, women are found to be wanting. Table 3.1 below shows that more women than men generally declare the investment process to be too complicated or that they were unwilling to take risk with their money.

Table 3.1. Female/Male Sentiments Towards Investing

General Statement	Women Agree	Men Agree
I find investing to be too complicated	66%	44%
I am unwilling to take risk with money	24%	11%
I am willing to take considerable risk	25%	40%

(Source: www.efmoody.com)

"Women have been taught to invest in lifestyle and children. Men have been taught to invest in things that hold value—a house, retirement," says Ruth Hayden, a financial counsellor and author of *For Richer, Not Poorer: The Money Book for Couples*. The author remarks that while most of what women spend money on makes the day work, the problem with that is that most of that stuff has no asset value (www.bankrate.com).

Women Can Do Better

Many studies, including those by Lily Fang, indicate that at the very worst, women do no worse than men when it comes to investment. Some studies in fact show that women perform better than men do.

A six-year academic study of 35,000 stock market accounts by American professors Terrance Odean and Brad Barber showed that the portfolios of female investors outperformed those of men by 1.4 per cent a year.

Two surveys by website Digital Look, one in 2001 and another in 2005, analysed 100,000 portfolios and discovered that women outperformed men in both periods. In the year to 27 May 2005, Digital Look discovered that women's portfolios averaged an 18 per cent return, while men averaged 11 per cent. Over the same period, the FTSE All-Share Index rose 13 per cent. In fact, studies shows that:

- Women bother with details and bother to do research.
- Women are more cautious than men.
- Women are more willing to ask for help and information.
- Women trade less often than men do.
- Women have less of an ego when it comes to investment. (Men's egos get in the way of sound financial judgment.)
- Women are less likely to repeat mistakes.

Contrary to conventional wisdom, research shows that women do make better investors than men, if they try. "Everyone makes mistakes," said Hannah Grove, chief marketing officer of Merrill Lynch Investment Managers, "but successful investors learn from theirs." According to a Merrill Lynch survey conducted in 2005, the ability of women to learn from their mistakes was one reason that women investors are more successful. Women are less likely to repeat their mistakes. Men, because of their ego, are more likely to keep doing something just so they can prove themselves right (www.sptimes.com).

So What Stops Women From Investing?
If women are good in investing, what stops them from doing so?

Lack of Confidence
A Charles Schwab survey, for example, found that only 52 per cent of women were confident about their investing ability, compared with 82 per cent of men. Why are women less confident?

- Reluctance to talk about money or investment issues. "I don't want to talk about it!" is a common refrain. Could this general reluctance to talk about financial matters be due to the fact that women do not understand investment jargon? Understanding investment terms and what they mean is important to growing your money. You need to be as comfortable talking about *making* money as you are comfortable about spending it. Talking about money matters allows you to tap into another person's brain and helps you think the investments through, whether for or against. For novice investors, learning through conversations with colleagues or friends is cheaper than making mistakes in the market. But be sure to do your own homework also before you invest.

- Negative self-image. We women set up negative self-images about our abilities. Most of us believe that we are poor at mathematics, and often because we believe that, it becomes hard for us to work at numbers. Research shows that it is negative self-talk, societal expectations and factors of the environment that make women underperform their potential in this area. According to a study of Brown University undergraduates, women perform as much as 12 per cent better on maths problems when tested in a setting without men. Brown University's research was not intended to determine whether or not females would benefit from single-sex education. The data, however, suggest that females may benefit from single-sex maths classes. Why do women underperform their potential in certain fields in the presence of men? Perhaps we are 'programmed' by our environment to believe that men are better.

Insufficient Motivation

Most married women I know leave investment decisions to their husbands. It seems many times easier for women to talk about Carats, Cut, Clarity and Colour than it is for them to talk about buying 20 lots of a blue-chip share. I see this in many of the women I speak to in the women development programmes that I run. The women who appeared to be more fashionably dressed more often seemed to reflect the 'my-husband-takes-care-of-that' atttitude. Or they say, "No time to do it."

But why is this so? Women are, after all, motivated hunters when it comes to shopping for things they really want. Here is an example. I was at Copenhagen Airport waiting for my flight out when my colleague shook me excitedly and said, "I must buy the Rolex at this airport." Out of breath and walking faster than she has ever walked to any board meeting, she said, 'Rolexes are cheapest here!" What struck me was how she knew exactly where to buy what.

Women *know* when and how long each sale would last. They know which shop in which street in Hong Kong sells what outfit at what price during which season. Women can find themselves all over the world shopping for the best deal in handbags, watches, clothes, even jewellery, but when it comes to financial products, women wear a glazed look. Why? Don't we know that we absolutely need financial products more than handbags? Don't we?

I'm going to draw an analogy between investment and football. Close to the same discomfort we feel about money talk is football talk. What on earth is a banana kick, a 4-4-2 formation or an offside trap? My friend Football Sandra decided one day to learn. She accompanied her husband to every football match, watched every single telecast game with him and dedicated this decision to him as her way of loving him. Today, Sandra can conduct a conversation on football with any man, and they love her for it.

See, if you are motivated to do something, you will learn. Sandra was motivated to learn about football. I am motivated to win on investments, so I spend time learning the jargon and whatever it takes to win. And the more I learn, the hungrier I am for more learning on this topic.

> Investing is not about being right or wrong. It's about making money. Women are able to put their egos aside in ways men have trouble doing so. This ability to set their ego aside makes women great investors.
>
> ~ Mike Hamilton, Editor and Founder of the Global Investment Institute

CHANGE AND BREAKTHROUGH

So, if you want to be successful, you may need to do some soul-searching to remodel your self-image and ask some tough questions on how you see yourself, women and their roles versus how you see men. Until you can resolve that being successful and financially independent is as important as having a happy family, you will find that you sabotage yourself along the way. Research shows that we sabotage our life goals if these goals and our value system or our beliefs are not aligned.

In the next chapter, we will take you to your first steps of finding your own self-vision.

Think about the last money trap you fell for. What did you buy? How long did the joy last? How much money did you spend? How useful was the purchase? What other money traps are there in the consumer market today that you can think of?
Do write and tell us about money traps you see and the ones you have fallen into. Please write to: norma@gorgeoussexyrich.com

4 A New Self

As in any business, working out our own lives should start with a VISION. Funny how we do that for companies but not for ourselves. Getting from vision to REALITY requires a series of carefully thought-out steps, determination and action. Every successful person has a vision of self. For entrepreneurs, self-vision is often tightly intertwined with the vision of their companies or businesses.

A Strong Self-Vision

A strong self-vision is critical to set our hearts and minds on what we want to be so that we work towards it. In many traditional and ancient cultures, the youths undergo a series of planned experiences that may include solitude, just so that they obtain clear self-visions to enable conscious living for the rest of their lives. This ritual of planned experiences, sometimes known as 'vision quest', has disappeared from urban living. In those ancient cultures, the ritual marks the transition from youth to adulthood.

A weak or non-existent vision of self results in purposeless living. When people live purposelessly, it is like getting into the car, starting the engine, going on the road, and driving until they hit something or something hits them.

A vision of one's self cannot be complete without a clear vision of how much money one has, where it comes from, how good one feels to have the money and how the money will be deployed for a great life.

Vision Does Not Equal Ambition

More often than not, our self-visions today are clouded by the self-judgement, critical voices and material images of keeping up with the Joneses. For the majority of us, we mistake ambition for self-vision. Self-vision is more powerful than ambition. Ambitions are single dimensioned. Self-visions are holistic; they cut across multiple facets of self and reposition the entire person in the mind's eye. Here's a simple self-visioning exercise for you to do.

- Give yourself two weeks to go through magazines. Cut out pictures or articles of things you love (including material things), places you want to go to, and of people you admire or like because they hold the qualities you want to have such as kindness, generosity, intelligence and humour.

- Take time in these two weeks to reflect. If you have your way in life, who is the ONE person you would want to emulate? Don't take this lightly. Do not think you want to be Victoria Beckham, for example, unless you also want the accompanying lifestyle, and if you do, write that down. There is no right or wrong, just what you really want in the deepest part of you. You may even want to take some time off to do this. Go for a walk on the beach. Reflect.

- Each day, close your eyes for two minutes and imagine yourself five, ten and 25 years from today. Who do you want to be? Now that you have a vision of yourself in five years' time, what is your financial vision of yourself? How much money do you want to have? What would be your net worth? Would you own your home? Your own car? What sort of financial freedom would you have? Can you see the means to get there?

- Hold those images in your head. Write them down on a clean sheet of paper. Paste the pictures you have cut out. Make a declaration board and place it somewhere prominent in your home so you can review it constantly. It can even be in a scrapbook that you keep by your bed.

- Every morning when you awaken and every night before bedtime, look at the pictures of the New You and review what you want for yourself. You should begin planning the steps to attain these things.

Breaking The Vision Down Into Itemised Steps

What comes after having a strong mental picture of the New You is setting out itemised steps to reach the vision. Like in any business plan, you can work out the steps backwards from the envisioned state to the present state to determine what it takes to get there.

Of course, life is not a bed of roses, and as you take those steps on a day-by-day basis, there will be detours and hiccups. What the plan does is that it helps you identify the major milestones or the major pre-qualifiers that you need for that success.

Do not be impatient with yourself as you do this exercise. To run a full self-visioning exercise will take several chapters of a book. Here, I have given you a doorway to your new self. It is an important doorway, but it's just a doorway. Please do more homework in this area. It is necessary to find out for yourself who you really want to be. For a more in-depth exercise of self-visioning, attend a good personal development workshop or visit my website: www.gorgeoussexyrich.com.

Self-Beliefs

Harv Eker in his series of talks and books on the Millionaire Mindset pointed to the financial blueprint of a person. We have these blueprints ingrained in us. It is so important to know what they are so we can change them and break the old patterns.

In a volunteer training programme that I conduct for lower-income women, I speak about the self-limiting images that we carry in our heads. On one slide, for example, I show pictures of a happy, financially secure family next to an impoverished family. I would then ask the participants which family they identify with in their hearts of hearts. Many of these women see themselves as impoverished and fighting for money all the time.

Which image do you carry in your head? That picture you hold has a way of becoming your reality. Many studies indicate how our dominant thoughts determine outcomes in our lives. Hardly surprising, right? Here are some mental models or self-beliefs that I have come across.

- *Pauper Pauline.* We are poor and will always be poor. There is not enough money to buy a new handbag. This broken handbag will do just as well.

- *Struggling Sue.* There is just enough every month to put food on the table for the family. I wish there's just a bit more.

- *Defending Diane.* I have to protect everything I own. I must be careful who I talk to and what I say. People are out to get things that belong to me. People are out to cheat me.

- *Fighting Fannie.* I have to fight for everything in my life. If I want a promotion, I must fight for it. If I want a pay rise, I must fight for it.

- *Winning Wanda.* I am successful. I look and feel fantastic. People listen when I speak because I am great!

These self-beliefs propel how we act. Pauper Pauline, for example, may never see an opportunity in front of her as she would not believe that such can exist. She would not notice the $100-note dropped on the floor in front of her. And if she did and picked it up, she would not invest it. She would probably spend it so that she is back to being poor. Self-beliefs make us what we believe ourselves to be.

You laugh at me for thinking that there is any opportunity around $100? I know a plucky woman, Aini, who was down and out. When given $100, she decided to change her life. She slaved away and made enough curry puffs to sell at a nearby food court. She made $700 that weekend. She now thinks of making curry puffs for a living and has plans for supplying her curry puffs to ten food courts in two years' time. See what $100 can do when you think positive?

Whether called financial styles or financial blueprints, how we view money is deep in our psyches. Much of this conditioning is due to the families we were born into. Harv Eker's and other very successful money programmes expound how people are conditioned from a young age to think about money. All of us are conditioned in one way or another. How are you conditioned? Do you know?

Here are some common examples of self-beliefs that we carry in our heads:

- Rich people are not happy. Their marriages break down. If you become rich, the chances are your husband will not be faithful and your marriage will break down.

- When you get a win, you were just lucky. You should celebrate your luck by buying yourself an extra nice present.

- When you have a win, you should give it all to charity as it is good for you.

- It is better to be poor and happy than rich and unhappy.

- Money is not everything. We do not need money to be happy.

- As long as we have enough food to eat and clothes to wear, we should be happy.

The list goes on. We hear these beliefs in our heads every day. Your financial end will be the outcome of the way you continue to think and behave towards money. Whether we are Britney Spears, Bill Gates, Warren Buffet or Jeffrey Skoll, we will act out our financial thoughts and pattern, with or without being conscious of doing it.

You Have The Power To Change

A large number of books in the market today already talk about the power of positive thinking, the power of attracting positive things into our lives through positive thoughts. Without repeating them in this book, I agree with most of them. Please invest time to read these books to change the way you see the world. There are timeless gems to be gleaned. Learn them well.

The best news in life is that anyone can change their self-beliefs and the way they behave. Studies show that if you do something consistently over a period of 30 days in a consistent, predictable manner, this new pattern will lodge in your synaptic processes and you will be on your way to a new learnt behaviour. Wow! We have the power to change! And yes, it can be done. We can teach ourselves to be different. We can reprogramme ourselves.

I read and reread the writings by Gandhi and his biographer, Louis Fisher. Fisher said that Gandhi was not always the person we now know him to have been. He started changing at the age of 37. Before the change, he had a bad temper and would often shout at his wife. Reading this gave me much hope that anyone can decide to change to become a New Self. Anyone.

ACTION AND MORE ACTION DOES THE WORK

Anyone can envision all they want. Anyone can draw up lots of plans and budgets. But until they have the will to carry them out, visions and plans are useless. Action is what enables reality in the end. In reading the wonderful motivational books by Napoleon Hill, Wallace Wattle and many others, what is clear is that DOING is as important as thinking. Furthermore, if you fail the first time, KEEP TRYING. Try doing it differently. Make it work no matter what. You will become financially independent if you are determined enough. Small failures will not stop you. Nothing can. If you are determined and act on your vision for your future, you will become unstoppable.

> Anyone can change their self-beliefs. Take the cue from Winning Wanda: I am successful. I look and feel fantastic. People listen when I speak because I am great!

YOU CANNOT DELEGATE FINANCIAL PLANNING AWAY!

I know some women who have never filled up a tax return form ever in their lives. They depend on their husbands to complete the tax filings for them. I remember filling the first form with my first husband. The experience, I admit, was quite intimidating the first time. But I decided thereafter that it made more sense to file separately and so I learnt.

Your Responsibility

If you are married, never get into the situation where you believe your husband knows best for the both of you when it comes to money. Especially if you are a homemaker or a stay-at-home mum. Always find out. Find a way to have your say on how the family money should be managed. Do it together.

Should your husband suddenly drop dead, you do not want shocks. It is pointless and too late to blame a dead man for his lack of care towards you. You owe it to yourself also to care for your own future by taking an interest in the financial affairs of your family unit. It is your responsibility to know and to plan while he is alive.

(If a man happens to be reading this, I urge you to do the responsible thing and to bring your wife up to speed on financial matters if she happens to be a homemaker. Not doing so is selfish.)

Mei, my gentle friend, is a wonderful woman. Her husband, Jonathan, was a successful owner of a renovation business. Mei used to work as his designer and project coordinator. When I met Mei by chance recently, I found out that Jonathan had passed away after fighting cancer for two years. Mei was left alone. She then discovered that their home had been used as guarantee for a company loan. The company bank account was depleted repaying the loan. The family bank account was also near zero. Medical bills had used up $200,000 of the family savings. If the house was sold, she would have no home, no money, and, in fact, she was the beneficiary of a company with a net debt position and a home that was still mortgaged to the bank.

Mei did not know all this when her husband was alive. He had kept the information from her. What was worse, after he passed away, she discovered that Jonathan had had an affair with his secretary when he was in his healthier years. Imagine her shock and sense of betrayal. Mei fell into depression. She finally struggled out of it after a few years. She also took steps to wind up the old company and settle the debts, and started her own renovation company. She rebuilt her life. But it took time and much emotional endurance. I admire Mei very much for her inner strength and beauty.

Take Charge

Having a husband or partner to take care of you is great. Having a father and a mother care for you is also great. But YOU need to take charge when it comes to YOUR money and YOUR financial future.

You need to plan for yourself, whether you are single or married. If you are divorced or widowed, I hope that you already have a plan in place. It is very painful for divorcees and widows who do not have financial plans, savings or investments. They are so alone. Losing their loved one is bad enough. Knowing that one is broke, and alone, is a double whammy. I would hate it if you wake up one day to find yourself alone and broke.

For those of you who still believe that you should just depend on your husband or partner to care for you, here are some questions to ask yourself:

- What if he drops dead suddenly? What if he leaves me when I am hospitalised?

- What if I fall ill suddenly? What if I am hospitalised for four months without income or I become pregnant tomorrow?

- What if he is retrenched? What if I am retrenched?

- What will happen to my children when they reach 18? Who will pay for their studies?

- How is the mortgage of our house insured? Who will the house belong to if either party died?

- Is there insurance? Who benefits?

- What is the net worth of my husband at any one time? What is the net worth of this family at any one time?

It's About Me, Myself and I!

Before a plane takes off, the crew explains emergency procedures. They instruct passengers to take care of themselves first before their children, in particular to put on the oxygen mask on themselves first before putting the mask on the children. Likewise, whether you are single, married or widowed, when it comes to financial planning and freedom, you need to be selfish. You need to think "It's about me, myself and I!" Only after you have helped yourself to become financially independent can you help others, including the people in your family.

Most women make the mistake of caring for everyone first and themselves last. Wrong, wrong, wrong! Take care of yourself first. After that, the others.

Thoughts For The New You

As we move on to the rest of this book, I have a few thoughts to share with you.

It's Your Birthright to be Wealthy

In the days of old, men went out to hunt, and women stayed home to cook, breed and till the land. In tilling the land, the women owned the land and the fruits of the land. Women planted the seeds and harvested the crops, and then they stored the yield. Women also domesticated and bred animals. It was women who built long-term sustenance for families. It was women who created 'income' and 'recurring income'. Barter trade came along later to enable transactions between families, tribes and villages. To me, therefore, women owned all the true wealth in those days of old.

Men were just the hunters then. They were the troops sent out to kill the mammoth tiger that threatened the village. It was only when weaponry was invented that men began to plunder and pillage for land tilled by other communities, and the power shift between men and women happened.

Going by anthropology, you have the right to be wealthy as a woman. It is your *birthright*. Did you know this?

Let me provoke you with the next question. If men historically, through weaponry, shifted wealth ownership from women to men, and between villages, states and nations, what should women do if women want a different future for humanity? I believe that women should arise to lead. Their leadership is required to balance values and thought. Thank goodness, the war for economic wealth today is no longer fought with just firepower but with *brain*power too.

Who Cares What the Broke Think!

As you start this journey towards building your new self, there will be people who will be envious. People will try to borrow from you since they now know you have money. Some will tell you horror stories of investment failures. A few will try to derail you.

Why do they do that? People do not like change. It is a lot of work to change successfully in the positive direction. They like it even less when someone changes to become more successful than they are. What you need to do is to stay on course. Stay firm.

Here is a story (rephrased) by financial guru Dave Ramsey:

> A young man called Luke married a beautiful bride. Both of them moved into a small apartment above a garage. They were earning $80,000 a year between them and could afford to buy a home on mortgage. They decided that they wanted to buy a home using cash and not take out a bank loan. Both worked hard at it. They cut their expenses to $30,000 a year. In a matter of three years, they had saved $150,000 between them. In some states in the US, $150,000 can buy you a decent home. They bought a home of their choice making full payment. Luke's wife was 26 years old when that happened.
>
> Over that period of saving, Luke's friends thought they were mad. They had houses on mortgage, and cars and all sorts of stuff on bank loans and credit card loans. It is not hard to imagine that after owning their first home, and having kept to a strict budget of $30,000 a year, and with rising incomes for both of them, they were able to accumulate wealth very rapidly. After the first home, they were able to buy their second, third, fourth properties, and with all that, accumulate wealth beyond the imagination of their friends.

Ramsey ended the story by asking, "Who cares what the broke thinks?" That's right. Who cares? Your job is to accumulate money so that you can become financially independent. Stay focused. Do it. No one else will.

Don't Sweat the Small Stuff

There are very many good people who are so bogged down by small things in their lives that they have no time to see the big picture. I know women who get flustered by a parking ticket or being snubbed at a dinner party.

This is what my former colleague Heng taught me. Having finished a department lunch, we were walking back to his car when, lo and behold, we found a parking ticket on his windscreen. He picked up the ticket, glanced at it, scrunched it up and tossed it away. Goody-two-shoes me, I was appalled. Heng said, "They will eventually write to me and I will pay. Small stuff. Don't let it spoil the great lunch we just had."

Each time I get a parking fine these days, I make a mental note to be careful the next time. I would then do a mental scrunching of the ticket, mentally toss it away and tell myself to move on. After all, I have to pay anyway. I have messed up already. Why get upset about the past? The event is over. Move on.

In financial management, 'don't sweat the small stuff' also translates to 'please do not spend time negotiating the 20-cent reduction in the price of fish unless you buy tons of fish for a restaurant and the 20 cents is for every kilogram or 100 grams'. Your time is money and you need to balance between finding the ideal buy at a few dollars less and the value of your time.

I shop online for the bulk of my groceries to free time for myself. Yes, I pay a few dollars for the delivery, but if I went to the store I would have to pay for petrol and parking. So I go online once a month and buy most of the non-perishables that way. It saves me much hassle. I adopt this time-consciousness philosophy for many things.

I would not spend half a day of my time to save $100 because I know that my time is theoretically worth more than that if I invest my time well to educate myself or to make money.

My mother calls me every other week to advise me that my helper, possibly one of the best in Singapore, is eating too much and helping herself to the best food from the fridge. My comment to her is that I am not about to spend time policing my helper on what she eats if the difference to my food bill is $10 per week.

Forget the Past, Move On

Everyone knows someone who is locked in past losses, lamenting each time you see them that they lost a huge amount of money.

One of the best things you can do for yourself is to forget the past, whether good or bad, and move forward. For this reason, I love the Walt Disney cartoon, *Meet the Robinsons*. The motto of the cartoon is 'Keep Moving Forward'. It is apparently the same motto that Walt Disney himself lived by.

Yes, you have heard this many times. But can you do it? Can you celebrate successes and then put them aside so you can focus on the next success? Can you learn from failures or non-successes, and once you have understood the lesson, set that aside so you can focus on the goal ahead of you?

I've made many financial blunders and have had to set them aside to continue moving forward in life. For instance, I sold a beautiful home once when the market was not right. Instead of making $1.5 million, I hardly broke even on the investment. On another occasion, I made close to a million in a property transaction, but I had sold too early and could have made another $500,000 or more. I have invested $100,000 in a start-up business and trusted the CEO to run it. When he defaulted, I had to sort out the mess as a founding director. I once loaned $10,000 to a colleague because he said his mother was ill. He gave me a few IOUs and post-dated cheques that bounced. Till today, he has not repaid me. I tried contacting him, but he does not return my calls or e-mails.

I do think back sometimes to these mistakes, but I do not let them hamper or discourage me. What is important was that in the ensuing years, I did not sit back. To me, it was a question of chasing the market and ensuring that I did not fall back. In other words, I had to ensure that my minimum success position is one that tracked the market.

As the New You, learn from past mistakes. And do not let your past haunt you. Forget the mistakes. Move on. Move forward.

Maintain the Balance

Keon and I emphasise that life should be balanced. Keon, more than I, emphasises that all the time.

Women attend seminars and workshops and get recharged and motivated to change. Often, this surge of energy is powerful enough to make them wish to clean up their lives completely. This is great. However, for change to last, the approach to change must be balanced. In your eagerness to be a brand new person, please remember 'balance'.

> If you have made a bad financial decision, take the lesson and move on. If you have never made a financial decision in your life and you regret your lack of self-empowerment, get off your feet today and start working towards your future. The only way to move forward is to start and then to keep moving forward.

> Don't sweat the small stuff.
> Focus on the big picture and larger goals.
> Value your time. Value yourself.
> Forget the past. Keep moving forward.
> This is the New You.

Part Two
Money Fundamentals

From Vision To Reality

In Part One, we discussed how having a strong self-vision, which includes a financial vision, is important for you to achieve your goals in life. We also stressed that the road from vision to reality is one of action. Ideally, like all great visionaries, you can plan backwards from your self-vision to determine the steps you need to take.

In Donald Trump's book, *How to Get Rich*, he made a point about being stubborn as he hunted down deals. He wrote about his vision to transform the Commodore Hotel in 1974 into a state-of-the-art hotel. He had a six-point plan. Each point clearly indicated what he needed to do to create wealth through the transformation.

The points listed out actions that are classified as 'must-dos', 'must-change' and 'must-leverage'. What is amazing is that this great man took a vision to reality in six points and in two years. This is what he wants. He creates a checklist to get there. Then he gets up and gets it done. Billionaire Peter Lim had the same thing to say about super billionaire Robert Kuok.

You want to get there? You need to identify what you want. You then work that backwards into a six-point, or a ten-point action plan. And then you just get up and go get it done. My job in this book is merely to give you some basic tools and pointers to kick you off.

Parts Two, Three and Four will be tough going. Part Five is easy; it covers the life passages a woman can expect to go through. If you want to be financially free, however, you have to go through the tough reading. You have to start wealth comprehension. Understanding 'money talk' helps you achieve your financial vision.

Basic Knowledge For Any Investor

You need to know or understand the following as you become an investor:

- Personal self-vision—life goals and financial goals.
- Personal finance management—budgeting and debt management.

- Investment and investment management.
- Investment fundamentals.
- Personal net worth.
- Investment diversification.
- Investment strategies.

In Part Two, we highlight the following concepts which provide a foundation for you to read the rest of the book:
- Budget.
- Net worth and the 'I Am Rich' number.
- Inflation.
- Risk and risk management.
- Investment strategies.

In Part Three, we will describe personal financial products.

In Part Four, we discuss:
- Investment management and diversification.
- Investment products.
- Personal investment psychology. This is an important topic for any investor. You must know yourself as an investor because you can be your own largest risk.

Read on. You are on your way to financial freedom.

5 A Budget To Spend Like Crazy

Your Emotional Relationship With Money

'Rich' people delight in reading financial statements to see how much money they have. 'Poor' people hate receiving financial statements as it usually says how little money they have. Which are you?

The problem is that we see money as a means to an end and not an end in itself. No wonder we end up spending and spending. We are just fulfilling our inner belief that money is the means to an end. And if our 'end' is to look fashionable, we will use money to achieve that goal, instead of keeping it and growing it.

If you do not have that simple joy of seeing money in your bank account, the odds are you would find a compelling need to fill your home and life with things instead. Some reprogramming of how you see money is probably needed. Until this underlying self-revisioning is done, it is too difficult and takes too much willpower on its own to save, budget and invest for your financial freedom.

You must want to be financially free. You must want to stop falling into money traps. You must want to be rich without any hidden inner self-talk and negative thinking that are unwittingly self-sabotaging. The way forward is to BUDGET.

Don't Tell Me How To Use My Money!

Most people don't like the word 'budget'. How can you blame them? To budget means NOT spending our money the way we want. Budgeting means we have to spend less, watch what we spend on and sometimes not spend at all.

But budgeting is necessary. It underpins anyone's financial freedom. The emphasis is anyone's, not just the working class which you and I are. Even the rich stick to their budgets to stay rich. The reason is simple. If you don't plan what you spend, you will overspend.

If you do overspend consistently, you will end up broke. It is reported that Britney Spears earned US$737,000 a month and she spent it all. The general opinion was that she was spending too wildly and if nothing changed, she would be broke. You see, it does not matter whether you earn $737, $7,370 or $73,700, you will be broke if you spend all of it.

REDEFINE, BE RESPONSIBLE AND EMBRACE

I hated budgeting until the day when I redefined it. Budgeting now helps me define what portion of my money I can throw away at gold-flaked mascara for the year-end party to match the very expensive Italian designer gold speckled dress I bought from an obscure shop in South Yarra, Melbourne.

Instead of thinking of budgeting as a control measure, I think of it now as *a means in which I can spend like crazy and without guilt*. But only AFTER I have taken two responsible actions:

- I set aside money for myself for investment and for my financial freedom.

- I pay my bills on time.

After taking these actions, I can spend what's left like crazy. You see, as long as I get to spend like crazy at some point, I am fine. It removes my unwillingness to budget and the feeling of being constrained. Of course, what I set aside for my financial freedom and what goes under the bills section determine what is left over for the crazy spending.

Naturally, it is ludicrous to set aside one cent a month for investment so that you make the rest available for crazy

The question to ask is: How much money must I set aside every month to achieve a desired amount of funds within a certain time frame so as to realise my financial self-vision?

spending. You need to be true to your self-vision and overall plan as you set aside the funds for investment.

The First Step: Do Up A Budget

Your budget is your first step to financial freedom. It is a simple financial plan itemising what you earn, what you spend and what you save. It can be likened to a simple income statement for companies.

A well-constructed budget tells you what goes in and what goes out. It must be easy enough for you to remember in your head or to work on, on a regular basis for discipline. One of the worst things to do, however, is to spend a lot of time creating an elaborate and detailed budget only to have it used once—the day it was created.

The trick about budgeting is first to ensure that your income is greater than your basic expenses which comprises fixed and committed expenses. If you don't earn enough to cover even your basic expenses, you really need to tighten up your spending, or earn more, or pray for a windfall from somewhere. Since windfalls are hard to come by, focus on the first two!

Components Of A Budget

Let's now look at the components of a budget. Refer to Table 5.1.

Table 5.1. Components of a Budget

	Income	Amount
	Salary	$
	Rentals and commissions	$
	Dividends and interest	$
	Others	$
A	Total Income	$
B1	Financial Independence Account	
	Savings for retirement	$
	Savings for investment	$
	Savings for children's education	$

B2	FIXED EXPENSES	
	Car loan	$
	Home mortgage	$
	Insurance	$
B3	REQUIRED EXPENSES	
	Groceries	$
	Utilities	$
	Phone	$
	Transport	$
	Domestic helper	$
	Others	$
B4	DISCRETIONARY EXPENSES	
	Clothing	$
	Entertainment	$
	Eating Out	$
	Hobbies/Sports	$
	Vacations	$
B	TOTAL SAVINGS & EXPENSES	$
A–B	ADDITIONAL CASH TO SPEND OR SAVE	$

Your Income

These are inflows into your bank account. They include salary, interest, dividends, commissions and rental income. Income does not comprise loans from the bank or via credit cards to boost spending.

Your Financial Independence Account

These are savings for your longer-term financial objectives such as retirement, buying a home or your children's university education. Remember to take care of yourself first. More about this later.

Your Expenses

When you first make a budget, you need to start by tracking your present expenditures. This will help you work out a realistic budget.

It is pointless to put down idealised numbers for any of these boxes without knowing your monthly habits.

So, take a shoe box and clearly mark 'budget box' on the cover. For a period of two or three months, track your income and expenses. Whatever receipts, bills, salary slips and credit card statements you receive, throw them into the box. At the end of the period, classify the receipts, bills, slips and statements into these categories.

For some of you doing this the first time, you might be shocked to realise that you had spent more on shoes in one month than on food bills. Aha! Now you know where your money truly went. And you had thought, like I used to, that the money went only to life's necessities! The painful, awful truth of how we have spent often comes out when we analyse our monthly expenditure.

Fixed expenses

Fixed expenses are pretty much the same amount every month. They include loan payments, insurance premiums, rental payments and taxes. These are probably the most difficult to cut. But if these expenses are burning a major hole in your pocket, you need to think about how to reduce your loan payments, perhaps by switching to a smaller car or downgrading to a smaller home.

Some years ago, a former colleague, Damien, asked to meet me. Over tea, he asked for a personal loan. His brother had refused to help him, he said. Damien wanted to borrow $5,000 to pay off his credit card debts which the bank was about to close in on. I was surprised. Damien and his family always looked so well-put together. He looked really desperate. I do not like lending money to anyone. But I liked Damien, his wife and his kid daughter. So I told him I would think about it.

The next day, I gave him a conditional 'yes'. The condition was that he let me help him plan his finances. He agreed. I wrote out a cheque for $5,000 and we fixed a meeting for the following week. Cheque in hand, Damien rushed off to pay his credit card bills.

When we worked through his expenses a week later, he told me that his wife was a homemaker and that he had just bought her a cute, metallic pink car to zip around in. Looking at his budget, I knew there was no way he would be able to balance the monies—one income, a beautiful wife, one lovely daughter, coordinated outfits, designer shirts and a cute, metallic pink car.

How did I know so quickly? By benchmarking his expenses to my own budgets through the years. I would have never bought a car if I was earning $7,000 per month with two dependants and a housing loan. After CPF (Central Provident Fund) deductions and tax deductions, he brought home slightly more than $5,000 per month.

Paying $700 for the car loan, and adding in petrol, road tax and maintenance, Damien had to set aside $1,000 every month just for the car, leaving about $4,000 every month. Four thousand dollars is a lot of money and can support families if they did not eat out, drink Starbucks coffee or dress so beautifully. For Damien, $4,000 was not enough. His lifestyle required him to earn close to $10,000 a month for it to be sustainable.

The great thing about Damien was that he repaid me. I don't know how he did it. He must have really tightened up expenses. Till today, I think he should not have bought a brand new car and committed to such a high car loan payout every month.

If you think your monthly cash flow is tight, look over your budget carefully. Look especially into the area called Fixed Expenses and ask if you have over-committed.

Required expenses

These are expenses for 'must-haves' or necessities, and they include food, clothing, transport and utilities. While their amount varies month to month, they tend to be quite predictable.

Discretionary expenses

These are the 'nice-to-have' expenses such as buying a pair of shoes you don't really need but must have, eating at nice restaurants and going for vacations.

Your Financial Independence Account

At the start of this discussion on budgeting, I said that there is a way of budgeting where you can spend like crazy. Look at Table 5.1 again. If you are to be financially independent, B1 IS THE MOST IMPORTANT PART OF YOUR BUDGET TO FOCUS ON.

Pay Yourself First

To make B1 happen effortlessly, create IMMEDIATE and AUTOMATIC deductions from your pay cheque every month on the day after you are paid. By setting aside a sum of money for your future, you can then spend whatever is left and not be neglecting your long-term financial goals.

Your B1 Financial Independence Account must come *before* expenses, and it must be budgeted in. It is too important to leave to chance. Some people think that they will save what they can for old age after current day expenses. In fact, they should start by saving first for their future self, and then look at the remainder as the cash left for today's spending.

When I was in my early twenties, I did not think about saving for my retirement. I only picked up on this later after my son was born. It is the rate and extent that you increase B1 that separate the financially free from those who will have to work all the way into their old age. I was able to increase my B1 account quite aggressively once I realised this, and then earned my financial freedom thanks to some investment decisions that were spot on.

Let's now discuss how to set up this B1 account.

Open A 'Pay Yourself' Account

Ensure you put in place your B1 Financial Independence Account. You can call it the Pay Yourself Account or your Freedom Account. To get on your way, start NOW.

- Go to the bank at the very next available timeslot you have. Open a new account. This is now your Financial Independence Account.

- Limit the access to that account. No cheque books. No ATM cards. Only over-the-counter withdrawals are to be allowed.

- Make it difficult to go to this bank. Choose a reputable bank with very few branches so it is a big hassle to get to the bank to withdraw money.

- Authorise the bank to Auto-GIRO an amount from your other 'everyday' account to this Financial Independence Account. (GIRO is money-transfer from one bank account to another, whether for the same or different payer-payee. The word 'giro' traces back to the Italian word for 'circulation'.)

Recognise Time As A Reality

If you think it is easy to be financially independent and you can do it anytime, ask yourself this: How long will it take me to save six months of salary if I save 10 per cent of my salary every month? The answer is 60 months or five years!

In other words, it takes time to achieve your financial goals. It requires diligence and self-discipline. It is, however, not impossible. But the longer you put it off, the worse off you are.

The good thing is that once we make up our minds to do something, we can somehow squeeze to make it happen. The difficulty is getting motivated sufficiently to start, and to start as soon as possible. Just as you cannot stop bad habits overnight, you cannot start good habits overnight. Avoid the smoker's mentality. If you have a friend who chain-smokes, you might have heard her say, "I can stop anytime." Of course, she never does stop and two years down, you are still breathing her cigarette puffs as you try to have a conversation with her.

The trick to doing anything important is to start NOW. This is the moment. START NOW. Get your budget together and your Financial Independence Account up and running. Then weather the toughness of making it a habit of keeping to the budget every day for a period of 30 days at least. Watch your new behaviour or attitude take root as a good habit. You are on your way to becoming rich.

Beware Pay Day Habits

Someone once said this: "The difference between the Rich and the Poor is what they do on pay day."

By 'rich', we mean those who are financially independent. When we say 'poor', we mean those who have to work for a long while yet, and possibly to the day they die. Sorry about this very harsh but true statement.

What the Poor Do on Their Pay Day

On pay day, the poor celebrate being paid. They dine out at a nice restaurant with their friends or family, or they buy the pair of shoes they have been eyeing since the 15th of the previous month. They then walk into their favourite boutique and buy the newest designed blouse. They tell themselves that they feel good with their purchases and that they deserve to shop because they have worked so hard.

What the Rich Do on Their Pay Day

On pay day, the rich put aside a sum of their money for investment. They carefully divide up their pay cheque into what should be spent and what should be saved or invested. Depending on their age and their family requirements, they might save between 10 to 30 per cent of their salary.

In other words, the poor buy stuff. *The rich buy income generating assets.* In fact, the rich transfer as much of their income as possible into income-producing assets. They continue to do this until the income from their assets alone is big enough for them to retire.

Beware Pay Day Loans

Retailers and product manufacturers have billions of dollars behind them to help you spend your tiny fortune on their products. This is an important realisation. The more you spend, the less you have, the more they have. It's not a coincidence that pay days and sale days often coincide.

A Budget To Spend Like Crazy

In the US, the insidious 'pay day' loan was introduced to help consumers extend their buying power. Repayments are scheduled for the following pay day with only the interest deemed payable. Over time, the consumer would have signed on several of these loans and would use all his pay servicing interest payments on pay day. The pay day loan sucks the poor person dry, all on the happy marketing promise, "Don't worry. You can pay us on your next pay day."

These loans are available through non-bank channels and are known by fancy brand names. Their advertisements are brightly coloured and most friendly. They make you feel like they are big brother helping you to achieve the small pleasures in life. Bombarding you with their attractive mail marketing and offers, they make you think you need those extra few thousand dollars for that new wardrobe or kitchen sink, presents for the boyfriend, your sister's wedding, your mother's 60th birthday and so on, without realising that the small, insignificant loan is the beginning of a horrible downward spiral.

> On pay day, the rich put aside some money for investment. The poor buy stuff. Which are you?

The loan amounts offered are small. They do not need to be large. If you and many others pay high interest on small loans indefinitely, the company will do extremely well. In fact, these companies do *not* want full repayment from you. Please just service the interest. Every month. A bit at a time.

We write more about these personal loans in Chapter 8 on Personal Borrowings and Debt. If you have such loans, turn to that chapter straightaway. We need to convince you what a slippery slope you have placed yourself on and that you need to get off fast!

Worse than these pay day loans are the increasing number of small, white signs I see stuck near shopping malls in Singapore and Malaysia with the words "Professional Financial Services" on them. These pieces of laminated A4 papers are tied to any form of metal railing near the malls. I shudder. Loan sharks have now climbed on-board to fuel wild spending and consumerism! We return to this topic on page 116.

Choose To Be Rich

Human psychology is strange. People buy emotionally and justify logically. Research shows that humans do that—they save $20 and they spend $40 in their elation that they had saved $20.

If you take away nothing else from this book other than the following two sentences, the book would have been worth your money spent.

- Stop shopping for things that make you poorer.

- Choose to buy financial products with returns that make you richer each year.

If out of ten shopping decisions you make, you change two of them, this means that about 20 per cent of your disposable income is now earmarked for investment. In other words, choose to stop spending. CHOOSE TO INVEST. CHOOSE TO BE RICH.

> Each time you decide to spend or buy anything other than a financial product,
> **STOP TO CHOOSE.**
> Choose between buying there and then ...
> and your future.

6 The 'I Am Rich' Number

Life Goals

One of the most important financial awakenings a person can have is when she realises how much money she needs to continue living for the rest of her life without working.

When I realised that I can be as happy retired in a developing country, living by the beach, I started to make mental notes of what it would take to achieve my retirement dream. In 1998, I found out that I needed less than S$100,000 to buy a small, 60-year leasehold house in Bali with leftover funds to live a quiet life with my books and the Internet. From that point on, it became glaringly clear to me that financial freedom was predicated on the lifestyle choices we make.

The most important task is for us to choose what we want for our lives. First, set our life goals. Then, with that clarity, work backwards from those goals to make them happen. Some examples of life goals:

- Live life in easy style by the beach on an island such as Bali.

- Have enough money to go shopping in Europe three times a year without concern or worry about money.

- Have a happy family in a nice suburban home.

- Own and run a $300-million-turnover company.

So When Can I Retire?

You may ask yourself, "So when can I retire?" You can retire when what you have equals what you need to retire in the lifestyle of your choice. What you *need* to retire in the lifestyle of your choice is called your Financial Independence Number or your Magic Number or what I like to call, your 'I Am Rich' Number. What you *have* is called your Net Worth.

You can retire when your Net Worth equals your 'I Am Rich' Number. When you reach that number, you know you have enough stashed away to turn bohemian artist and hang out as you wish. You no longer have to fight tooth and nail with that back-stabbing colleague for the next promotion.

Life Expectancy And Your Retirement Years

How long you will live after you retire is a critical question. Imagine if you retired at 40, and you projected to live 20 years longer but ended up living 55 years longer. That would be horrible. You projected to live comfortably and die well. But instead the last 35 years of your life would be one of poverty and utter misery. No thanks!

Life expectancy tables show that where you are born and live makes a big difference to how long—and possibly how well—you live. According to the CIA World Factbook, Singaporeans have one of the highest life expectancies in the world. At birth, we are expected to live till 82 years old. Andorra has the highest life expectancy at 83.5 years. Many of the countries with the lowest life expectancies, namely Swaziland, Botswana and Zimbabwe, suffer from very high rates of HIV/AIDS infection of up to nearly 40 per cent of the population.

Our advice is that you should plan to live longer than expected. At your retirement, you should plan to have more money rather than less. Add medical bills to the lump sum. A health care industry expert told me that more than 80 per cent of a person's medical bills are spent in the last five years of his/her life! It was a shocking revelation.

The 'I Am Rich' Number

You can set life goals in terms of a sum of money paid to you monthly without your having to work. That sum can be $3,000, $6,000 or $12,000 a month in today's dollar terms, so that you can live the lifestyle corresponding to that income. This is your Desired Lifestyle Income Number.

The 'I Am Rich' Number is your Desired Lifestyle Income Number translated into a lump sum number today. It is also your Financial Independence Number. If you are worth this much today by way of your Net Worth, you can stop working today forever! We will explain net worth on the next page.

'I Am Rich' numbers are different for each of us because we have different needs. Let's use $10,000 per month as the magic number. Supposing you plan to retire at age 60 and you want to have $10,000 a month for the next 25 years till you are 85 when your bank account will be drawn down to zero. If you can park your money in an account that generates 3 per cent per annum, then you must have $2,114,036[1] at age 60 to make that happen. (See Table 6.1 below) If you wish to have a more lavish monthly expenditure of $25,000 for instance, you can multiply $2,114,036 by 2.5 to get $10,570,182.

Those who are wealthy can live off the interest generated by their investments alone, meaning that instead of drawing down on their capital sum to zero at death, their capital stays intact and they live off the interest generated. To do that at 3 per cent interest and drawing $10,000 a month or $120,000 a year, you would need to have set aside a total sum of $4 million! This is the 'I Am Super Rich Number'. I am working towards my 'I Am Super Rich Number'.

Table 6.1. How Much You Will Need in Your Retirement Years

Monthly Expenditure	Number of Years in Retirement				
	20	25	30	35	40
$1,000	180,762	211,404	237,782	260,491	280,040
$2,000	361,523	422,807	475,565	520,982	560,080
$3,000	542,285	634,211	713,347	781,473	840,120
$4,000	723,047	845,615	951,129	1,041,964	1,120,160
$5,000	903,808	1,057,018	1,188,912	1,302,455	1,400,201
$6,000	1,084,570	1,268,422	1,426,694	1,562,946	1,680,241
$7,000	1,285,332	1,479,826	1,664,476	1,823,437	1,960,281
$8,000	1,446,094	1,691,229	1,902,259	2,083,928	2,240,321
$9,000	1,626,855	1,902,633	2,140,041	2,344,419	2,520,361
$10,000	1,807,617	2,114,036	2,377,824	2,604,910	2,800,401

---

[1] This is based on a calculation called Present Value that your financial adviser should be able to perform easily for you based on your situation.

Net Worth

The net worth of a person in financial terms is the balance sheet view of her financial position. In a company, a balance sheet compares what a company owns (called assets) versus what it owes (called liabilities). Your net worth is the difference between what you own (your asests) and what you owe (your liabilities). Net worth tells you how rich or poor you are at a specific point in time.

If you own $5 million worth of assets and you owe the bank $3 million, then your net worth is $2 million. This means that if you were to pay off what you owe with what you own, you would be left with $2 million, whch is then your net worth. The balance sheet must comply with the following formula with assets on the left side and liabilities plus net worth on the right side:

Assets = Liabilities + Net Worth

To understand how the balance sheet works in practice, let's look at an example. Suppose you own the following assets:

C1	ASSETS		
	Cash	$100,000	
	Car	$200,000	
	Home	$600,000	
	Investments	$100,000	
	TOTAL ASSETS		$1,000,000
C2	LIABILITIES		
C2.1	Long-term liabilities: Housing loan Car loan	 $450,000 $150,000	
C2.2	Short-term liabilities: Credit card loan Personal loan	 $0 $0	
	TOTAL LIABILITIES		$600,000
C3 (C1 − C2)	NET WORTH		$400,000

By deducting your liabilities from your assets, you get a net worth of $400,000. This is the actual amount of money you will have if you were to pay off all your liabilities with your assets.

Your Net Worth Can Go Up and Down

To become and stay financially independent, it is your job to increase your net worth. Your net worth generally goes up when:

- The value of your assets goes up. For example, if the value of your home rises to $200,000, then your net worth rises by $200,000.

- You generate a positive balance after deducting your expenses from your earnings. If you earn $50,000 per annum and you auto-deduct $10,000 per annum to your freedom account, and you still somehow managed to save $5,000 after all your expenses, then your net worth that year would have increased by $15,000.

What goes up can also come down. There are many ways in which your net worth can drop, for example, when you dip into your savings to buy a $20,000 Alaskan cruise, when the value of your home falls by 30 per cent and when your car depreciates in value.

How Much Should You Be Worth?

Thomas Stanley and William Danko, authors of *The Millionaire Next Door*, propose this:

> Take your current pre-tax annual household income (include investment income but exclude inheritances). Multiply that by your age. Divide it by 10.

In other words, if your last drawn income is $60,000 per annum, and if you are 40 years old, you should be worth $240,000 ($60,000 × 40/10). The authors go on to say that people should try to double this expected amount. In other words, to be really well positioned as a "prodigious accumulator of wealth", you need to have twice this benchmark amount.

In Singapore, the general scarcity and correspondingly rising value of property throws this benchmark off. Because of the increased value of their properties, most people would easily meet this net worth benchmark through no effort of their own. The number is, therefore, only useful as an indicator. It does not say how financially free you are because if you need to move out of your property to release monetary value, you still need to live somewhere.

Another benchmark of being well off, used often in press reporting, is your net asset, excluding the home you live in. According to various reports in *The Straits Times* (2008), more than 77,000 people in Singapore are considered high net worth individuals because they have more than $1 million in net assets excluding the home they live in.

What the reports do not ask is whether the home people live in is paid for in full. For example, a person can be living in a $5 million home, leveraging a bank loan of $3.5 million while having 'net' assets of $1 million. In reality, the person has negative net worth compared with a person who owns her home in full without mortgage, and has a bank balance of $300,000.

> The magic numbers for financial independence are the 'I Am Rich' and Net Worth Numbers. Finding out these numbers is just mathematics. Realising those numbers takes discipline.

Achieving 'I Am Rich'

How can you achieve the 'I Am Rich' Number? There are no short cuts. You need to:

- Develop an investment road map and follow it. We will cover this in Part Four.

- Find a role model. The fastest way to achieve the kind of success of someone we admire is to study the person and ask how that person became successful. We then emulate the methods in so far as possible while inventing our own solutions to new problems along the way. My friend Frederic understood role-modelling in his twenties. He started studying the habits of the old tycoons of Asia immediately after leaving university. I think his net worth today is close to between $30 and $50 million.

Unfortunately, most schools do not teach this to youths. We leave school thinking that we will figure it all out ourselves, or we somehow muddle through without clarity of goal or purpose.

OVER TO YOU

Now it's your turn to find out how much you will need to achieve your life goals. Using the charts on the next page, answer the questions below. Take your time to fill up the charts.

1. I will need $_____ per month to retire. Based on inflation and bank interest rates alone, I will need $_____ in my retirement account or as net worth to retire.

2. Using Stanley and Danko's model, how much should I be worth today? How much am I *really* worth today?

You need to ask yourself: How much of my present net worth is due to property appreciation of the home I am staying in? Since you need to stay on in a property after retirement, you need to calculate net worth, net of the property you are residing in, to give you an idea of how much cash you have managed to stash aside for retirement.

What is your current Net Worth?
What is your 'I Am Rich Number'?
What is your plan to become 'I Am Rich'?

Chart 1: How Much Should I Be Worth?

How Much Should I Be Worth?		$
My annual salary (Income before tax)	A1	
My annual investment (Income before tax)	A2	
My Total Income Before Tax	B	
My age	C	
My Total Income Before Tax × My Age	B × C = D	
My 'Should Be' Net Worth (according to Stanley and Danko) is: My total income before tax × my age/10	D/10	

Chart 2: How Much I Am Worth

My Present Net Worth		$
My Assets		
House or apartment at market value		
Investments (stocks or bonds)		
Bank accounts and insurance, if drawn		
Car		
Other Assets: for e.g. jewellery at resale price		
Total Assets	A	
My Liabilities		
Housing loan		
Bank loan		
Car loan		
Other loans		
Total Liabilities	B	
Net Worth	A − B	

7 The Disappearing Dollar And The Magic Of Risk

Why can't you do nothing? Why can't you just sit still with a pile of money saved in the bank? We can, and indeed, sometimes we should, for instance in highly uncertain periods when the investment market has gone erratic. The Asian currency crisis of 1998 was one such period. The 2008 global market crisis is another.

Over any other period when investment markets are functioning well, we need to remember that putting the money in the bank has an undesired effect. Money tends to diminish in value over time because of inflation. Here's how and why.

The Evils Of Inflation And The Diminishing Dollar

Inflation says that the price of everything goes up over time. Whenever I take Aunt Penny to her favourite noodle shop in Singapore, she will say it used to cost 10 cents a plate when she was in her teens. At the time of my writing this book, Aunt Penny is 85 years old and it pains her to fork out $3 each time.

If one were to calculate the rate of inflation of a plate of fried noodles according to Aunt Penny's estimates, then inflation would be 5 per cent over 70 years. No wonder Aunt Penny is upset; the 10 cents she has today won't buy even one fried cockle from the stall.

The crux of the matter is this. Money loses its buying power over time due to inflation. The only time to be rich in cash and low in investments is when the market is unpredictable.

Let's look at another example of inflation. Suppose you have $100,000 in a fixed deposit that you want to use for your retirement in 30 years' time. If we were to take 3 per cent as the rate of inflation we would expect going forward (Singapore's inflation rate has been less than 3 per cent on average over the past 40 years), how much is your $100,000 going to buy you in 30 years' time? The answer is $41,199, almost a 60 per cent drop in value. See the table below.

Table 7.1. What Your Money is Worth

Time	What Your Money is Worth in Future at 3% Inflation Per Year					
Today	$20,000	$40,000	$60,000	$80,000	$100,000	$120,000
+10 years	$14,882	$29,764	$44,646	$59,528	$74,409	$89,291
+20 years	$11,074	$22,147	$33,221	$44,294	$55,368	$66,441
+30 years	$8,240	$16,479	$24,719	$32,959	$41,199	$49,438
+40 years	$6,131	$12,262	$18,393	$24,525	$30,656	$36,787
+50 years	$4,562	$9,124	$13,686	$18,249	$22,811	$27,373

Inflation itself is not a bad thing if it is stable, low and predictable. Most countries, such as Singapore, try to maintain an inflation rate of 2–3 per cent per year. If you do not know what your local inflation rate is, find out. Google it. In anomaly cases, some countries experience high double-digit inflation rates. Beyond personal finance issues, high inflation can create economic chaos. Businesses find it hard to plan and price in such economies.

As you can see, inflation is why making your money work for you is so critical. Inflation means that even if you did nothing but put your money under your mattress, you will be able to buy fewer and fewer things with the money you have.

Inflation is the reason you MUST learn to invest, besides budgeting and getting your net worth together. You need to look for places to invest in, and at the very least, park your money in some place that gives you rates of return that are greater than the rate of inflation.

Money loses its buying power over time because of inflation. The only time to be rich in cash and low in investments are in times when the market is unpredictable.

The Effect Of Inflation On Nominal And Real Interest Rates

There are tons of material written on the topic of nominal and real interest rates. It is important for you to know the difference between them because of inflation.

Suppose you went to the bank at the beginning of the year to deposit $10,000 at a fixed deposit rate of 3.5 per cent interest per annum. You were quite happy about it, thinking that you would get $350 at the end of the year in interest. You told yourself that you would buy a nice handbag with the $350 or take a holiday in Phuket that was advertised for $350.

At the end of the year, you take your $10,000 out from the bank and the $350 interest accumulated. You go shopping with the $350. To your surprise, the $350 trip to Phuket now costs $367.50 and the handbag you have been eyeing now also costs $367.50. You now cannot buy either without eating into your base capital of $10,000.

What happened? You rang up your friend in the financial services industry. She explained that in the last one year, inflation was super high at 5 per cent instead of the usual 2 per cent. She said that the raised prices were because of inflation and not because the retailers were making higher profits.

In this one incident, you learnt two things:

- The interest rate that you received from the bank before factoring inflation is the *nominal* rate.

- The *real* interest rate for your deposited money was -1.5 per cent (3.5% − 5% = -1.5%).

Inflation had chomped up your earnings from the fixed deposit and the interest you earned was, in fact, insufficient to cover the rise in prices. You have lost value on your capital sum of $10,000 by putting it in a bank account with a fixed interest rate that did not track inflation rates.

In countries where inflation goes up by double digits, people find it difficult to comprehend savings and investment since the investment vehicles themselves (companies and businesses) cannot plan progress. Capital flight, when money and assets rapidly flow out of an economy, and black market currencies happen in these unstable monetary regimes.

So, How Big A Stash Do I Need To Retire?

Let's go back to what we covered in the last chapter. What is your 'I Am Rich' Number, taking into account inflation? Or, "how much money must I have before I stop working completely?"

This is the most basic investment question and target that anyone has to ask and know the answer to. In other words, given expected inflation rates and the safest place to park money, how much do you need to have before you can retire?

Suppose that you are 55 years old today and you want to retire with $5,000 every month. You believe that your savings can earn you a rate of return of 2 per cent after inflation. How much will you need for a retirement period of 35 years till you are 90 years old? According to our calculations, you would need $1.5 million[1]. (See Table 7.2.)

Whether you will need $5,000 or $2,000 a month at retirement to accommodate your desired lifestyle is for you to decide. You may want to consider the type of vacations you want to take, the medical care you need and the insurance policies you have. If you need help doing this, consider the services of a certified financial adviser.

Table 7.2. Amount of Money Needed to Retire

Monthly Allowance	Year in Retirement								
	10	15	20	25	30	35	40	45	50
1,000	108,680	155,398	197,930	235,930	270,549	301,875	330,223	355,875	379,089
2,000	217,360	310,795	395,348	471,860	541,097	603,750	660,416	711,751	758,177
5,000	543,399	776,980	988,370	1,179,651	1,352,743	1,509,376	1,651,115	1,779,377	1,895,443
10,000	1,086,788	1,553,981	1,976,740	2,359,301	2,705,485	3,018,752	3,302,230	3,558,754	3,790,885
15,000	1,630,196	2,330,961	2,965,111	3,538,952	4,058,228	4,528,127	4,953,345	5,338,131	5,686,328
20,000	2,173,595	3,107,961	3,953,481	4,718,602	5,410,970	6,037,503	6,604,461	7,117,508	7,581,770

[1] This is based on a calculation called Present Value that your financial adviser should easily be able to perform for you based on your situation.

Investment Risk And The Possibility Of Earning (And Losing) Money

Risk in the financial textbook is a measure of the potential fluctuation in price of the investment instrument you have bought, or the potential fluctuation in earnings. While most people think of risk as the possibility of losing money on the original investment, risk is also the POSSIBILITY OF EARNING money. This is an important clarification.

Most people run away when they hear that an investment or a venture is risky. But for those who understand and who can also find ways to manage the risk exposure in any specific investment, their eyes will brighten up and they ask, "Where is this risky venture that I should look at?" In other words, when you hear the word 'risk', you should see the words 'an investment opportunity to make a profit, as well as a loss, with the need for risk management'.

The Return on Your Investment

When you make an investment, your gain or loss is called the return on your investment. For example, when you buy an investment for $10 that pays a 50-cent dividend (this is a portion of a company's profits that is paid to a shareholder), and you sell it for $12 one year later, the $2.50 gain is your return. If you sell the investment for $9 instead, you will have suffered a $0.50-cent loss after netting off the $0.50 cents dividend income.

The Risk-Return Trade-Off

One of the most fundamental assumptions in the investing world is the risk-return trade-off. It works on the premise that any investor who bears a higher risk should be rewarded with better returns, that is, he should be compensated for bearing that additional degree of risk.

The risk-return trade-off could simply be called the 'ability-to-sleep-at-night' test. While some people can handle the equivalent of financial bungee jumping without breaking out into a sweat, others are terrified to climb a six-foot ladder without a secure harness. Deciding what amount of risk you can take while remaining comfortable with your investments is one of the keys to investing successfully. So,

- Lower levels of uncertainty or risk are associated with lower potential returns.

- Higher levels of uncertainty or risk are associated with higher potential returns.

Put another way, the general rule is that the higher the expected return on any investment, the higher the risk. The word 'expected' is an important word. It means that you can expect it, but it may *not* happen. Financial analysts spend years in schools and in financial sweatshops (the backrooms of investment houses) looking at risk-returns and constructing baskets of investments that will give the optimal expected return against identified risk.

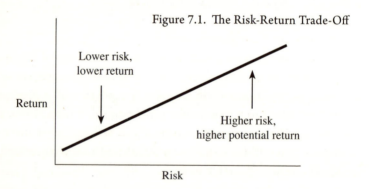

Figure 7.1. The Risk-Return Trade-Off

Why does this equation hold? Let's explain with an example. A Singapore government bond is considered to be a very safe investment. So when the Singapore government issues a bond, it is asking: "Will you lend me some money?" Because of how secure Singapore is, the government does not need to promise a high return for the money you lend it, unlike the case for a developing country or an emerging economy that issues bonds. The market views the two bonds and believes that Singapore is more likely to pay out the promised interest rate as well as buy back the bonds on the maturity date. Singapore needs only to promise a low rate of return then for its bonds. To put it another way, any fixed interest rate bonds sold by Singapore would fetch a higher price than other fixed interest rate bonds sold by some emerging economies.

How Much Control?

Every investment carries risk with controllable and non-controllable items. A good investor identifies these upfront and has a strategy to deal with the 'unexpected'. That strategy when executed is called risk management. Companies and banks, in particular, pay risk managers big salaries to identify and manage risks.

The degree of control you want in any investment is important. If you want absolute control, you might start your own business. All businesses, however, face risks that are both controllable and non-controllable. *The extent to which you can manage risks will be your key to success.*

Say you own a gourmet coffee stall. Overnight your customers have fallen for bubble tea, a strange concoction containing gelatinous tapioca pearls. Now, that sort of a market risk is not predictable as the consumer market changes all the time. As the owner of the stall, you might decide to offer bubble tea to soften the impact on your business. But to your shock, you find that instead of the market responding to your initiative and flocking to your stall for the choices offered— bubble tea and gourmet coffee—the market rejects you. Your old customers have decided that you have 'sold out' to new fangled drinks and new customers see you as just a copycat. In business, you cannot predict outcomes or market responses.

Warren Buffet invests in companies where he can have a say on how the company is being steered for the future. His stakes are usually strategic with a board seat. Most of us do not fall into that category. Some of us, however, are investors in a friend's business or a private company where we have some say on how the business is run.

You will have no control, however, if you invest in a public company either directly or through a fund or unit trust. But if you manage your portfolio yourself, you have control over which companies you want in the portfolio. If you invest through a fund or unit trust, you are not able to choose the companies you want to invest in. The professional fund manager does that for you. You can only decide whether or not you wish to pull your money out completely from the fund.

To summarise, here are the main types of investments, beginning with the type where you have the least degree of control:

- Managed portfolios/unit trusts looked after by a professional fund manager.

- Self-managed/self-constructed portfolios.

- Strategic and significant investor.

- Business owner.

Investment Philosophies

As an investor, you should develop your own investment philosophy and stick closely to it. You do not want to be shifting from strategy to strategy based on a strong sales pitch or recent business cycle upturns. With a strong sense of core beliefs, you will have far more control. Otherwise, your portfolio will be a group of unrelated assets that you will find very difficult to manage.

Most people gravitate towards one of these five main investment strategies—Value Investing, Growth Investing, Index Investing, Technical Investing and Portfolio Investing. Let's use stock XYZ to help illustrate what these investment strategies mean. Suppose it closed yesterday on the exchange at $10.00 per share. How you analyse whether there is an opportunity depends on your investment strategy.

Value Investing

The most famous investor in the world, Warren Buffet, is a value investor. To the value investor, value and price are different. Value investors first assess the value of XYZ by forecasting cash flows and examining fundamental information, such as financial reports, and analysing the industry. They then compare what they assess as being the stock's intrinsic or actual value with its market price. The value investor may buy the stock if it is valued at say, $12.50 or more. The $2.50 difference between value and price indicates a 25 per cent 'margin of safety' ($2.50/$10.00). A more conservative value investor would insist on an even larger margin, such as 30 per cent.

Growth Investing
Peter Lynch, former Magellan fund manager in the 1980s, was one of the most famous growth investors of all time. Growth investors seek companies whose earnings potential promises to boost intrinsic value rapidly. They would buy stock XYZ if they believe its value and price will grow by $3.00 in the near future.

Index Investing
John Bogle, founder of The Vanguard Group, one of the world's largest fund groups, popularised index investing in the 1980s. Index investors buy shares that replicate a large market segment such as the Straits Times Index. Index investors are not sure they can figure out the relationship between value and price, and so believe that the best and safest strategy is to buy stocks representing substantially the whole market. As such, index investors wouldn't be interested in XYZ unless it forms part of a portfolio that is invested broadly across the whole market. No special skill or homework is required. Returns will reflect overall index performance rather than that of selected stocks.

Technical Investing
Technical investors use mathematical indicators and charts to study market price data to look for imbalances in supply and demand. They care little for fundamental data such as earnings and cash flow. Technical investors care only about price, not value. They would be interested in XYZ if technical indicators and trend lines show its stock price is headed for a bullish run. Technical investment is often seen as speculation, not investment.

Portfolio Investing

Portfolio investors determine their appetite for investment risk and then create a diversified investment portfolio that supports that risk level. Portfolio investing won its backers the Nobel Prize in economics in the 1970s. Portfolio investors pay less attention to the difference between price and value. Instead, they believe that price changes reflect risk and that investors should pick a mix of securities bearing the desired risk level. To portfolio investors, the important question is whether XYZ's risk suits an investor's risk profile and how the stock would complement the risk in a diversified portfolio.

The emphasis of this book is on PORTFOLIO INVESTING, and how to combine assets in a portfolio that minimises risk and maximises returns, according to your risk profile and financial objectives.

For myself, I use a combination of strategies while ensuring that my risk is contained overall in my portfolio. The 3-baskets approach that you will read about in Part Four is precisely what I do. I do like risk and I do like some fun when I invest. Sticking to one method only would be unexciting for me. However, if you are new to investing, I strongly suggest you stick to the portfolio strategy for now.

Using your Start State and your Desired State, and the time frame that you have from now to achieve your Desired State, you need to design your investment strategy based on your risk profile.

> When you start to invest, it's important to determine your end-game or what we call in Part One of this book, your Desired State. You will need to ask yourself:
> What kind of risk profile do I have?
> Am I a risk-fearing or a risk-loving investor?
> Based on my risk profile, what type of investments should I invest in?
> How much do I have to invest each month?
> How much do I want per month in retirement?

Part Three
Personal Financial Products

Back To Basics
The simplest yet most comprehensive financial advice I know are:
- Learn to live within your means.

- Invest your savings wisely.

- Protect yourself against the unforeseen.

These three points are the basis for Parts Three and Four.

Products With Different Functions
There are only a few basic categories of personal financial products in the market but myriad variations. Each product is designed to satisfy different consumer needs. Many have bells and whistles attached, for example, free gifts and personal services. Some products even provide personal concierge services including helping you to remember the birthdays of your loved ones!

We cannot describe or compare all the financial products on offer. We advise that you do your homework with the banks. Shop around for financial products and do not simply accept what is generally used. If you are still with the same bank your parents set up your first bank account with the little Donald Duck piggy-bank, it is time for you to check out if other banks have better products to offer. It is also time for you to UNDERSTAND the terms accompanying the various products.

Financial products serve a few functions. These are are listed in the table opposite. We will not explain Savings or Current Accounts in this book as you already know what they are, but we will describe the rest. As you can see, the credit card can be used both as a payment product as well as a loan product. Using it to make payment is a very convenient way to shop. Using it to borrow money from the bank is another story. We will talk about this in the next chapter.

Insurance products tend to have investment characteristics. The reverse is also true; some investment products have insurance linked to them.

We have classified investment products separately from personal financial products and discuss them in Part Four. Anyone with a healthy financial profile needs personal financial products to function in life. Investment products are the icing on the cake. They come in only after a person has sorted out how to use personal financial products well.

Financial Products and Their Functions

Product	Function	Reference in This Book
Savings account	Save or store	PERSONAL FINANCIAL PRODUCTS (covered in Part Three) These products are for your present day and day-to-day needs.
• Current account • Credit card	Make payments	
• Credit card • Car loan • Personal loan • Mortgage • Other types of exotic loans, eg., from pawnshops or loan sharks, personal loans, and pay day loans	Borrow or loan	
Insurance • Term • Life • Acccident • Health (and long term) • Investment linked	Protect	
Investment	Grow	INVESTMENT PRODUCTS (covered in Part Four) These products are for your future needs.

8 Personal Borrowings And Debt

Do you know anyone who is debt free? There are different definitions of being debt free, ranging from being 'credit card' debt free to being absolutely debt free with no car or housing loan to service. What I mean is 100 per cent completely debt free.

Can I Afford To Borrow?

Just about everyone we know owes the bank or someone money. Being completely debt free is not necessarily the ideal financial state to be in, although during any financial crisis being debt free is empowering.

In the midst of the 2008 credit crunch when bank lending rates started to climb, home owners with large mortgages began to worry. I remember the 1980s when mortgage rates climbed to about 12 per cent. As a young executive working in Singapore Airlines then, I saw how worried and anxious some of my older colleagues were over their housing loans.

Let's now look at some macro indicators for debt. According to US statistics, the average American is rather prone to debt.

- Of the 70 per cent of homeowners who currently have a mortgage, 22 per cent also carry either a second mortgage or a home equity loan.

- The average American spends roughly 10 per cent more than what he/she earns per year.

- Although 40 per cent of credit card users pay off their balance in full each month, 60 per cent carry a balance of between US$12,000 and US$14,000.

- Almost 90 per cent of couples who divorce say arguments over finances were a significant factor for ending their marriage.

It can be seen from the US numbers that owing money may appear to become a way of life the more developed an economy gets. Therefore, it is important that we understand how to *owe money smartly*, and not let 'stupid debt' jeopardise our plans for financial independence.

When women shop, it seems we always encounter salesgirls who are trained to say: "Go on, you can afford it. You worked hard for it. Reward yourself. Spoil yourself a little. You look so nice in it." At almost every other shop, salesgirls mouth these words. And the words work like magic on women. Out pops our credit card from the wallet. Then it's swiped and signed. You are some tens or hundreds of dollars poorer because you can afford it and you look nice in it.

The salesgirls never ever say: "Go on, you can afford to borrow to buy this. You can always work very hard to pay off your credit card loan. It doesn't matter if your loan makes you a slave to your job indefinitely. Looking nice is more important." They never ever tell you the truth.

Borrowing costs money. People know this, but they don't take it seriously. They have a tendency to borrow too much, without being able to repay it in a timely fashion. This gets them into a lot of financial trouble. How so?

- They could end up using a lot of their income each month towards paying off interest. When they can't save, they cannot make progress towards financial independence. They end up servicing debt payments for items bought a long time ago which have little or no value left. They have little left to buy more useful things with investment value that is for their future.

- They may not even be able to pay what is required of them. As a result, they might go into default on their obligation. At this point, they may lose the collateral for their loan (for example, their car may be repossessed due to missed payments). They may be sued by credit card companies or other lenders. They may even be forced into bankruptcy, a court-supervised process of settling your debts with existing assets. Bankruptcy can stain a person's financial record for many years.

THE COST OF MONEY

If someone merrily 'lends' you money, you must ask questions regarding the cost of that money. What are the costs? Are they hidden?

If it was a loved one lending you money, the cost of lending to you is potentially the relationship, should you not return the loan. I have lost good friends this way. They disappeared fast after I lent them the money. Phone calls are not returned. The friendship is gone. It is a horrible thing. I dread the words: "May I ask you a personal favour?"

In the money world, everything is measurable. The simplest way to understand the cost of money is to ask the cost of using money TODAY versus using money tomorrow.

A second generation tycoon told me how his Shanghainese mother would, in his youth, give him pocket money every month. For every dollar that he saved rather than spent, she would double that dollar for him in his savings account. He was not allowed to withdraw the funds for use. He quickly learnt the power of savings from an early age. His mother programmed it into him. Today he owns a well known chain of retail stores in Asia. Most of us do not have such far-sighted parents. The only people who would pay us to consume tomorrow rather than today are the people behind investment products!

Let me offer you two new ways to think about debt. One, unless you are borrowing the money to improve your personal wealth situation tomorrow, you are using someone's money to pay for something that you probably don't need, today. Someone will make you pay for it, whether immediately or in the future.

There is always a cost to debt or anyone giving you money. The only exception is money from parents to children. It does not matter what the lender, close friends included, says to you. Look out for that cost. The lender is forgoing her opportunity to enjoy her money today. There must be compensation for the 'sacrifice'. Interest is the price of her having to wait to enjoy her money that she lent to you.

Two, when you borrow, you are asking your future self to pay off that loan. In so doing, you are depriving your future self of the sum of money you are spending today. Plus you are making your future self pay for the associated borrowing costs.

In my view, there is nothing in any shopping mall anywhere in the world to justify credit card debt. There is also no service, other than medical services, that anyone can sell to me to justify my owing a credit card company or taking a personal loan to finance the service.

> Smart debt is any debt that makes your future self richer. Stupid debt is any debt that makes your future self poorer.

Money is not free. It is never free. I repeat, *for every borrowed dollar today, you are asking your future self to pay for the dollar borrowed plus borrowing costs.* So unless that dollar grows money for you, you are making your future self poorer with your debt. Since money is not free, what is the cost of debt? What sort of debt do you have? Are they good (smart) debts or bad (stupid) debts?

Now let's go back to basics to understand debt.

Types Of Personal Debt

The following are personal debt choices that are available in the market today:

- Credit card loans.

- Car loans and housing loans.

- Small personal loans ('easy' credit products from non-bank institutions such as finance and credit card companies).

- Loans from pawn shops and loan sharks.

- Friendship loans.

CREDIT CARD LOANS

Credit card loans are unsecured loans. The lender, usually a bank, expects a percentage of borrowers to default on their payments. In order to make a profit, the cost of lending to you must, therefore, be commensurate with the risk of default.

However, despite credit card interest rates being high, there are always plenty of borrowers! In the US, credit card debt is at all time highs. In Singapore, the credit card is acknowledged to be a potential financial hazard for families, and credit card debt is closely monitored by the government. Thankfully, it is said, Singapore families predominantly still only use the credit card as a payment instrument, rather than a debt instrument.

The most alarming financial news I heard in 2008 was that small businesses in the US that were facing borrowing difficulties in the credit crunch were opting to borrow on their owners' credit cards. My goodness! I don't know many businesses that can give a total of 24–30 per cent return on equity or investment to cover the cost of a credit card loan. I am cringing at the interest rate pain these business owners face. If they cannot borrow at business loan rates and things are so bad, some fundamental business questions must be asked. Should the business continue?

Borrowing on credit cards to cover a business' shortfall is a death knell. Businesses cannot run that fast in a downward economy to cover the cost of such funds.

Do we stop to ask: Can I afford to borrow to buy this item?

The credit card is an incredibly stupid way to borrow money. Let me repeat this— *the credit card is an incredibly stupid way to borrow money*. Table 8.1 opposite shows the interest rates of various consumer loan products. The credit card is by far the highest, and by four times. The only other more stupid way to borrow money is to borrow from a loan shark, which is illegal in the first place.

Table 8.1. Loans and Their Corresponding Interest Rate

Consumer Loan	Annual Interest Rate
Neighbourhood loan shark	1,200–2,400% (about 10–20% a month)
Credit card loan	24% *
5-year car loan	6%
15-year mortgage loan	6–7% **

The word 'stupid' is a very strong word. And people who borrow using credit cards are incredibly stupid especially if they have not exhausted other borrowing means. So while I should apologise for calling some of you 'stupid', how else can I stress your folly to you if you have decked yourself with bling to party but face a pile of debt and private self-despair at the end of each month?

How do the card companies catch the unwary? What are some of the traps that people fall for?

Freebies Are Not Free! Beware the Rollover Debt
I used to teach life skills to youths at secondary schools. One of the lessons I tried to impart was the danger of credit card spending without control. The lessons helped the youths understand credit card interest and the impact of rolling debts. When the students did the calculations on rolled over payments, their eyes widened. Some began to realise why their parents were broke.

In one lesson, I asked them, "Credit card companies give away lots of freebies to sign up new cardholders! Ever wondered why? How many people in the world would give you a free X-Box, a free latest PDA, a free latest designer bag for NOTHING?"

---

*A check with HSBC, Maybank, OCBC, StanChart, UOB and DBS shows that they all charge 24 per cent per annum. **This was the rate at the end of 2007. It is a variable rate which typically changes based on a short-term rate called SIBOR (Singapore Interbank Offered Rate). Finance companies were also charging around this rate at the time for 15-year mortgage loans.

The answer to why credit card companies give away expensive gifts is rollover debt. They expect every so many customers to roll over their debt and not pay in full. One smart 15-year-old asked, "So how come people don't take the freebies and NOT use the card?"'

"You are a smart boy! Of course these people can," I replied. "But you know what? The day that most people end up not using the card after claiming the gifts, the credit card companies will change the claim conditions. They will say that the gifts can only be claimed after the first $10-purchase on the card."

These companies know that if someone spends $10 on the card, the same person will likely spend $50, and soon the credit card bill will pile up. They do not need all cardholders to roll over their debt. Only some. For those of you who do, interest will soon pile up to make the credit card product a hugely profitable business for the card issuing bank. It is only common sense.

There really is no free lunch. No free X-box. No free PDA or free anything. Anytime anything is free, someone somewhere is making money from someone else. Just ensure that they are not making money from you. If they are, stop your behaviour. Clean up your mistakes and move forward.

What Is Rollover Debt?

When you cannot pay your balance during the 'free credit' period, the balance is rolled over and is subject to interest charges.

In October 2007, there were about 5.5 million credit cards in circulation in Singapore and about S$3 billion in rolled over balances. At an interest rate of 24 per cent per year, these card holders are paying $720 million in interest every year. Assuming that each person owns about 2.5 cards, this means that the average interest paid per person is about $327. This excludes any principal repayment, and the penalty and late payment charge if the minimum sum is not paid.

Balance Transfer From One Card to Another
My friend Credit Card Paul had four credit cards. He withdrew cash from one credit card to pay off another, and transferred accounts from one credit card to another like musical chairs. Doing this is just not sustainable because no one is that rich to pay interest at 24 per cent per annum. Remember I said that a return of 20 per cent per annum is a fantastic return? Most excellent companies only hope to generate a consistent rate of return of between 8 and 15 per cent.

The simple lesson here is that if you are living a *borrowed lifestyle* through credit cards, the borrowings will catch up unless you have the means to repay, or a rich relative dies, or you strike it rich somehow. If you are thinking of getting another card to reduce your interest rate and to pay off your other credit card—STOP! Unless you change your buying behaviour, you will get to six credit cards before long. Becoming Credit Card Paul is so easy.

But isn't balance transfer a good deal?
But isn't it a good deal to transfer my credit card debt to another card that offers lower rates, you ask? You know those advertisements that tell you that if you transfer your outstanding balance from some credit card to THIS new credit card, you need only pay a significantly lower interest rate on the outstanding amount?

Instead of giving you the X-box and the PDA for a new account, all these advertisements ask of you is to get unstuck from high interest rates by transferring loans to lower interest rates. Wow! Doesn't it sound like a great deal?

The answer is yes, it looks like a good deal, it does look like you save some money on interest. But what are you doing, trying to save money on an extremely high interest rate debt product when that debt should never have been incurred in the first instance!

Let's go through an example now to show you your 'savings'. Say you have a balance of $10,000 with ABC Bank. You see a DEF Bank advertisement offering a balance transfer of 0 per cent interest for six months if you transfer your balance to them for a 2.5 per cent one-time processing fee. If you made the transfer, you would save $950 in interest payments over six months:

Balance transferred: $10,000
Interest payable with ABC @ 24% for 6 months: $1,200
Interest payable with DEF @ 0% for 6 months: $0
Processing fee of 2.5%: $250
Savings: $950 ($1,200 − $250)

So, what's the catch? These ads are targeting people who are *already in debt*. How *cheap* for them to sell this way! They know that the people who respond are people who are already in debt and do not have the financial discipline to clear those debts on a monthly basis. That is,

- After the initial savings in interest, you still owe the second credit card company at the same, high interest rate as before. Only this time, it is a different company you owe money to.

- The second credit card company is willing to offer you the 'savings' because it knows that after the six-month period, you will have to start paying 24 per cent interest on whatever new balance you have. It also knows that if you were a debt defaulter, it is unlikely that you would bother to make the debt transfer. People only bother to make transfers if they have some intention of paying, and if they still want the credit card and not be declared a bankrupt.

- The second company is pleased that you were tried and tested by the first credit card company. If you have not been sued into bankruptcy, it means that you have been dutifully servicing your interest payments and, therefore, you are a good customer!

- The second company also knows that if it raised the borrowing limit for you with a carrot to do so, you are likely to add to the amount borrowed. Soon your $10,000 loan will become a $15,000 loan. Soon you will be paying interest on the larger

$15,000 loan. All because you thought interest free for six months to do a transfer is a good deal!

The right question to ask is not whether the transfer is a good deal, but how many times can you do this? And if you did not have the discipline with the first credit card company to bring the debt balance to zero, what makes you think you will have the discipline with the second company?

How Many Cards do You Really Need?

You do not need ten credit cards from ten different banks! I have never had more than two credit cards. Why two? It is for the just-in-case when I travel and when one of the cards does not work for whatever reason. You need two different card brands as they use different processing hubs and separate networks. You do not want to be in Tokyo without access to funds when you need it.

Master the Card or it Will Master You

I love credit cards, not least because it's a neat way to carry money in my purse. While the credit card is a stupid way to borrow funds, it is one of the best and most convenient ways to make payment. I use my credit cards to make payments, never for taking out a loan. I pay all balances each time they are due. The amount is automatically deducted from my operating bank account to make the payment.

However, you must have self-control and you must understand the product. You need to find ways to master yourself. There are two types of people you need to be aware of in your relationship with your credit card—your 'buddy' and your 'enemy'.

Your credit card buddy

A credit card buddy is someone who will take away your credit card when you are on a buying spree for incoherent reasons. Keon is my credit card buddy. He stops me whenever I go into a shopping seizure or am blinded by sales. Once, while shopping for a gift for a friend, I also bought three long, jersey blouses and tiny wedge-heel shoes.

Keon asked if I was buying because I was reacting emotionally to some recent incident in my life. He then offered to take away my credit card until the phase passed. He is what every woman needs. A financial conscience! I ended up keeping the credit card in my wardrobe, right under boxes of old clothes. The spending demon left fast! I loved my new shoes and blouses, but enough was enough.

Your credit card enemy
At the risk of being a friend-buster, I want to wake you up to what I call our 'worst money enemy'. All of us have a friend like this. This is the girlfriend who goes out with us, praises us for our choices in everything we buy—yes, everything! She encourages us to buy the item and tells us we look wonderful even if it's in a colour that she knows we will probably wear just once.

She is Ms Hole Burn. She burns a hole in your bank account each time you go out with her. Perhaps Ms Hole Burn does not intend to kill your bank balance. She does it anyway with amazing panache. Everything looks great when you go out with her. You want to buy everything, even that big brand grey, shapeless, sack dress with square buttons. "It's so YOU!" she gushes. You fall for it. $1,700 lost. You walk out believing you look like Kate Moss.

Two weeks later, you see your sister-in-law in that sack. You nearly choke. On the way home, you ask your ever supportive husband, "Do I look like her when I wear my big brand dress?" His answer is evasive and vague, and he says almost too quickly, "No dear, you look much better! You have style." You bozo! How can anyone think they look good in a grey, shapeless, sack dress with square buttons? Only Twiggy and Kate Moss would look stunning in that sack.

Ms Hole Burn is bad news! Get away fast! Recognise her and run! Whatever her intent, the bottom line is that you are always more broke after going out with Ms Hole Burn than before you went out with her. My advice? Maintain your friendship with her. Play badminton with her. Skate with her. Go for English tea and hot scones. Shampoo each other's dog. But do not go near any shop with Ms Hole Burn. The three of you together—you, Ms Hole Burn and the credit card—in a shopping centre is very bad news for you financially.

Car Loans

Car loans carry lower interest rates than credit cards, but the lender can repossess the car should payments not be made. If you have ever been in a situation where the car you are driving is in the process of being repossessed, you find out two things.

One, it can be a terrifying experience. Once, in the 1980s, when one of my father's businesses went bust, he did not make payment for my little sports car. I was at a very busy traffic junction in Kuala Lumpur waiting for the light to turn when someone yanked the car door open and demanded that I get out. He said he was repossessing the car. I was very afraid and sped off with the door still opened. I then found out what repossession was all about.

Two, even after the car is repossessed and sold off at the best possible price, you might still owe the Hire Purchase Company the balance. You are obliged to make good. If you are like most people who buy cars, you would probably get a car loan. In Singapore, car loans are hire-purchase arrangements. This means that the bank owns the car until you have paid up your loan.

Flat Rate and Effective Interest Rate

Let's see what Susie, who has just graduated and got her first job, pays when she gets her first car, a yellow VW convertible. Even with some help from her dad, Susie still has to borrow $60,000. A bank has offered a flat rate loan of 3 per cent over five years.

Here's one of the more confusing aspects of a car loan. The flat rate is not the actual rate she is paying. The flat rate is used to calculate how much interest she would pay over the five years and her monthly instalment. In Susie's case, she would be paying total interest of $9,000.

Total interest = Loan amount × flat rate × duration
= $60,000 × 3% × 5 years = $9,000

From here, we can calculate her monthly instalment:

Monthly instalment = ($60,000 + 9,000)/60 months = $1,150

Is Susie really paying 3 per cent interest a year? Not really. As we said, the flat rate is a convenient way to illustrate the interest and instalment amounts. The actual rate (technically called the Effective Interest Rate) uses a fairly complicated formula that requires a financial calculator, and is about two times more.

Table 8.2 shows the various flat rates (2 to 5 per cent) charged, the loan durations (one to ten years), and the actual interest rate incurred. For Susie, the actual rate of interest she is paying is 5.84 per cent or slightly less than two times the flat rate of 3 per cent.

Table 8.2. Various Flat Rates, Loan Durations and Effective Interest Rates

		Flat Rates						
		2%	2.5%	3%	3.5%	4%	4.5%	5%
Duration in Years	1	4.35%	5.43%	6.50%	7.58%	8.66%	9.73%	10.80%
	2	4.13%	5.15%	6.16%	7.17%	8.17%	9.17%	10.17%
	3	4.04%	5.03%	6.02%	6.99%	7.96%	8.92%	9.87%
	4	3.99%	4.96%	5.92%	6.87%	7.81%	8.74%	9.66%
	5	3.95%	4.90%	5.84%	6.77%	7.69%	8.60%	9.49%
	6	3.91%	4.85%	5.78%	6.69%	7.58%	8.47%	9.34%
	7	3.88%	4.81%	5.72%	6.61%	7.49%	8.36%	9.21%
	8	3.86%	4.77%	5.66%	6.54%	7.40%	8.25%	9.08%
	9	3.83%	4.73%	5.61%	6.47%	7.32%	8.15%	8.97%
	10	3.80%	4.69%	5.56%	6.41%	7.24%	8.06%	8.86%

Table 8.3 opposite is another useful table. It shows the expected monthly instalments for every $1,000 borrowed. Using the table, we see that Susie's loan of $60,000 at 3 per cent for five years requires a monthly instalment of $1,150.

Monthly instalment = 60 × 19.17 = $1,150

Table 8.3. Expected Monthly Instalments for Every $1,000 Borrowed

Duration in Years	Flat Rates							
		2%	2.5%	3%	3.5%	4%	4.5%	5%
	1	85.00	85.42	85.83	86.25	86.67	87.08	87.50
	2	43.33	43.75	44.17	44.58	45.00	45.42	45.83
	3	29.44	29.86	30.28	30.69	31.11	31.53	31.94
	4	22.50	22.92	23.33	23.75	24.17	24.58	25.00
	5	18.33	18.75	19.17	19.58	20.00	20.42	20.83
	6	15.56	15.97	16.39	16.81	17.22	17.64	18.06
	7	13.57	13.99	14.40	14.82	15.24	15.65	16.07
	8	12.08	12.50	12.92	13.33	13.75	14.17	14.58
	9	10.93	11.34	11.76	12.18	12.59	13.01	13.43
	10	10.00	10.42	10.83	11.25	11.67	12.08	12.50

If Susie finds that the amount is too much to pay per month, she can consider another bank offering her a seven-year loan at 3.5 per cent flat rate. What is her monthly instalment? It would be $889.

Monthly instalment = 60 × 14.82 = $889

A car loan is a major financial commitment. Before you sign any agreement, these are the important questions you must answer:

- What is the actual interest rate I am paying? Whatever the flat rate is, multiply it by two as a rough guide.

- What is my monthly instalment and what happens if I cannot pay? If you pay late, you will face additional interest charges and fees. If you fail to pay, the bank has the right to take legal action and repossess your car. Do your sums.

- What if I pay up the loan ahead of time or refinance? There may be charges for early repayment. Also, you will be faced with another set of calculations using something called the Rule of 78, which you should have the bank officer explain to you. The reason is that most of a car loan's interest is paid in the early years of the loan. It is a good idea to pay early just to get rid of the loan. But if you are paying early to refinance, you have to be very clear as to whether there is an advantage.

Beyond the Car Loan: Four Important Things to Know
The day you sign on the dotted line is the same day the car depreciates 15 to 20 per cent in market value!

- A car is a medium-term purchase. The rule of thumb is to sell it when it is about five years old, as cars tend to give problems from their fifth year, and if you don't want a car that is in the workshop eating up your monthly income.

- Find out when the car maker changed the design for your particular model and when the next design is due out. I once owned a BMW 3-series that I bought in the last year its lights were square-shaped. The next year the lights were changed to a rounder shape. The price dropped drastically as the old square-shaped lights classified the car into an earlier release of that 3-series generation. Car salesmen are smart people. They told me this when I bought a new car in the 5-series: "Of course we don't release every feature all at the same time. Otherwise, next year, we have nothing new to offer." So know what you are *not* buying when you make your decision. And ask: "Is this the year to buy this car from this car maker? When is the next design change?"

- Read the Classifieds and find out how much the model is selling for brand new, second hand and third hand. Look at the resale value against the purchase value. Some car brands have higher resale value in percentage terms of the original price paid. Some cars are not desired. You may think that the car you are eyeing has a great shape, colour and interior, but does the market think so? If not, are you willing to bear the difference in market perception when it comes to selling the car? Do study the resale market and depreciation trends.

- Find out about car maintenance. I once had a lovely second-hand midnight blue Porsche 924. As the car neared its eighth year, it was sitting in the workshop every month for a week. The bill came up to about $1,000 or so each time. The Porche was chomping up nearly half my take-home pay then. My first baby came along, and soon I could not climb out of the car. The car was the fourth baby in my home: The Husband, The Pregnant Me, The Baby Inside Me and The Porche. We sold it fast. Cheap, beautiful old car. Extremely high maintenance.

Housing Loans

My favourite kind of a loan is a housing loan. It is one of the cheaper personal loans that anyone can get and I love it for the same reason that the banks love it. Banks love it because it is large, long term and secured. I love it because it is long term and secured, and generally cost the least.

Imagine having ten credit cards and rolling $10,000 on each card. That's $100,000 at 24 per cent per annum. For the $100,000, you can have some bling and plenty of designer shoes, clothes and accessories. For the same $100,000, you might own a one-tenth share of a $1 million home. Which would you choose? I choose to put my money into homes and real estate. These are huge commitments, but they pay off, *if* you did your homework and *if* you got your timing right.

If you decide to buy a property, your money is likely to come from a combination of your personal savings and a bank loan. For Singaporeans, you can also call on your compulsory savings in your CPF (Central Provident Fund). Generally, you can borrow up to 80 per cent of the purchase price or market value of the property, whichever is lower, if your income can support the loan structure. This means, for example, if the purchase price of the property is $1 million and the market value is $1.1 million, then you can borrow up to 80 per cent of $1 million, the lower number, or $800,000.

Therefore, consider borrowing to the maximum on your home loan. Borrow as much as possible and for as long as possible if you can service the loan. But I need to put a caveat on this statement.

The caveat is to ensure you know what you are buying when you invest into property. Getting a large loan to buy a bad property is a bad decision. Do not borrow right only to buy wrong.

Taking on a Housing Loan

A housing loan is a large debt. It's worthwhile thinking about your loan and what you are getting into.

- Understand the loan. Most loans in Singapore are variable-rate loans where banks fix the interest for the first one to two years at a usually attractive rate. After that period, the loan becomes pegged to something called the board rate, which is a rate fixed by the bank. Each bank has a series of board rates. Borrowers find these board rates confusing because of the lack of transparency on how it is calculated by the banks other than that it is pegged to some interbank rate. An interbank rate is the interest rate at which banks can borrow funds from other banks. (In Asia, the SIBOR, the Singapore Interbank Offered Rate, is used more commonly, and serves as a reference rate for borrowers and lenders). Home owners often complain that loan rates are jacked up promptly whenever the reference rate goes up but are cut slowly when the reference rate drops.

- Banks now offer adjustable-rate mortgages (ARMs), which are pegged to a variable interest rate such as SIBOR. Different from a board rate, an ARM rate is truly variable and changes whenever the peg rate goes up or down. They are transparent and fairer, and overcome the drawbacks of the board rate system. When interest rates go lower in the economy, ARMs automatically adjust rates lower. It, therefore, no longer requires customers to take action to refinance their home loans to get the lower rates. But it requires customers to be educated and to plan for a range of rates over the tenure of the loan. A housing loan of 3 per cent impacts on disposable incomes very differently from a 5 per cent loan.

- Refinance where possible. Always look for opportunities to transfer your outstanding balance to cheaper alternatives through refinancing. If interest rates are falling in your favour, it would be foolish not to consider refinancing. Bear in mind, though, that refinancing your loan incurs additional costs, such as legal, transfer and processing fees. You may also have to pay penalty charges that could cancel out any savings from refinancing. On the other hand, your existing bank may offer you better terms if they know you are thinking of refinancing and may switch to another bank. So try to negotiate a better package for yourself first with your current bank.

- Look at alternative sources for loans. In Singapore, borrowers have recourse to HDB (Housing and Development Board) loans if they qualify to buy a government flat. These concessionary rate loans are almost always lower than bank home loan rates and the terms are more flexible. HDB imposes a list of requirements for such loans, including maximum household income, CPF withdrawal limits and private home ownership conditions.

- Get mortgage insurance. This is an effective and cheap way to safeguard your investment. Most banks today will not allow you to borrow without mortgage insurance. Banks may have the house as the loan collateral, but they still want to know that the loan will be paid should you die unexpectedly. The great news is that mortgage insurance is not expensive and it can be carried to cover a new home if you should change homes, and if the terms are outlined that way.

- Pay your loan instalments on time to avoid late fees and extra interest. If you cannot pay your instalments at any time, the bank has the right to sell the property to recover the balance, but they will usually work with you first. So do not ignore calls or letters asking for repayment. If you have difficulty repaying, contact a bank officer to discuss your problem. The bank officer will advise you on how best the loan can be restructured to help you to continue servicing your loan. For example, if you have been retrenched and are looking for a new job or you are recovering from a major illness, the bank may extend the tenure of the loan to lower the monthly instalment or have you pay interest only for a specified period of time until you regain your ability to repay. Or the bank may ask that you add a joint borrower or a guarantor with good income and credit profile.

Beyond the Housing Loan: Four Important Things to Know
I have discussed why it is important to get into property as early as possible so you can track the market. We won't go through all the advice on buying property here. That is a book in itself. I am also not a property investment expert although I have made money from my investments. Here are a few more tips when looking for a home:

- You can change the inside of the home but not the environment. If the neighbourhood is not a great one, the value of your property will be weighed down, no matter how much you redecorate. Location is important.

- Some homeowners do not mind living next to a main road. I do. I once bought a home with a main arterial road running behind it. With about 20 per cent of Singapore being covered with a super efficient road system, many landed homes are next to main roads, and high rise apartments next to flyovers and expressways. For myself, I find the noise difficult to live with on a day-to-day basis even if I were to leave the air-conditioner running the whole day. You do need to check out the noise level at different times of the day and from different spots within the apartment or house. The agents will hardly show you the home at peak traffic hours so keep your eyes and ears opened, and demand to see the home at other times. Yes, even if it means taking leave to check it out.

- Think of the amenities around the area. Schools, shopping malls, libraries in easy reach do affect the value of the property.

- Is your property leasehold or freehold? I do not like leasehold property. I have stuck consistently with freehold and 999 years. There was a time when I was given an opportunity to buy a beautiful 99-year leasehold home in its twentieth year. In those days, getting a bank loan for the 99-year leasehold home in its twentieth year was difficult. That quickly showed me that 99-year properties have resale limitations. This is not to say that you cannot make money from 99-year leaseholds or that you do not enjoy higher rental yields. On average, the 99-year leasehold property would cost less to purchase than a 999-year property next door to it. In a market such as Singapore, however, I prefer to think of capital gains rather than rental yields. You might prefer rental yields.

Calls for Top-Ups and Falling Property Markets

Some years ago, my friend Sally was suddenly widowed. She was 45 years old when her husband passed away from liver cancer. They had just bought a brand new home but unfortunately did not buy mortgage insurance. Sally had a good job and could afford the $5,000-mortgage instalment. The property market then went south and the market value of her home fell by 30 per cent almost overnight. As the value fell below the loan value, she was asked to top up her account so that the outstanding loan amount can be covered by the asset value of the property. Sally had just enough savings to do so, but the top-up took a big hit on her. She had to replan her life finances as a result. She prayed for the property market to recover so that she would be able to sell her home.

While housing loans offer the lowest interest rates available to individual borrowers, they are not 100 per cent fail-safe. During the 1998 Asian financial crisis, many homes in Hong Kong rapidly lost up to one third of their value when the property bubble burst. House 'owners' were reportedly walking up to lending banks and dropping off the keys to their apartments over the counter, saying they could no longer manage the mortgage in a downward spiralling market.

I too was caught. I bought a nice apartment in Malaysia. When the ringgit fell during the financial crisis, the apartment lost value in exchange as well as its price. It was a double whammy and I ended up losing about half my investment. I cut my losses and moved on. It was just too depressing to worry about the property and to take care of the rentals, which were small due to the market and currency impact. What a lesson to swallow!

The 2008 sub-prime mortgage crisis in the US is an example of how lending institutions went overboard in lending to customers with poor credit ratings, and how the public and institutions believed that property prices would go up indefinitely and without limit, without grounding in reality. It shows how much the lending institutions love mortgage loans, over believing and over relying on the underlying collateral and the upward price trend of the property market. Part of the problems in the sub-prime mortgage crisis is due to lack of understanding by the borrowers. Loans were packaged very attractively and some borrowers did not expect or plan for the higher quantum payments that were expected from them once the 'honeymoon' period was over. There were no cheaper loans made available to which these house owners could transfer their loans. Defaults started to happen.

In the long run, however, if one has the holding power, property values in prime areas and in cities recover. (Currency is another thing, so be careful of the double exposure!) While any particular company's stock may not recover to its previous glory, having suffered deep blows to operations and plans in market crises, properties are different. Once the market recovers, property price patterns tend to reestablish themselves. A property in the prime districts of 9, 10 and 11 in Singapore will remain crème-de-la-crème for a long time, just like Kensington will be Kensington in London.

SMALL PERSONAL LOANS

Small personal loans, also known as easy credit products, are unsecured and typically offered by credit card and finance companies with very attractive terms. To give you an idea of how attractive these loans look, here are some marketing messages you might see bundled with their super friendly brand names:

- No guarantors needed.

- We deliver cash to your doorstep 24/7, as easy as ordering pizza.

- Get up to $100,000 ready cash or up to four months of your monthly salary PLUS a free cheque book PLUS insurance coverage in the event of accidental death and even work retrenchment!

- Flexible payment schemes. You can pay interest only; not pay anything for up to two months a year; pay more the first few months and pay less later; pay less the first few months and pay more later; and other payment combinations.

- Use your ready cash right away with discounts at 150 select merchants.

With all these features, it's easy to see why so many people sign up, spend and overspend.

The interest rates set for such loans can be confusing. I was at a major shopping mall recently. One of the promotion booths was offering ready credit deals at a special interest rate of 6.5 per cent per annum, which certainly sounds attractive. But on closer examination, the 6.5 per cent turned out to be a flat rate. We discussed how flat rates worked in the section under car loans. Upon working it through, the effective loan rate was between 12 and 20 per cent.

LOANS FROM PAWNSHOPS

A pawnbroker offers monetary loans in exchange for an item of value. The word 'pawn' comes from the Latin word *pignus*, meaning 'pledge'. The items that are pawned to the broker are called pledges, pawns, or simply, the collateral. The borrower may have different redemption periods to redeem their items of value. Naturally, the pawnbroker offers a loan at a value significantly lower than the value he can sell the item for, in case you do not turn up to redeem the item at the end of the redemption period.

Borrowing $30,000 and Losing $70,000

Despite the financial ups and downs my father went through as I was growing up, he would buy beautiful, expensive gifts for my mother whenever he did well. Once he bought her a stunning emerald-cut diamond ring with all the four Cs. He paid close to $100,000 for it.

When business was bad, my mother had to pawn the ring because the shop they had bought it from was not interested in discussing a buy-back. The pawnshop gave my mother $30,000 for the ring with a redemption period of six months. Six months later, my mother sadly lost the ring as we did not have the means to redeem it. Since then, my father has more than made up to her for her 'sacrifice', but she still remembers how she lost her beautiful diamond ring.

What that episode taught me was that jewellery cannot be sold for the value they were bought. Jewellers who tell you that you are making an 'investment' are referring to the rising prices of *new* jewellery at the stores. These same jewellers will never tell you how much they will pay to buy back your 'bling' piece. How can anything be an investment if you cannot sell it for at least what you paid for it?

THE LOAN SHARK

Looking at the outrageous interest rates of borrowing from loan sharks, one can say that such loans should only be considered when in total desperation.

My relative in Malaysia once made the mistake of borrowing from a loan shark to send his son to an overseas university. The interest rate agreed on was 10 per cent per month on the loan amount. Uncle Bobby thought that he would only need the loan for six months as he was waiting for a late, large payment from a client. He just needed to manage a cash flow situation for a few months.

At the end of a year, when repayment was not in sight, the loan shark turned up at Uncle Bobby's house at 6 o'clock in the morning. She shouted shameful things from the front gate, then climbed over it and banged on the wooden front door until it broke open. She then signalled to some men to follow her. Soon there were six huge men in the house, hauling out the sofa set, the TV set, the hi-fi set and anything else that was of any value. Uncle Bobby was frozen in shock. The family lodged a police report, but that did not help. Painfully and slowly, he repaid the debt.

Never ever borrow from a loan shark. They come in all shapes and sizes. Some may even appear to be humane, justifying why they need 10 per cent per month as interest. Don't be fooled. Once the deal is done, the blood-sucking teeth are bared. And should you not be able to repay the loan, the loan shark will have no qualms resorting to strong-arm tactics to make you pay up.

FRIENDSHIP LOANS

A good friend of mine is incredibly kind. Kenneth has a weakness for lending money to 'friends-in-need'. And he seems to have friends perpetually in need. When I found out that he had lent close to $50,000 to one of his friends, I nearly screamed at him for his blind trust. I told him that he would probably never get any of it back. He kept saying then that his friends were unable to repay as they were all down and out, but he was sure they would. The loans were six years old then. The last I met him, Kenneth himself became down and out. He probably lent his net worth away through the years!

I do not believe in borrowing from, or lending money to, anyone. This makes me sound extremely harsh. I told Kenneth in no uncertain terms to wake up as his friends, in my opinion, will NEVER pay him back. Why?

One. I believe that if a borrower did not have the basic discipline of making the first few payments back, little by little, no matter how hard he tried, that borrower would not have the discipline to save. Worse, he would never become anyone of substance. His down-and-out situation was really his own doing. It is the personal loan borrower's curse.

Two. If someone cannot borrow from the bank, the credit card company or some personal finance company, the reason is that he has exhausted those avenues already, no matter what he tells you.

So, never feel sorry if you cannot lend to a friend. If the situation is dire and if you have the money to spare, give the money away. If you cannot give it away, rethink the lending decision. Generally, personal loan borrowers are unlikely to make repayment. It is not in their character make-up. Recognise that these people have flaws and that it is not your job to patch it up for them.

In the same vein, if you are about to approach someone for a personal loan, STOP. In situations where a family member is ill and needing treatment, I might support your decision to ask a friend for a loan. In any other situation, I don't think personal loans are merited. There has to be other ways to resolve financial problems, including selling treasured items for whatever value they will fetch, driving a taxi part-time at night, or working as a part-time cashier at a 7-Eleven store.

> Never borrow on the credit card.
> Never borrow from loan sharks.
> Never believe that buying jewellery is an investment.
> Buy jewellery because you like the piece for its beauty.

9 Managing Debt

Debt management is an imperative for anyone seeking financial freedom. Being debt free is also one of the most satisfying states to be in. The day you finish paying off your home mortgage and your car loan and have zero debt, you feel an amazing lift in spirit from the knowledge that you do not owe anyone anything.

It may not always be a clever thing to pay off all debts since some debt is good for most people as long as they can service the debt. Mortgage loans, for example, are good debts to have if you bought the right property at the right time and signed a good mortgage deal with low interest rates.

Smart Debt And Stupid Debt

We described smart (good) and stupid (bad) debts earlier. The difference between these cannot be emphasised more. So I am writing it again here.

- Smart debt is debt you incur for purchases of assets that have the potential for capital appreciation or income generation. Such types of debts are for education and in some countries, housing and property.

- Stupid debt is debt that you have assumed for junk purchase. The word 'junk' is very strong, but it is a good word to use. What has happened to the glossy baubles you bought two years ago for that fabulous dinner at which you had to look perfect? Same thing as mine, I bet—no longer used or thrown away by now. I hope you have paid off for the item and the purchase sum is not sitting on your credit card as a loan.

Most People Are Broke

In a recent Singapore survey, it was found that 62 per cent of Singaporeans could not survive more than three months if they stopped working. That is the case whether the person has worked for three years or 30 years. Worse, most are in debt. Americans appear to be doing worse, going by the excerpts taken from *Land of the Broke* (www.mdmproofing.com). More than 70 per cent of Americans live from pay cheque to pay cheque. Singaporeans are better, but not by much.

To survive in the post-retirement years, most people compromise on lifestyles to get by. Or they depend on their children to care for them. While it is an Asian tradition for children to look after their parents, there used to be *more* children looking after two parents who used to die *younger*.

These days, we have either one or two children to look after two ageing parents. It makes life tough for the children to hold up obligations to their parents, their wives and their own children. We are already called the Sandwich Generation. I am not sure if we want our children to be called the 'Crushed Generation' or the 'Walk-Out Generation', meaning our children either get crushed by the financial pressures of looking after us, or they walk out because they cannot take it anymore.

Broke with Junk

In 2005, BBC reported that bankruptcy amongst women was on the increase. More women were willing to borrow using the credit card, and one in ten women was spending more than 50 per cent of her salary to repay credit card debt every month.

Reading some of the blogs online, I am amazed at the number of young women who are stuck in credit card debt. Read what one man had to say about this in a blog:

> *"Are there any single women over the age of 25 that don't have mammoth credit card (or otherwise) debt? After discussing this with several friends and based on personal experiences, I have never met*

one. Many men probably have the same problem, but I don't date them. My one friend's wife had £125k in miscellaneous debt when they got married ... that's a house! They struggle.

My last GF had over £40k in credit debt and my present one has over £75k. I don't have a huge income, live modestly, don't have a bunch of shiny things, and haven't used a credit card in over eight years. I manage my money. It just makes it hard thinking long term. I've worked hard to accumulate the money I have by sacrificing, and this would vanish the day I got married in order to pay off her debt. I don't believe in having separate pots of money (or separate debt) in a marriage and I'm fine sharing. I know I sound selfish, but actually I'm more than generous to friends and family. I just can't help thinking if things don't work out, she makes out great (free ride out of her 75k debt + part of my future earnings) ... and I've spent the last decade 'saving' for nothing. Funny when I started accumulating some wealth, women were much more available.

I know we just need to get on the same page and all that financial-guru stuff. Basically, I'm just curious if there are ladies out there without massive debt ... particularly credit card debt for miscellaneous junk?"

(Source: www.enotalone.com)

In my time, as a single woman, guys would ask if a girl was high or low maintenance. By that, a guy was asking whether the girl was someone who spent a lot of money on how she looks. As a potential husband, he knew that he would eventually be expected to foot her bills. Smart guys stayed away from high maintenance girls.

When I was working at Singapore Airlines years ago, some of my high-flying male colleagues were very clear that they were on the lookout to marry schoolteachers. When I asked them why, they said: "We are expected to be mobile on this job and to be posted overseas as we climb the Singapore Airlines corporate ladder. Schoolteachers are good with children, so they can stay at home if required to look after the children. They can also come with us on our postings and easily get another teaching job when we return to Singapore. They also tend not to be big spenders as they are conservative." And we thought that people married for 'love' and chemistry!

What Has Financial Independence Got To Do With Debt?

Earlier, we defined the various levels of financial independence. Let's use the diagram below to recap and explain why you must take care of debt. Imagine trying to fill a sink with water. Turning on the water tap all the way does not help if your outflow outlet drains away all that your inflow tap lets in. Your sink will never fill. Get it?

Excessive debt interest servicing is an outflow you can do without. Imagine that the interest rate is 24 per cent per annum. It means that for every dollar you borrow for a year, you need to return the capital with a debt interest servicing of 24 cents.

When you put that in the context of the rate of return on capital invested in most investments or companies, that 24 per cent is very hard to match. For most investments, you might earn between 2 to 15 cents to every dollar invested for a year. There are very few companies that can earn a rate of return of 24 per cent to a dollar invested.

What this means is credit card borrowing is one of the more lucrative businesses for banks and, therefore, one of the worst kind of loans you can have. Can you see the extrapolation that until and unless you pay off unwanted loans such as credit card debt, you can never gather enough in your financial reservoir to gain financial independence?

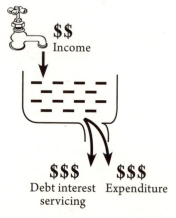

Repaying Your Debt

Let's work on a few possible situations of how big a debt-hole you need to crawl out of. Let's assume that some of you owe the credit card company 10 per cent of your annual salary in credit card debt. Or you might owe 50 per cent of your annual salary, or horrors, 100 per cent! The last is possible; you can owe up to 100 per cent of your annual salary if you have taken out five credit cards, each with a spending limit of up to two to three months of your salary. Let's hope none of you owes 200 per cent of your annual salary, which can be the case if you had lost your job earlier and now have a lower paying job compared with the time you went on that spending spree.

Look at Table 9.1 below. It shows how long it would take you to pay off your debt, using a percentage of your monthly salary to make the repayment without considering loan interest. Whenever I look at this table, I get the chills. If I owe the credit card company that much money, I would be miserable trying to figure out how to pay it off. It is tough enough to save to get into a *positive* cash position to enable investment. Now, imagine working to pay off a *negative* cash position. It's extremely hard work.

Table 9.1. Time Needed to Repay Debt

	Your Savings as a % of Your Monthly Salary to Repay Debt				
	10%	20%	30%	40%	50%
Your Bad Debt as a % of Your Annual Salary	Number of Months it Will Take to Save to Repay Your Debt				
10%	12	6	4	3	2
50%	60	30	20	15	12
100%	120	60	40	30	24
200%	240	120	80	60	48

There are only a few ways to get out of debt:
- Pay off the debt either in full or in part, negotiating with the lender for a reduction.
- Declare yourself a bankrupt or become sued to become bankrupt.
- Get someone to pay it off.

I hope none of you are in a situation that would take you months to repay your debt. But I know that some of you, oh dear, are. I have never consciously owed money to credit card companies, and for as long as I can remember, I shy away from credit card debt. I have also always paid off my debts! In fact, this is the reason a very well known credit card issuer refused to take me as a customer when they had a special promotion for their cards that gave away a small Samsonite luggage bag with every new card approved! My credit history was sterling. I did not meet their requirement of a customer who would 'roll over' their debt every month. If you have stupid debts, you must get out—fast.

Put In Place A Debt Reduction Plan

A debt reduction plan is crucial to getting your finances under control. Ranking your debts from stupid to smart, you need to have a plan to repay ALL money you owe. A debt reduction plan comprises the following steps:

- Step 1: Write down all your debts. Write down the debts that charge the highest interest rates and the debts that have the highest quantum payment amounts. Table 9.2 opposite is an example of how you might write out all the loans you have, the interest rates and the interest payments expected by the banks.
- Step 2: Work out the debt repayment into your budget.
- Step 3: Pay off the stupid debts first, please.

At all times, KEEP TO YOUR BUDGET!

Table 9.2. My Loans and Interest Rates and Payments Expected by Banks

Type of Loan	Total Loan Outstanding	Effective Interest Rate per Annum	Interest Payment Alone per Month
Car	$30,000	6%	$150
Credit card	$2,000	24%	$40
Housing	$500,000	5%	$2,083
Personal	$10,000	20%	$167
Loan shark	$5,000	100%	$417

Pay Off Stupid Debts First

Next, look at your budget. Reviewing the past months, be firm with yourself. SLASH AWAY UNNECESSARY SPENDING. DO NOT MAKE ALLOWANCES FOR UNNECESSARY SPENDING VIA CASH OR DEBIT TRANSACTIONS.

The necessary expenses every month are housing, simple meals and transportation. Other necessary expenses may be insurance premiums, education fees and monies for parental support. What is the total cash flow that you can release to pay off your debts?

Based on the loan examples in Table 9.2, say you have worked out a release of 20 per cent of your salary every month for paying off your debts. Say this figure is $1,000 for now. Ranking the debts, you look at the ones with the highest interest rates. Note that we have not included capital repayment (paying down the full debt) in this table as it will make the sums come out differently.

- Use the $1,000 to make the minimum payment for all debts. Putting aside the housing loan that we shall assume you pay using CPF, the rest is a total of $774 = $(150 + 40 + 167 + 417).

- With the $1,000, please pay off all interest so that they do not cumulate with penalties. With the remaining balance of $226 ($1000 − $774), pay off the loan from the loan shark first. In fact, pay it down as soon as you can. Once you have paid off the loan of $5,000, you can then work on paying off the personal loan of $10,000 with its interest rate of 20 per cent.

- In other words, start with the debt item with the highest interest rate. When you have finished paying off this heavy-debt item, move to the next debt item with the second highest interest rate. Work out how long it will take to repay that debt. Do it. When completed, move on to the item with the third highest interest rate, and so on until you have completed paying off all your debt. (See Table 9.3 below.)

If you receive any bonus payments, or any windfall cash, use it to pay down the debt. You are in NO position to celebrate with a new handbag. Remember, you are still in debt. If you feel you need to celebrate, you can treat yourself to something small, with say 5 per cent of the total value of the bonus payment you received. No more than that.

Table 9.3. My Loans and How I Intend to Pay Them Off

Type of Loan	Total Loan Outstanding	Effective Interest Rate per Annum	Interest Payment Alone per Month	Immediate Action	Total Number of Months Until Full Repayment
Car	$30,000	6%	$150	Wait	
Credit card	$2,000	24%	$40	Wait	
Housing	$500,000	5%	$2,083	CPF	
Personal	$10,000	20%	$167	Wait	
Loan shark	$5,000	100%	$417	Pay $226 to reduce loan principal	22 months if non-reducing loan / 18 months if reducing loan

*(Table 9.4 opposite—see Housing loans) Note that the 2008/2009 property crash is a market anomaly that will reset. Watch for the market reset when prices stabilise. There are more opportunities than threats.

Table 9.4. Smart Debts and Stupid Debts At A Glance

	Types of Loan	Remarks
SMART DEBTS	Housing loans	Good loan as long as you can service it. Home ownership is a basic milestone to financial independence. Importantly, in most markets, property prices tend to go up in the medium to long term as long as the economy is growing.*
	Education loans	Good loan provided you are not a full-time student for the rest of your life without any intent to earn your keep. As your educational level increases, so too does your earning potential.
	Car loans	Cars are liabilities, hardly ever assets. Loans for liabilities are not good loans. If you don't have a good reason to own a car, you shouldn't.
	Loans for financial investments	Such loans can be very profitable or very dangerous because your profits and losses can be magnified many times. For example, some brokerage accounts offer you a margin that is 3.5 times your deposit. So instead of investing $1,000, you'll have 3.5 times more and you can see how you can be easily overleveraged.
STUPID DEBTS	Personal unsecured loans from banks for renovation or other expenses	Borrowing to renovate is fine if you have a repayment plan and can implement it. If you already have housing, car and credit card loans to repay, I would suggest that your loan to renovate your home can wait.
	Personal loans from friends	I do not like such loans unless one is pushed to a corner in life. Basic rule: Do not borrow from, or lend to, friends.
	Credit card loans	One of the most expensive loans you can get. Use the card only to make payments on items you can pay for, NOT as a means to borrow.
	Loan from loan sharks	This is DANGER. All your alarm bells should ring. Stay away.

10 *L*ove-Hate Insurance

Gosh, I Used To Hate The Agents!

There was a time in my life when I would hang up the phone faster on insurance agents than you can say "Happy Holidays". Even worse, I would give them wrong personal contact information when asked. I hated their sales pitches! I also hated saying "No, thank you", followed by "I don't believe in insurance".

Now years later, I know that one of my biggest financial mistakes was discontinuing my term insurance policy when I was 35. I was young, healthy and happy. I had a new home, a small child and the growing needs of a young family. I thought I could save on an insurance policy and take it up later. Besides which, could I not earn that amount in any case somehow? I also thought I could begin saving it regularly off my income and invest that into something that would give me a good rate of return. So, never mind the insurance, I thought then, I really needed the money for other things. I was wrong.

In my forties, I tried to take up health insurance. I realised that my age and the fact that I had been unwell in earlier years had changed my risk profile drastically for the insurers. I discovered that insurance companies shared a common repository of information. They referred to my last doctor's appointment which I had missed because I was well. It was more than seven years ago, but they traced the records. And because I missed that appointment, I was rejected. To be considered, the insurer insisted on an extensive medical check-up.

After the check-ups, the premium payment required of me was ridiculous. It didn't matter how I felt or what the doctors said. The insurer said that I was lucky to be considered 'insurable'. It was difficult to find a product that made financial sense. As a result, for a while and until I started my own businesses, I had no health insurance other than that through my employers.

So, when and if I am asked for my biggest financial mistake, it would not be that I lost a lot of money in an apartment in Malaysia I bought just before the Asian currency crisis, or that I lost money investing in that Internet start-up that had to close down because of a character-flawed CEO who defaulted. It would be that I discontinued my term insurance policy. The truth of my folly hit home when I became a single mother. If I should fall sick, I would deplete whatever cash I had, and if I died, my children would be penniless! It was a terrifying few years for me!

The Best Thing To Do When Young

I urge you, if you are young and healthy, GET INSURED. It is not boring and it is not a waste of money. Get in when the premiums are low and add to the coverage as you get older. Your early insured base helps give you an averaged down cost.

We know that even as we recommend that you look at insurance for yourself, you are unlikely to do so. Most of us give ourselves reasons for not needing insurance. The common ones are:

- It's too expensive. I prefer to invest my money and watch it grow.
- I'm already covered by my employer. I'll get it later, but not now.
- I have other policies already and I don't know which is which by now. I also have no one to ask to help me rationalise.
- I don't understand how it works and I don't want to ask.
- I don't want to think about death.
- I'm too lazy to find out.
- I'm terrified of agents. They never stop selling! The last one had body odour.

I can rebut these reasons, one by one. But I started this chapter by saying that stopping my insurance plan was the worst financial mistake I have made. It is, therefore, sufficient for me to stress to you to get insurance coverage if you have none, and to review if you have sufficient or too much if you already have some.

The Financial Adviser

Once upon a time, the people who sold financial products (mainly insurance policies then) were called insurance agents. Insurance agents were employed by insurance companies to sell their products to the mass consumer market. The sales commission structure of agents in those days, with overrides for managers, was probably the forerunners of multilevel marketing.

Then deregulation of the financial sector and disintermediation of the financial services supply chain happened. Today, there are many distribution channels for financial products and you need not buy from 'tied' agents. A 'tied' agent is one who is contracted to sell financial products from the company he is tied to.

The word 'financial adviser representative' or FAR was legislated to mean an individual representing a financial adviser or FA, which is the company. FARs today come from banks, insurance companies and smaller, independent companies. Compared with the agents of yesteryear, many FARs today are highly educated, with some holding Masters degrees. FARs sell more than insurance. Their array of financial products may include unit trusts and investment-linked policies. Some enterprising FARs have set up alliances to sell hedge funds, mortgages and even land parcels.

How FARs are Rewarded

For your FAR, selling is his job. Money is his reward. So if you are going to use a FAR, you should know how he is rewarded.

Sales commissions

Most FARs are rewarded by sales commissions. It is for this reason that I do not like talking to most of them much. Often, they are only interested in selling you something ... anything. In recent years, these FARs started to attend neural linguistic programming courses and applying what they learnt to gain their clients' trust. Some of them started to pace their speed of talking to mine, tap my shoulder to show familiarity or imitate my body posture in an attempt to propagate a sense of friendship.

Please learn to spot the agent who is only interested in your commission, and not in your welfare. There is a case for supporting commission-based FARs if the products they sell are simple, and if you as the buyer already know exactly what you want. Paying commissions is cheap when compared with fee-based services.

Fees

Some FARs are paid a fee for providing advisory services. To me, paying for advisory services or advice from a financial planner makes much sense. I recently paid a tax consultant $5,000 for advice and was very happy to have made out the cheque to her. Just as how we pay lawyers or accountants for advice, paying for financial advice, independent of purchase of services, should be encouraged. In Singapore and most Asian countries today, this consultancy model is lesser known and used. Asians by and large do not like paying for advisory service or information. We tend to believe, erroneously, that information and advice can be given free.

Licensed to Give Advice

In Singapore, FARs and FA companies have to be licensed by the Monetary Authority of Singapore (MAS) before they can give advice on investment products to consumers. There are three categories:

- Licensed Financial Advisers (Licensed FAs). These are typically independent financial adviser companies that must have a minimum paid-up capital of either $150,000 or $300,000, depending on the activities they conduct and professional indemnity insurance.

- Exempt Financial Advisers (Exempt FAs). These are banks, merchant banks, finance companies, insurance companies, insurance brokers and holders of a capital markets services licence. Exempt FAs are exempt from holding an FA licence because MAS already regulates them under separate legislation. However, they must meet similar business conduct rules as the licensed FAs.

- Financial Adviser's (FA) Representatives. These are employees or agents appointed to provide financial advice on investment products on behalf of licensed FAs and exempt FAs.

If you are not from Singapore, find out what the categories are in your home country. Financial advisories in most developed economies tend to be regulated by the equivalent authorities. Ensure you are speaking to someone qualified to give advice and help you structure your investments.

Choosing a Financial Adviser

Neither Keon nor I are FARs. We both have good friends from the industry. Oh yes, I have changed much from my early days of hating agents. While I still am occasionally rude to agents who are over-persistent in trying to sell to me, I have come to appreciate the value they bring to my life. These are my guidelines for choosing an agent:

- If you do not have an agent, don't rush this decision. Get to know a few first. Ask your buddies to recommend their agents. Tell them you are interested in investing, but do not buy from the first agent you meet with, no matter how smart, good-looking, dashing, sweet, wonderful or great he is. They will be there and they will continue to be smart, good-looking, dashing, sweet, wonderful and great. Take your time. Choose.

- The agent is not there to tell you what to invest in, but should care what you buy *for your sake*. Any agent who pushes any one particular product to you is not someone you want to listen to. An agent should be able to give you a range of products and explain them to you with equal clarity and passion. When an agent is particularly passionate about a product, I would always ask, "Why?"

- I dislike agents who make me feel stupid and afraid to ask questions, no matter how stupid or dumb my questions may sound. If you feel you cannot ask your agent questions about anything under the sun, you should walk away. Anthonia, a friend of mine, is a super successful money manager for the Really Rich. She told me that she had once helped a client mend a difficult marriage; she pulled the wife to one side to explain to her that her husband was going through male menopause! A relationship with your agent or financial planner can be lifelong, and you should not be afraid to ask questions.

- If you do not like the way your agent smells or dresses, rethink the relationship. Some agents have halitosis and some have body odour. There are few of us who want to listen to someone who smells. Your instinct to flee will overcome you and you will hardly be able to have any deep discussion with her. If you know the agent well and if she is very good, you may want to advise her. She will probably be grateful for the advice. It's simple— you must like your agent.

Over the years, I've come to know a handful of agents whom I like and trust. Here's what I like about them:

- When they say they would do something for me, they get it done. Promptly, without excuse or tardiness. Sometimes, the agent is required to help me with some 'menial' job such as getting a financial standing report or making a phone call. The agent who does these unpaid activities for you without too much expectation is an agent worth listening to.

- They are truthful. If they do not know something, they say so. If they cannot get the information, they say so. If they are not representing a product you are looking for, they say so. Ideally, they even introduce you to their friends who are selling those products, thereby giving you choices.

- They are good human beings in themselves, with high morals and ideals.

What FARs Sell and How You Should Pay

FARs provide financial advice but only on the products for which they are licensed to sell. FARs today do not sell stocks and bonds, other than packaged products that include stocks and bonds. Perhaps it is just a matter of time before they do. Make sure you find out what your FAR is allowed to advise you on.

The market is rich with a wide range of insurance products with variations of benefits. There are almost endless product permutations matching age, gender, triggering events and risk appetite. The key products are: Benefit on Death, Benefit on Illness, Benefit on Event, and Investment-linked gains.

Note that FARs are not allowed to receive payments in their own name for the products sold. That is, if you are writing a cheque, ensure that the cheque is made out to the name of the product provider. It should not be written in favour of the FAR who sells you the product. If you do not have a cheque book or you prefer to pay in cash, you should get a receipt from the product provider as proof of payment.

> Some of the best people I know today are financial advisers. It is rare but possible to find such advisers. They take great pride in their work and they are passionate about helping others achieve financial freedom. They see this as their mission on earth.

Recourse on Complaint

If you have a complaint about your financial adviser or insurance policy, you should first refer the matter to your insurer or the insurance adviser who sold you the insurance policy. However, if you fail to reach an agreement, you should contact the relevant body that oversees such matters. In Singapore, the Financial Industry Disputes Resolution Centre (FIDReC) provides an independent, alternative dispute resolution scheme. It is like the Consumer Association of Singapore (CASE) for the financial services industry. If you are not from Singapore, this information can be readily found online.

Now that you know some of the main do's and don'ts regarding FARs, let's work on the nuts and bolts of insurance.

Getting Life Insurance

Life insurance answers a very difficult but necessary question: How will my family take care of themselves financially if I die?

Starkly put, if you have dependants, you need life insurance. Unless your family is already extremely wealthy and none of your relatives needs money on your death, you have to insure yourself for your dependants' sake. Should you pass away, life insurance payouts can be used to cover daily living expenses, mortgage payments, outstanding loans, university fees and other essential expenses. Even if you have worked hard to establish a solid financial framework for your family through other means, life insurance is the bedrock on which it all rest. It supports your plans if and when the unexpected occurs.

Why Life Insurance?

Here are some examples of life situations that should trigger the need for life insurance, should you pass away:

- If you are married, will your spouse have enough money to cover your funeral expenses, credit card balances, outstanding loans and daily living expenses?

- If you have children, will there be enough money to pay for day care, a college education and everything in between?

- If you own a house and were to pass away, can your family pay off the mortgage? What about present debt? Do you have large loans that you don't want your family to be burdened with?

- Will your ageing parents have enough money to live on?

- If you own a business, what will happen to your business if you or one of your key employees died?

Figuring out how much insurance you need is tricky because everyone's financial situation and goals are different and these change over time. There is no rule of thumb that can tell you exactly how much to buy. I recommend that you sit down with your insurance or financial adviser to go through what is called a Financial Needs Analysis to find out. Be aware that some advisers will try to sell you everything and the kitchen sink. You might then become overinsured!

Here is what you can expect to go through with the adviser. You will need to gather your personal financial information and estimate what your family members would need, after you are gone, to meet their current and future financial needs. Then add up the financial resources they can access to support themselves.

The difference between their needs and their resources equals the additional life insurance you need. Your adviser should also go through assumptions about inflation and investment returns in the long run.

Types of Life Insurance

There are really just two main types of life insurance: term life and permanent life.

Term life insurance

Term life insurance pays only a death benefit. It provides protection for a specific period of time or term. The period can be from one year to as long as 30 years. This type of insurance makes sense when your need for coverage disappears at some point in time, for example, when your children are grown up or the house mortgage is paid off. Because term insurance offers just coverage against death, it is cheaper than other types of insurance and is a good choice for young families on a tight budget.

Permanent life insurance

Permanent life insurance offers lifelong protection and accumulates cash values. The cash values can be withdrawn for a variety of purposes, such as for an emergency or for supplementing your retirement income. Compared with term life policies, however, premiums are higher, although premiums generally remain fixed for life.

The most basic feature of both types of life insurance is the DEATH BENEFIT, which is the lump sum payment your beneficiaries receive if you die. While this is one main reason to own life insurance, it is not the only one. Some policies have health insurance tag-alongs and others are investment-linked.

Naming Your Beneficiaries

In your life insurance contract, you should name at least one beneficiary, the person who will receive the benefits the policy provides. It is common practice to name someone who has a great deal to lose if you are not around anymore, such as your spouse and children. But choose your words carefully when naming your beneficiary.

> Life insurance is the bedrock upon which all other financial planning should rest. It is *the* responsible thing to do for your loved ones.

As an example, consider Henry, whose policy states the beneficiary as Mary Tan, his wife. If Mary became unfaithful and they divorced, and Henry subsequently passes away, Mary will still get the money even though she is no longer Henry's wife! Henry, of course, could change the beneficiary's name after the divorce. But if the policy came from an insurer that is governed under the Insurance Act, such as Prudential and AIA, you must seek your ex-spouse's permission to revoke her beneficiary status! What do you think Mary would say?

One exception in Singapore is NTUC Income which operates under the Co-operative Societies Act, a different legislation from other insurers. With an NTUC Income policy, you can name anyone you wish and revoke the nomination if you change your mind later.

In Singapore, regulations relating to the naming of beneficiaries in insurance policies are being changed as we write so we won't get into any kind of long-drawn discussion on the matter. Suffice it to say, please get your adviser to review what you have today to make sure that is what you really want. You do not want to benefit the wrong person after you are dead and gone.

Getting Health Insurance

Health insurance is one type of insurance you are guaranteed to use. If you do not have this insurance cover, you need to run out and get one as fast as you can. My suggestion is to sign up for the first reasonable package you understand. To be covered is better than not to be, especially in view of the potential disasters of insufficient coverage or non-coverage. You can always choose again as packages change from time to time. There are many types of health insurance products, depending on what you want protection against. Check Table 10.1 below to see what you can buy in the market today.

Table 10.1. Types of Health Insurance

If you want to…	You should consider…
Have your medical expenses paid	Medical expense insurance
Receive a fixed amount of cash when you are in hospital	Hospital cash insurance
Reduce your financial burden when you are diagnosed with a major illness (for example, cancer)	Critical illness insurance
Protect your income when you are unable to work	Disability income insurance
Pay the cost of any care you need when you are too weak to look after yourself	Long-term care insurance

(Source: Your Guide to Health Insurance, published by MoneySENSE)

Group Medical Insurance for Your Business
If you are the owner of a small business and you have not made use of group insurance to cover yourself and your staff, you are foolish. Group medical benefits using health insurance through a company is cheap. Staff members appreciate it, and it can be shown as a benefit to attract staff to stay with you. A small company I know spends about $2,000 a year in health insurance to cover its full-time staff. The year it bought the coverage, the company's owner was hospitalised with a bill of $10,000. The owner was relieved that she was smart enough to have bought insurance for herself and her team.

Health Insurance Pointers
Look out for these when you are buying health insurance:
- Age limit. Most products are not available to people over a certain age, so sign up early while you are still healthy.
- Premium type. Plans can be single-premium or regular-premium. If you have to pay regular premiums, the amount of the premiums will rise at each renewal as you grow older.
- Policy renewal. Some products guarantee that your cover will stay in force as long as you pay the premiums on time, while others give insurers the right to cancel your cover by giving you written notice.
- Policy termination. Your policy may end when you reach the maximum age stated in the policy, or you have received the maximum benefits that can be paid, or the insurer cancels your cover, or you fail to pay your premiums.
- Policy exclusions. All health policies contain some 'exclusions' which set out the circumstances under which benefits will not be paid. The most common exclusion is a 'pre-existing condition' exclusion. This exclusion means that any illness or disability that you have, or have had, when you sign up for the product will not be covered.

- Free look period. You have 14 days to review your policy. If you cancel the policy during this period, the insurer will refund all your premiums, less any expenses the insurer incurred, such as for your medical check-up.

- Extent of medical coverage. The cost of healthcare differs greatly between private and public hospitals, and between different types of ward. Make sure you check the ward charges and the costs of medical treatment recommended by your doctor. Check whether the benefits under your health insurance will cover the costs.

- Worldwide cover. Health insurance products generally provide cover anywhere in the world. However, some products have geographic limits.

Importantly, when buying health insurance, provide accurate and truthful information. An insurance contract is based on trust. When you apply for health insurance, you must provide all the information asked for. Such information would include your age and occupation, and any history of illnesses, medical conditions or disabilities. When you provide false information, and you are found to have provided false information, the contract is revoked even if you have paid the premiums. Insurance companies do check, and when they do, your policy must stand solid on the information you provide.

Long-Term Care Insurance

Long-term care goes beyond medical care and nursing care. It includes all the assistance you might need if you ever have a chronic illness or disability that leaves you unable to care for yourself for an extended period of time, whether in a nursing home or in your own home.

If you think such a day will never happen, consider this. Statistics show that about 19 per cent of Americans aged 65 and older will experience some degree of chronic physical impairment. Among those aged 85 or older, the proportion of people who are impaired and require long-term care is about 55 per cent.

In Singapore, there is a government backed programme called ElderShield which provides $300 cash every month, for up to five years, to those who are not able to do at least three of six activities of daily living (ADLs): washing, dressing, feeding, toileting, mobility and transferring. Private schemes are also available; some of these require you to be unable to perform just two of the six ADLs before benefits are provided.

You should also be thinking of long-term care insurance for your parents when they are insurable. I met a very jolly ex-civil servant while warded in a hospital three years ago. She said to me that it was by a stroke of luck that she insured her parents when they were younger. According to her, if she had not insured them when she did, she would have been wiped clean of her savings when they suddenly required expensive treatments in their old age.

Insurance for Women's Needs

Long-term care for women is particularly important. We tend to live longer, have shorter careers and earn less. We absolutely cannot afford to be caught out with insufficient insurance just as we are reaching our goal of financial independence.

We are also more susceptible to physical disabilities arising from conditions such as osteoporosis. We should, therefore, get as comprehensive an amount of coverage as we can get and afford. It should cover death, total and permanent disability, major illnesses, female-related illnesses, maternity complications, loss of income, accidental death, hospital and surgical expenses, and long-term care.

Some questions women should ask:

- Does the plan cover female cancers such as breast, ovarian and cervical cancer?

- Does the plan cover carcinoma-in-situ, which is an early form of cancer where there is an absence of invasion of surrounding tissues? This benefit differs from the cancer coverage in a critical illness plan, which requires the condition to be malignant and invasive before a claim may be made.

This benefit is particularly relevant to women susceptible to breast cancer.

- Does the plan cover surgical procedures for reconstructive surgery due to mastectomy, skin cancer, accidents and burns?

- Does the plan cover maternity complications that include babies diagnosed with congenital anomalies such as Down's Syndrome and the infant's death soon after birth?

These questions are unique to women and, therefore, you must take care to ask them and get covered. If you are married and your husband takes care of insurance matters for the home, ensure you get involved. Your husband may not realise what you need!

INSURANCE FOR SMALL BUSINESSES

Owning your own business can be one of the most satisfying experiences of your life. More women than men become small business owners at one point or other in their lives. Perhaps women do this because they want to spend more time with their families or they have hit a ceiling at work or they are just plain tired of adopting male values in male-dominated workplaces.

In your own business, whether small or large, you can follow your dream, earn a good living, provide employment for others, and maybe even make a difference in the world. But owning a business also entails a lot of responsibilities to your business, your employees and your family. I do not recommend it for everyone. It is tough! I own three small businesses today. Just about every day I worry about what will happen to my businesses if I become disabled or, worse, die? Can I sell them one day and retire? What can I do to make sure my most important employees stay with me?

With the help of a few financial advisers who have experience helping small businesses, I have started to put some plans in place to answer these critical questions. If you own a business, here are some important matters that you should attend to:

- Have a business continuation plan. One of the first things any business owner needs to consider is how to protect against events that may threaten the future of the business, such as the death of the owner, a partner or key employee. Business continuation plans protect family and partners from unwanted debts and responsibilities when an owner dies.

- Protect your family from personal guarantees. Many small business owners take out loans to help grow their businesses, and often secure these loans with personal assets and on a personal basis. If you have business loans and you were to pass away before the loans are paid off, you might think your family could liquidate the business to cover the debts and provide financial security for themselves. In reality, this rarely happens. When the family is forced to sell the business quickly, they would normally have to sell it at a discount or under poor market conditions. In other cases, the business may be worth very little without the owner or partner. Individual life insurance can protect your family by providing funds to cover guaranteed debts and living expenses should something happen to you.

- Protect your partners and family. When you die, your family would most likely not be able to run the business themselves as they may not have the skills or the desire for the job. One solution is to construct a buy-sell agreement between shareholders to buy out a deceased owner's share of the business in the event of the co-owner's retirement, disability or death. Buy-sell agreements are typically funded by a life insurance benefit sufficient to buy out the deceased's share, thus providing financial security for the surviving family.

- Protect your business. In your business, you probably would have certain employees who play a particularly critical role for the bottom line. Key person insurance can be purchased by the business on the life of such an employee and payable to the business. The death benefit can help make up for lost sales or cover the cost of finding and training a replacement.

- Take care of your employees. An adequate employee benefits programme is essential no matter how small or big your company is. It is a necessary tool for attracting new employees and retaining current ones. In fact, when it comes to retaining employees, benefits can make or break the deal. These benefits include life insurance and retirement plans (which could be co-funded by you and your employees).

Insurance is fundamental to the financial well-being of both your business and family. So, please get it done and do not neglect something this basic.

Consider Accident Coverage

Two years after I completed my MBA programme in Australia, I received the shocking news that my classmate Joanna had had a skiing accident which paralysed her from the neck downwards. She never recovered and became a paraplegic. When she visited Singapore five years later, she came with her full-time nurse who spoon-fed and babysat her 24 hours a day. Joanna's insurance covered the long-term care she required to ensure she would be well looked after.

Insurance ... Last Words

I started this chapter saying how much I hated FARS. Today, some of my good friends are FARs. My biggest financial regret in life is that I discontinued my insurance policy when I needed the money as a young woman with a young family. Getting back a policy years later was incredibly difficult and expensive. Please, don't do what I did.

> Befriend an agent today. Buy insurance as it is a sensible basic financial product to protect yourself and your loved ones. And it is certainly much more lasting and important than some over-advertised, famous black-eye-ring prevention cream that costs $200 or more for a small tube. Insurance, unlike those miracle creams, work, and are cheap for the peace of mind they offer.

Interview With
Michael Lee, Insurance Veteran

Michael Lee is a 25-year veteran of the insurance industry and the CEO of Cornerstone Planners Pte. Ltd. in Singapore. We asked him what he thought about insurance for women.

Q What must women absolutely have?
A Whether a woman is 20 or 60, she will definitely need health care insurance and very likely, life insurance coverage as well. By health care, I mean she needs to be adequately covered for hospitalisation and surgery, dental care, disability income, long-term care, women's illnesses and major illnesses. This may seem like a long list, but there are insurance policies that can offer all this packaged into one.

You might ask why a healthy 20-year-old would want health and life insurance. I can tell you that illnesses and death do not discriminate by age. I have seen healthy women in their twenties and thirties suddenly become afflicted with cancer and other major illnesses, and subsequently pass away.

Moreover, a woman needs to get health insurance when she is healthy in order to lock in her eligibility for insurance. You see, when she becomes unhealthy, not only would her premiums become exorbitant, she may not even be offered insurance. Life insurance is absolutely important for a woman especially when she has children and other dependants who need money to survive on should something happen to her. Or when she has liabilities that she does not want to pass on to her family. Or she wants to gift an amount of money to her favourite charity.

Many young women still question the need for life insurance. Once I had a client who was half my age and she said that when she needs to make a claim, I probably wouldn't be around anymore to help her. I told her that coffins contain dead people and not old people. Dead people can be young and old. She bought insurance from me soon after that.

One more thing to remember. If you are covered by your company or are included in your spouse's company plan, remember that once retirement or retrenchment happens, such coverage is lost. This means you better have your own private insurance plan to complement what your workplace or spouse's workplace offers.

Q My family is already insured generously through my company. Should I bother with my own?
A As answered above, you must have your own insurance. Your spouse can lose his job, he can pass away, or the two of you could separate and divorce. Do not depend on your spouse totally for your insurance needs.

Q What can I do if my parents are not insurable?
A Have you exhausted your options? There are health care policies that allow entry up to age 75. If your parents are beyond that age or have illnesses that preclude them from getting any coverage, then you'll have to self-fund. One of the first things to self-fund is for you and your siblings to top up your parents' Medisave funds from which they can draw down for medical expenses. Your contributions are tax deductible. If that option is not available, then it would also be good to sit down with your siblings and family to set aside a fund today for their future needs. You would want to do this so that when the money is needed, there won't be a mad and stressful scramble to gather funds from everyone.

Q Any other advice for women?
A Medical needs are complex. And they are not cheap. You do need a financial adviser to help you make sense of your personal situation and advise you on the type of coverage you need. And you should do this right away and make every attempt to understand what's happening. So get a financial adviser who is willing to counsel you on your entire family's situation, including even your parents', especially if they are not insurable. Just think of a medical emergency happening today, and you'll be glad that you did the planning ahead of time.

Part Four
Investment Products

Venturing Into The World Of Investment Products

It is just not possible for anyone wanting to become rich and financially independent not to invest.

Putting your money in a biscuit tin—while perhaps advisable in times of severe financial crises, and only if inflation was still predictable—will never make you rich. In fact, you lose buying power because of the effects of inflation. Given the risk-return relationship, it is insufficient to play safe by parking all your available funds in fixed deposits and savings accounts.

TO BECOME RICH OR FINANCIALLY INDEPENDENT, YOU NEED TO BE INVESTED.

Stocks and bonds are the more basic investment products. Derivatives are more complex as are other exotic products. We discuss all these and our '3-basket' approach to investing in this section.

As you embark on your investment journey, remember that you must invest with both eyes opened. In other words, do not trust until you have some understanding of what you are buying and the industry benchmarks.

You must also understand yourself. Investment knowledge grows with experience and mistakes. You will make mistakes in your quest to invest. But you can keep your mistakes small by investing in what you understand. Add to your understanding over time.

Finally, keep focused on the overall return of your portfolio rather than making decisions on single investments.

11 Stocks, Bonds And Unit Trusts

When companies such as Singapore Telecommunications (SingTel) need funds for new business projects, they usually raise money by issuing stocks and bonds. Stocks and bonds are the two most basic investment products for any investor. In this chapter, we will discuss these as well as a third type of investment product—unit trusts.

What Are Stocks?

When you invest in a company's stock, you have an ownership interest in the company. Companies sell their stock to the public on a stock exchange to raise additional capital. The returns you get from owning stock come from two sources:

- Cash dividends (the money paid regularly by the company to you, its shareholder).
- Capital gains (rise in share price and the profit you get from selling the stock when the company performs well).

Stocks do not guarantee the timing or the amount of dividends paid out. At any time, the dividends can be increased, decreased or taken away altogether.

So You Want To Be A Stock Investor

When you buy a stock, you become part owner of the company. In fact, one of the best reasons you may want to own stocks of a company is that you are very interested in the business and you understand why it might fail or succeed, BUT you do not want to show up for work. Stocks give you a chance to own the company and as well its success (and failure).

When you buy stocks, you are buying into the future performance of the company. You should therefore understand the dynamics of the business and the kinds of information in the marketplace that may cause the business to lose its value.

The best way to understand the prospects behind a stock is to understand how it will be affected by changing conditions in the economy, people's tastes, general price levels, and yes, even the weather. One of the best stock investment advice I have come across was from Peter Lynch, who used to run the famous Magellan Fund. He said: "Never invest in any idea you can't illustrate with a crayon." For the same reason possibly, Warren Buffett said that he does not invest in technology companies as he does not understand them sufficiently.

Perhaps for most women, one of the reasons in the past that could have kept them from investing in stocks was that most listed companies then tended to be companies in industries which women thought they could not understand, such as shipbuilding, aeronautical engineering and construction. But if investment is predicated on understanding the business of the company before an investment is made, there are many listed companies that women can use as a beginner's kit to investing. Try The Hour Glass (great watches), Food Empire (great 3-in-1 beverages) and FJ Benjamin (great brands) on the Singapore Stock Exchange. Internationally, companies such as the Vendome Luxury Group (maker of Cartier, Piaget and Montblanc) produce luxury handbags and watches.

In a sense, investment is easy. If a company sells great shoes, people buy those great shoes, you yourself desire those shoes, and you know there is rising affluence in Asia with an increasing group of brand-conscious wannabes, perhaps such a stock is worth looking at. I say 'perhaps' because a company's financial performance is not just dependent on its ability to sell but also its ability to make a profit.

You might then have questions as to whether the company's board and the management are people to whom you want to entrust your investment. For when you invest in a company, the board and the management are the people paid to look after your investment. You have become the company's shareholder. Companies take great pains to put together top management teams that are robust and board members who are able to stand up to market scrutiny.

But if you think you know that the person at the helm of a specific company is not all she seems, you might want to stay away to avoid an unpleasant surprise. Imagine a scenario where your father happened to be the chauffeur of the majority shareholder of a listed company, and he tells you that his boss is probably involved in 'funny business' because he had overheard the boss' phone calls. Imagine your father tells you that he is sure the boss is up to no good. Would you make an investment in that company even if the share price appears to be going through the roof?

> Understanding yourself and how you would react to financial information is as important as understanding the financial information.

In the ideal world, stock prices go up when companies do well and make a profit, or if a company promises to do well through its performance projections. But stock prices change every day as a result of market forces and investor psychology. Understanding these market forces and predicting mass behaviour often stump the best investor, even highly trained and experienced ones. Understanding yourself and how you would react to information and price changes is therefore even more important for you. If you are a knee-jerk investor, you need to exercise some level of restraint and self-control. If, however, nothing moves you even when the company is in a bad shape, because you never cut ties or relationships, you might want to rethink being an investor. Investment is not sentimentalism.

Two Main Types of Stocks
There are generally two main types of stocks: growth stocks and dividend stocks.
- Growth stocks. These are issued by companies with high growth potential needing cash for market expansion. People who invest

into Google, for example, may be investing for capital gains (rise in share price) as opposed to dividends. Growth stocks tend to be in industries that are expanding and performance might vary. Growth companies tend to have higher Price Earnings ratios. The higher ratio reflects the market expectations for the stock to grow its earnings faster than those in mature industries.

- Dividend stocks. These are issued by companies with high dividend payouts. Such companies do not need cash generated for market expansion and, therefore, tend to be in mature businesses where growth is steady and profits are predictable, and they are sitting on a fat cash cow. In Singapore, for example, Singapore Post is known to be a dividend stock, promising to pay good dividends every year. Dividend stocks tend to be companies in a mature industry.

Both types of stocks are good. Which is right for you?

Before you Invest in Stocks

Know the Company's Value–The P/E Ratio

How does one analyse a company's value? There are many techniques that can be used to determine value, some subjective and others objective. For example, you can value a company by looking at its management, or its prospects for future earnings and the market value of its assets. Judging the contributions of a company's management would be more subjective while calculating its value based on future earnings would be a more objective technique. Any analysis should answer the simple question: "What is something worth?"

Many types of valuation methods are used. One of the most common is the Price/Earnings ratio (or P/E ratio or PER for short). The reason is clear—you get to the bottom line. That is what investors want to know: How much money the company is making and how much it is expected to make in the future.

Calculating The P/E Ratio

The P/E ratio looks at the relationship between stock price and the company's earnings. You calculate the ratio by taking the share price and dividing it by the company's earnings per share (EPS). A company's EPS is the amount of earnings the company made divided by the number of shares the company has issued. So if a company's earnings is $1 million and it has issued two million shares, then its EPS is $1m/2m = 50 cents.

To see how this works: If company A has a stock price of $5 and its EPS is 50 cents, then its P/E ratio is 10 times:

$$\text{P/E ratio} = \text{Stock Price}/\text{EPS}$$
$$\text{P/E ratio} = \$5/\$0.50 = 10 \text{ times}$$

The P/E ratio gives you an idea of what the market is willing to pay for the company's earnings. The higher the P/E ratio, the more willing the market.

A high P/E ratio can also be read as an overpriced stock. But while 'overpricing' may be true, a high P/E ratio stock can also indicate that the market has high hopes for the future prospects of this stock and has bid up the price. A P/E ratio can also be quite high and still be considered 'cheap' by the market. Such stocks are called growth stocks.

On the other hand, a low P/E ratio stock may indicate the market's lack of confidence in the stock. Its future prospects are dim and the market is depressing its stock price relative to its earnings. Or, a low P/E ratio can indicate a value stock—an underpriced stock that the market has overlooked. Investors can make fortunes by spotting these sleepers before the rest of the market discovers their true worth.

At the very least, a company's P/E ratio should be compared with:

- P/E ratios of the same company over past several years. If the ratio of company A is currently 10 and its P/E ratio averaged over the last ten years is 15, we can say that the stock is cheap compared with its past.

- P/E ratios of other companies in the same business. If company A has a P/E ratio of 10 and is in the chemicals industry that, as a whole, has a P/E ratio of 5, we can say that the stock is expensive compared with its peers.

Know What Factors Affect Stock Price

When you buy a company's stock, you are investing in the future growth of the company. Yet, the stock's price may go up or down based on other broad economic factors that may only indirectly affect the company.

For example, concerns about a recession can send the overall market into a decline while strong economic growth is generally good news for the country and the market. The tricky thing is that some of these factors can be positive at times, yet negative at other times. Strong economic growth, for instance, can be 'too' strong and cause shortages of goods and services that drive up prices and inflation. As you know, inflation is bad because higher prices will make people stop spending and slow down the economy.

So the trick is for you to understand which market-moving factors may affect the company and its stock. Our suggestion is that you get into the habit of reading the business section of newspapers, and if that is too boring for you, watch CNBC or Bloomberg on TV. The TV, the newspapers and other financial reports I receive are indispensable in helping me monitor what is going on in the real world and how that affects financial markets.

While day-to-day economic news can affect a company's daily stock price, we should be more interested in *longer-term* trends. Many of these trends you already know and a little bit of common sense will help you get a good sense of the underlying factors. To name three:

- The boomer market. Singapore has one of the fastest ageing populations in the world. If you are in the 45–60 age group, ask yourself what you'll need more than ever before. How about vitamins, medical care, healthy food, exercise machines and travel packages? Watch the industries that provide these services and try to pick out the good companies to invest in.

- The high net worth market. Have you seen the greater number of Lamborghinis on Asian roads these days? The rich club is growing not just in Singapore but in major cities in Asia and the Middle East. So too will their appetite for luxury goods, wealth management services, spa treatments and great food.

- The education market. We are aiming to be the major education hub in Asia. Many established universities from the US and Europe have set up campuses and facilities here. International students come to Singapore for a truly cosmopolitan experience. All over Asia, people are in a hurry to study English and Mandarin. The education market will be a booming market for many years to come.

All said, however, you do need to do your homework. Figure out what the long-term underlying trends are. Then find the companies you like and learn about their products and markets.

What Are Bonds?

Bonds are loans issued by companies or governments to borrow money. Bonds have two main characteristics.

- They have lifespans greater than 12 months at the time of issue.

- They typically promise to make fixed interest payments according to a given schedule. Bonds are hence also called fixed income securities.

The returns you get from owning bonds come from two sources:
- Fixed interest payments at regular intervals.

- Final payment of the principal sum at maturity.

Three Common Bond Categories
Three common ways to categorise bonds are:

- By duration. If a bond is issued for five years, then we say that the maturity of the bond is five years, after which the borrower will pay you back the principal.

- By borrower. This is the issuer of the bond. The main issuers are companies and government offices.

- By the quality of the borrower. This is the investment grade of the bond. If the issuer has an excellent financial standing, the bond may have a grade such as AAA. It means that it is very likely to pay you when it is time to pay you. AAA bonds are lower risk and thus offer lower returns. Lesser-grade issuers may have their bonds rated C or even lower. Of course, C-grade bonds carry higher risk and have to pay you more. These are the junk bonds, also known as high-yield bonds.

STOCK AND BOND PERFORMANCE

Stocks have historically outperformed most other investments in the long run. And most people know that in the long run, stock returns beat bonds in total return. But stocks are considered more risky than bonds because stock returns are more uncertain in the short and medium term. While bonds do not have the appeal of stocks, bonds have two features that stocks cannot match.

Firstly, bonds return a known amount at the end of a stated period. When you buy a bond, you are lending money to the company that promises to pay you back what you lent when the bond matures, plus interest every six months or a year. For example, if you buy a 5 per cent Microsoft bond, you can expect to receive 5 per cent in interest every year and whatever principal you put down at the end of the period. Unless the borrower goes bankrupt, a bond investor can almost be certain that the capital originally invested will be returned. This certainty is less if the bond falls into the category of junk bonds.

With stocks, the loss of your capital into the investment is not only possible, it happens every time the share price dips below the price you bought the stock at. With bonds, if you wait out the stated period, you get back exactly what you put in.

Secondly, bonds pay interest according to a fixed schedule, typically twice a year. This interest can provide valuable income for retired couples and individuals, or for those who want a predictable cash flow.

Also, if you are not careful about which company you invest in, the company may have disappeared when you next review your investments. This last statement is particularly true for the global financial crisis in 2008 when Lehman Brothers declared bankruptcy and other companies looked weak enough to go under anytime.

Let's suppose you bought $10,000 worth of stock in Charlie and Ken Co., a company that sells fashionable women's shoes, and sold the stock after five years. Your returns are not certain because of a few key parameters.

- Companies are not legally obliged to pay dividends even if they make a profit. They may choose to reinvest their profits. So, you may get dividends some years and none in other years.

- Companies' earnings are seldom stable. They can be high in some years and low in others. This causes a company's stock price to fluctuate from year to year. In the end, your stocks may sell for $15,000 or $8,000 or anything in between.

Bond returns, on the other hand, are more stable. Suppose you bought bonds in Charlie and Ken Co., and the bond's rate of interest is 5 per cent and expires in five years' time. In other words, the company is borrowing money from you for which it promises to pay you 5 per cent interest every year. It also promises to give you back your capital in five years' time. This means that if you buy $10,000 of bonds, Charlie and Ken Co. will pay you interest of $500 a year for five years. After five years, your $10,000 is returned to you.

With a bond investment, you will know from the start exactly how much money you will receive. For this reason, bonds are generally safer than stocks if both are issued by the same entity. You cannot compare bonds issued by a junk bond issuer to a blue-chip stock. The risk profile and returns of the two products are different.

This Thing Called Unit Trusts

This book has become increasingly tough for some of you. But don't give up. Not yet. We have a solution for those who find all this too complex—unit trusts. Did you know you can hire a group of full-time investment professionals to analyse, select, buy and sell stocks and bonds on your behalf?

Yes, you can. When you invest in unit trusts, a team of professionals is there for you. They are paid a management fee through a percentage taken from your investment monies. For as little as $1,000, you can invest in any one of about 600 Singapore-registered funds. The funds are managed by professional fund managers whose jobs are hinged on how much they make for you. What you must look out for, however, is the size of the management fee.

Most times, the distributor of the unit trust will not highlight the management fee to you in her sales pitch. She would talk about past returns or expected returns of the fund. So watch out! Some unit trusts ask for higher fees than others. Higher fees are justifiable if the expected performance is above market average. But if the expected performance barely covers the fees, your takeaway will be marginal. So most importantly, what do you expect to take away from the unit trust investment?

You should also remember that both past and expected returns do not mean guaranteed returns. You must still ask the right questions and if the fund fits into your investment portfolio or strategy. Otherwise, you will be buying blindly just because the seller is in front of you pushing you a financial product and promising you a great outcome.

Unit trusts fall into two main categories: equity funds (or stock funds) and fixed income funds (or bond funds).

Equity Funds (Stock Funds)
Equity funds are unit trusts consisting of stocks. Here are some examples of equity funds:

- Global equity funds. These invest in promising companies anywhere in the world.

- Regional equity funds. These invest in the stocks of a single geographic region, such as Asia, Europe or Latin America. The share prices of these funds typically fluctuate more than the share prices of broadly diversified global equity funds.

- Single-country equity funds. These invest in the stocks of a single foreign country such as China, Singapore or the US. These funds are considered riskier than regional funds because of their narrower focus.

- Emerging market equity funds. These invest in countries that are moving to an industrialised economy or a free market economy. These markets offer the potential for faster economic growth than established markets, but they also present substantial risks. Examples of such countries are Brazil, Mexico, Indonesia and South Africa.

- Sector funds. These invest in a specific industry such as technology and health care. Investing in a narrow segment is higher risk because if fortunes in that sector fall, the whole portfolio is vulnerable. Sector funds are attractive if you already hold a diversified portfolio and you want to take on more risk because these funds can sometimes achieve spectacular returns.

- Index funds. Also called ETFs (Exchange-Traded Funds), these funds closely track and replicate market indexes such as the Straits Times Index. Unlike the other equity funds, index funds trade on the stock exchange. They are cheaper to own in terms of lower operating expenses.

Fixed Income Funds (Bond Funds)

Fixed income funds are unit trusts consisting of bonds. Fixed income funds invest in bonds issued by companies and governments. Like equity funds, there are fixed income funds that invest globally, regionally, in emerging markets and in individual countries. Some examples of fixed income funds are:

- High-yield fixed income funds. These seek higher returns by investing in high-yielding, lower-quality corporate bonds.

- Mortgage-backed funds. These seek to maximise income by investing in mortgage-backed securities, bonds backed with a claim on specific property. The bonds are thus of lower risk than unsecured bonds that are not backed by any asset.

Why Buy Unit Trusts And Not Invest Directly?

Ken Fisher, a leading investment professional in the US, advises that anyone with less than US$200,000 to invest should be investing primarily through funds. His advice is to look into index funds as he believes that most managers have a hard time trying to beat the market. For the majority of us then, going by Ken Fisher's advice, index linked unit trusts are a good vehicle for investment.

For those of you with more than US$200,000 cash to invest, first, I am surprised you are reading this book. Second, please read Ken Fisher's *The Only Three Questions that Count*. Third, please also spend time reading what Warren Buffet thinks and how he invests.

In the meantime, as you work out your investment strategies, you can stay invested in unit trusts. But do look carefully into timing and management fees.

Choosing A Unit Trust

There are several hundred funds available in Singapore. Choose carefully. Funds are sold like consumer goods these days. Banks and financial advisers who sell funds often have slick brochures and impressive fund performance numbers to show. But not all funds are good and even if you have someone advising you, it's best you do your own homework.

We recommend you do some fund analysis research through www.fundsingapore.com, an industry-sponsored website. All the images (11.1–11.4) are taken from Lipper, a Thomson Reuters Company.

Here's what you can do as a start:

- Go to www.fundsingapore.com. Click on Basic Search. Click on the various box options as shown below in Image 11.1. During this search, 198 equity unit trust matches will be found that could be invested into and that are offered by all the fund managers tracked by the database. If you have a CPF (Central Providend Fund) account, you can use your funds in there to invest. The page should look like Image 11.1.

Basic Search	Quick Search	Advance Screening

Fund Type

Universe	CPF Included
Unit Trusts	All

CPF Account type	Select An Asset Type
CPF INCLUDED OA	All Funds

CPF Risk Classification	Fund Manager
HIGHER RISK	Aberdeen Asset Management Asia Limited
MEDIUM TO HIGH RISK	AIG Global Investment Corporation (Singapore) Ltd
LOW TO MEDIUM RISK	AllianceBernstein (Luxembourg) SA
LOWER RISK	Allianz Global Investors KAG mbH

Ctrl+click selects multiple options

Fund Type Matches: **198**

Image 11.1. Basic Search on www.fundsingapore.com

You can narrow your search based on selective criteria. For example, suppose you want to look further at equity unit trusts that have consistent returns and favourable expense ratios compared with its peers (funds of the same type in the same group).

- Next, click for Consistent Return and Expense on the boxes below as seen in Image 11.2.

- Clicking on the Matches button reveals the funds that meet your criteria. (Image 11.3)

- At this point, we clicked on the last fund on the list, the United International Growth Fund. A whole lot of fund information appears (Image 11.4). The nice thing is that the same information format is used for all funds in the database. So after you get used to the format, going from fund to fund is easy.

This is just a sample to give you an idea of the kind of resources available to help you invest. We won't go through each and every technical detail in the database. You need either to put in the time to learn by going to the website, or get hold of a financial adviser to explain it to you.

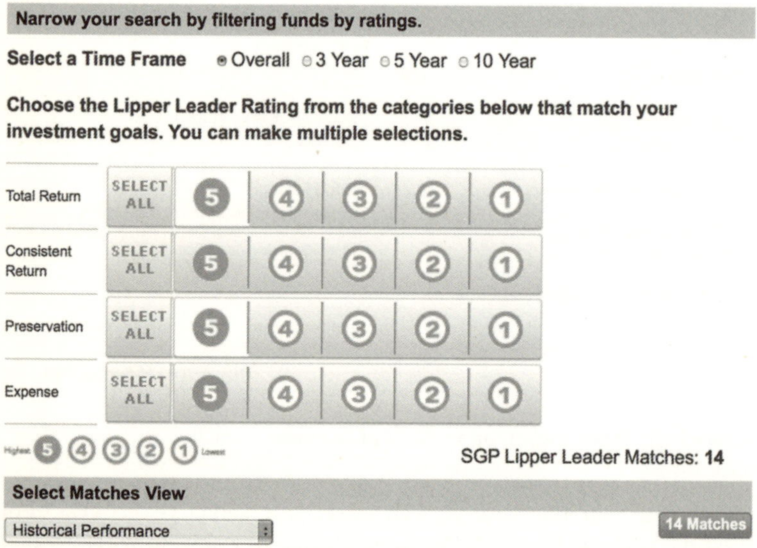

Image 11.2. Filtering Search to Match Criteria

Name	Class	Currency	Latest NAV
Aberdeen Global Technology	Equity Sector Information Tech	SGD	0.25
Accumulator	Equity Global	SGD	1.07
DBS Japan Growth	Equity Japan	SGD	0.59
DWS China Equity A SGD	Equity China	SGD	1.73
Eight Portfolio E	Equity Global	SGD	0.52
LionGlobal Thailand SGD	Equity Thailand	SGD	1.14
United International Growth Fund	Equity Global	SGD	1.09

Image 11.3. Seven Funds Matched to Search Criteria

United International Growth Fund

Overview

Fund Type	Equity
Geographical Focus	Global
Launch Date	07/04/1995
Domicile	Singapore
Currency	Singapore Dollar
Legal Structure	UNITTRST
NAV as of 09/03/2009	1.0940
TNA (Total Net Assets) as of 27/02/2009	127.08 Mil

Objective 29/04/2008

The Fund aims to achieve long-term capital appreciation through investing mainly in shares in global emerging and developed markets, identified by the Managers as having good prospects for growth.

Benchmarks

Technical Indicator	MSCI World TR USD
Risk Free	SIBOR SGD 3 Months
Fund Manager	Cust Benchm UOB United International Growth Fund

Management

Administrator	UOB Asset Management Ltd
Custodian	HSBC Institutional Trust Services (Singapore) Ltd
Investment Advisor	UOB Asset Management Ltd
Fund Management Company	UOB Asset Management Ltd

Minimum Investment (SGD) as of 29/04/2008

Initial	Regular	Irregular
500	100	500

Charges (%) as of 29/04/2008

Type	Retail	CPF
Initial	5.00	--
Annual	1.00	1.00
Redemption	1.00	--

Other

Income Distribution	--
Ex-dividend date	--
Dividend Payment	--
Dividends Per Year	1

Image 11.4. United International Growth Fund

We like this website because Lipper provides third-party evaluation that is independent of fund managers. The Lipper Leaders Rating System is also very simple to understand—the highest 20 per cent in its peer group are rated 5, and the lowest 20 per cent are rated 1 for each measure.

The Lipper Leaders Rating System scores funds according to several filters: total return, consistent return, preservation of capital, tax efficiency and expenses. For example, the Consistent Return rating not only shows how frequently the fund beats other funds in its peer group, but also takes into account the fund's overall volatility. In general, funds with high rankings tend to beat their peers and they do so without roller-coaster volatility.

Note that these ratings measure past performance which begs the question, "*Can you count on past performance?*", since we are investing for future results, not past. Some experts say that past performance is pretty much worthless when it comes to trying to figure out the future. Unlike reports that measure the reliability of washing machines, investment performance is very difficult to predict. While you may have a good prediction on hand today, things can change the next day as economies go up and down. Not only that, funds can change managers overnight.

In fact, *underperformance* of a once hot fund is common. Nobel prize winner William Sharpe cited a study which showed how funds that finished in the top 20 per cent over five years were the least likely to finish in the top 50 per cent over the next five years.

We believe that while the past is not indicative of the future, it still does a decent job of telling us what a good fund is. Here are some rules of thumb to consider:

- Buy funds with good track records with as long a history as possible. If fund A is the top performer over the last three years and fund B is the top performer over the last ten years, we would choose B.

- Buy funds with lower expense ratios, everything else being equal, because expenses will eat into your returns. If fund A's expense ratio is 2.5 per cent and fund B's is 1 per cent, fund A will cost 1.5 per cent more to run year in and year out. If you hold the fund for ten years, you lose 15 per cent of returns.

Now let's talk about your fund manager.

Choosing A Fund Manager

Choose the best. Look at who is consistently near the top of the performance table. Fund managers don't necessarily have to be number one every time, but they certainly should be close.

Choose a fund manager who has her money in the fund with you. The best fund managers generally invest their money in the fund they are recommending.

Listen to what they say. What does the fund manager say about performance? Where does he expect returns to come from? Read what they have to say in industry newsletters, magazines and the newspapers. Compare what they say to what you know. What is worse than losing money is losing money in something that you did not start off believing in, but you accidentally invested in. So read, read, read, and take time to understand the new game.

Ask about costs. Management charges can eat away returns. There is no point choosing a great fund manager if his fees are too high. And finally, look at the fund manager's short-term and long-term performance track record over all time periods.

Last Words ... Price And Value

The PRICE of any investment is what it would sell between buyer and seller, whether in a private sale or an open market sale. On one extreme of an open market sale, stock market prices fluctuate on daily buyer-seller transactions.

The VALUE of a stock is based on its underlying business, which for the majority of businesses do not change drastically from day to day, and may not even change drastically from quarter to quarter despite quarterly reporting for many companies, especially in the US. There are many ways to value companies. As some experts say, valuation is both an art and a science.

The investment fundamentalist way would be to try to understand the dynamics of an underlying business, and the strength of the business' management and board. Value it and then, invest. Most of us would not have the devotion of a Warren Buffet to understand an investment or to work out asset allocation. Most of us will research, analyse and plan. But none of us would do it as thoroughly as we would have to if investment management were our full-time job, and if we had billions at our disposal to change the future of companies through investments. Compared with Warren Buffet, our investments are, therefore, 'speculative' to a large extent.

OVER TO YOU

- Read a book or a website on understanding unit trusts and the numbers behind them.

- Attend financial talks. The Singapore Stock Exchange (SGX) holds regular talks and so do brokerage houses. You do not need to buy anything or be afraid of asking dumb questions. Remember it is better to look stupid asking dumb questions than it is to lose money because you were too proud to ask.

- Talk to banks about the unit trusts they market. Do not buy immediately. Understand what you are buying. Here's a list of questions to ask the unit trust reseller:

    - Who is the manager of the fund? What are the historical results? What is the management fee? What other funds do they manage and how do these other funds perform?

    - In what situations will I lose money? Is my capital protected? How? Can I lose my capital?

    - What are the expected returns?

Your exercise on reading this chapter is to watch Bloomberg or CNBC television for a month. I specially recommend "Bloomberg Morning Call" and "Bloomberg Asia Confidential". Watch these channels before you make your first investment. Although Bloomberg is more US- and UK-centric, you will gain a much better understanding of the stock market just by watching these channels.

12 Exotic, Intriguing, Complex and Alternative

Human Beings And Innovation

The earliest stocks and securities revolved around shipping and the spice trade. First, it was the maritime empires of the Netherlands and Portugal, then later Spain, France and England. The Dutch later started joint stock companies (which allowed shareholders to invest in business ventures) to get a share of their profits or losses.

The Dutch East India Company was the first company to issue stocks and on the Amsterdam Stock Exchange in 1602. The Dutch East India Company furthered Dutch colonisation of Asian domains, changing the political landscape and the development of their colonies with an impact lasting to the present day.

The history of how money was made in the early mercantile economy is the reason we have the saying today—"Your ship has come in!"—when someone strikes a good deal and makes a lot of money.

During his term from 1789 to 1795 as the first US Secretary of the Treasury, Alexander Hamilton started the first stock markets in America. Today, the US stock market is the largest, and most actively and internationally traded stock market in the world. To me, it is the most exciting market to be in.

Exoticism, Blind Speculation And Investment Bubbles

Although stocks and bonds form the backbone of all investments, they are not mankind's only investment inventions.

We humans innovate all the time. In a matter of 300 years, with most of the changes happening over the last 30 or so years, new financial products were developed largely due to information technology and new mathematics. These new products are complex and sophisticated. Topping off the complexity is a lot of speculation, giving rise to market performance that sometimes does not make sense. In this chapter, we will cover the different types of new products in the market, and we ask that you think *very* hard before you leap (into investments that you do not understand).

In a sense, all investments are speculative since people invest in the hope of gain and cannot absolutely predict the future. Some investments are, however, more speculative than others. We are amazed at how, throughout history, people have made investments in all kinds of objects in the hope of financial gain.

In the early days, colonies were founded on the back of trading companies supported by the British Crown and military might. Fortunes were made and lost at sea. For every ship that left harbour, only some would return laden with tea chests and other great treasures from faraway lands. Examples of past exotic investments include black tulips and tea leaves.

Today, people invest in a wide array of products, ranging from oil pods to ostrich farms, and for a range of reasons and justifications. Investments in Internet stocks followed by biotechnology stocks were also speculative to a large degree. Depending on which you choose and when, you either win big or lose big ... and painfully.

OSTRICHES AND THE INTERNET

Once, my childhood best friend, SC, said he needed $15,000 to buy some shares in ostrich farming. I did not know what ostrich farms were about, but I did know that I would not eat ostrich meat. I also could not imagine anyone else who would. When I asked him who would buy the ostriches from the farm, he said that ostrich eggs could be eaten, the egg-shells could be made into lampshades, the feathers into feather boas, and the meat served in Chinese restaurants.

I thought of the ostrich lampshade and decided that ostrich farming was a product seeking a market. I told SC that the ostriches were the only ones benefiting from the investment, provided the farmers did not run away with his investment money. Till today, I still would not invest in ostrich farming even if you showed me ten successful farms.

At around the same time, I invested $100,000 into an Internet start-up company. The difference, I thought, was that I would be involved in it. Our appointed CEO defaulted. It was difficult to sue him and not worth the effort. To clean up the mess he left, I had to plough in another $30,000.

SC did not invest in the ostrich farm after our discussion. He kept his $15,000 safe. Sometimes, I think if he had invested, he might still have the ostriches albeit old and bald ones today. I, however, have lost $130,000 on my Internet bet.

INVESTING IN DERIVATIVES—THE OPTIONS MARKET

Derivatives are a fascinating financial innovation. An investment into a derivative is not an investment per se, but it is the purchase of a right to buy (or sell) an underlying asset within a specific time frame. We call this 'right' an option.

An option that everyone is familiar with is the housing option —the right to buy a house at a pre-agreed price by a certain time or date, failing which the option lapses. The price for that option is considered to be the 'deposit' for the house. Options such as housing options are legal instruments, and the seller is obligated to sell the house to you should you decide to exercise your right to buy.

For the financial market, however, what started off as a simple 'right' to buy or sell has become incredibly complex for most people to understand well. Financial experts determine the actual buy or sell decisions based on computations in powerful systems that run multiple parameters for price determination. Legal experts draw up detailed contracts that bind selling or buying at appointed times.

Two Main Types of Options: Call and Put Options

A call option gives you the right to BUY at a specified price whereas a put option gives you the right to SELL at a specified price. These rights are sold at a price.

For any given financial asset, there are people who believe that the asset would fall in price and people who believe that the asset would rise in price. The options market is created by trading among such people.

The attractiveness of the options market is that it allows investors and speculators to buy and sell into prospective gains in financial assets, reaping gains (and bearing losses) at a fraction of the asset price. Owning and paying in full for the actual asset while waiting for the gain would tie up a higher amount of capital than buying into the option for the expected future price. Here's a make-belief example to show how call and put options work.

The Birkin Handbag

The Birkin handbag by Hermes is considered a prized possession. Actresses, models and society ladies pay top dollar just to carry one on their arm. Inspired by the French actress, Jane Birkin, the standard Birkin bag costs between US$6,000 and US$15,000 (enough to feed a family of four comfortably for a year). If you want to own a Birkin, you will have to join a long waiting list. If someone wanted the top of the line Birkin, it might be the Crocodile Birkin with its breathtaking price of US$120,000. What makes this bag so special are the ten carats of diamonds set in white gold and placed on its clasp. Every year, there are only two such bags available for purchase in the world.

Hermes has created a market for this bag by limiting the supply. For the economists among us, we know that the Hermes market is not a 'bag' market. No one would rationally pay US$120,000 for a bag. People, however, would rationally pay US$120,000 to be identified as *someone who carries* a US$120,000 bag, that is, someone who is able to own a Birkin. The Hermes market is one of *desire* and *status*, not of bags.

For this example, let us suppose that Hermes wanted to capture the emotions of the people desiring the Birkin bag. Let's say they want the world to know how much the bag is desired. Besides letting it be known how long the waiting list is, Hermes can start a Hermes Bag Futures Market. Let's say it has identified that there is a group of people who would gladly pay at least US$130,000 for the bag if they knew that the price would go up. This is what Hermes could do.

- Hermes develops an investment proxy known as an option and releases this in the market. The option gives someone the right to buy the bag at US$130,000 at any time for a period of a year. The price of the option is US$5,000.

- You do your sums. You know that the bag is sold today at US$120,000. If the bag should rise in price to US$150,000, then buying the bag at US$130,000 is not a bad deal as the same bag can be sold at US$150,000 in the market.

- If the price of the bag should rise to US$200,000, the same option becomes even more valuable. But if the price falls to US$100,000, you do not need to buy the bag. You can forgo the option. Remember, it is the right to buy, not the obligation to buy!

- Knowing that the price of Birkin bags has been rising steadily through the years, you decide to buy the $5,000 option and not the US$120,000 bag. You know that if the price goes up higher than US$135,000, you would make a profit. You feel the chance of that happening is high as you know the next season's fashion will look very good with the Crocodile Birkin and that Vogue will be featuring Birkin in a ten-page story next quarter.

Derivatives fluctuate in price in the open market because of future price expectations of the underlying asset.

- The option that you bought at $5,000 can be sold for at least $5,000 if someone believes that the price of the bag will rise above US$135,000. With the option in hand, the buyer can exercise the option and pay US$130,000 to Hermes to get the bag. People without the option will have to pay US$135,000 or more.

- The option can be sold for at most $3,000 if people generally believe that the bag might only rise to US$133,000. In other words, you have lost $2,000 in buying the option believing that prices will go up.

Investing In Currency

Whenever I visit my relatives in Malaysia, I will change some money. Changing SGD1,000 will give me MYR2,300 based on a SGD/MYR rate of 2.3. I remember when I was growing up, the SGD/MYR rate was 1. Changing SGD1,000 then would give me MYR1,000.

Through the years, the SGD (Singapore dollar) has strengthened relative to the MYR (Malaysian ringgit). One SGD exchanges for more MYR today than a few years ago. That's good news if you are a shopper in Malaysia or have expenses to pay in MYR. But if you had a business in Malaysia and your revenues are in MYR, you would then be converting MYR into fewer and fewer SGD over the years if you lived in Singapore.

Most of us earn and spend in one currency. There are many people, though, who earn in one and spend in another, like my friend, Penelope, who earned in USD (US dollar) and spent in SGD. Her contract with the multinational corporation was written out of Hong Kong and her salary was paid into a Hong Kong bank account. I was once offered a job that paid a nice six figure sum in USD. I wanted the company to peg the employment contract to a pre-agreed foreign exchange (forex) band, but they could not as their budget was in USD. I decided not to take the job. If I did, my earnings in SGD would have fluctuated with the swings in the foreign exchange market.

Depending on what currency you earn in and what you spend in, forex matters very much. Table 12.1 explains.

Table 12.1. Why Forex Matters

	If you Earn in MYR	If you Spend in MYR
SGD strengthens against MYR	Not favourable. You get fewer SGD when you exchange MYR for SGD.	Favourable. You get more MYR when you exchange SGD for MYR.
SGD weakens against MYR	Favourable. You get more SGD when you exchange MYR for SGD.	Not favourable. You get fewer MYR when you exchange SGD for MYR.

Fixing Rates Ahead of Time

If you are expecting a large sum, such as MYR1 million in 12 months' time, you can fix the rate one year ahead of time. By doing so, you will know in advance what rate you will pay for SGD, thus removing the uncertainty of rates moving against you. Banks offer this service although the amount to fix has to be fairly large, such as USD100,000. Banks are able to do this by locating a counterparty that has the opposite need of wanting to sell SGD for MYR in one year's time. As you can see, foreign exchange rates clearly affect the bottom line.

Should I Put my Money in High-Interest Rate Foreign Currency Fixed Deposits?

If you put $100,000 in any one of the local banks today, you will get just 1 to 2 per cent interest. This is very miserable interest earnings when compared with inflation which has been over 5 per cent in recent years. Putting $100,000 in the bank's fixed deposit would give you less spending power in 12 months' time even if you will be getting more dollars in absolute terms.

It is no wonder that many people are attracted to the high interest rates offered by Australian (AUD) and New Zealand (NZD) dollar fixed deposit accounts, which until the recent global credit crunch, paid up to about 8 per cent per annum, especially in Australia and New Zealand. But what are the risks of a NZD fixed deposit? That depends a lot on the SGD/NZD exchange rate when you enter and exit the deposit. The rates in Table 12.2 are actual rates although we simplified them for easier comparison.

Table 12.2. NZD/SGD Exchange Rate and % Change

Date	NZD/SGD	% change
A: Oct 05	1.18	
B: Apr 06	0.98	-17%
C: Jun 07	1.18	+20%
D: Sep 08	0.98	-17%

Suppose you invest SGD100,000 in such a six-month deposit that pays 8 per cent interest. Say you invested at Point A when the NZD/SGD was 1.18. This would put NZD84,747 into your account:

$$SGD100,000 / 1.18 = NZD84,747$$

In six months' time, at Point B, your account with interest would add up to NZD88,136:

$$NZD84,747 + 4\% \text{ interest} = NZD88,136[1]$$

Now when you convert the NZD back to SGD, when NZD/SGD is 0.98, you would be in for a surprise as you would get back only SGD86,373, an overall loss of 13.6 per cent despite a high rate of interest:

$$NZD88,136 \times 0.98 = SGD86,373$$

If the exchange rate had stayed the same at 1.18, you would get back SGD104,000:

$$NZD88,136 \times 1.18 = SGD104,000$$

People have gone into foreign currency deposits only to lose their pants when the exchange rate moved against them. But is there a way to have your cake and eat it too by earning the high interest and getting protection from the exchange rate?

You could if you have financial obligations in New Zealand. If you own a home and have to pay for maintaining it every year, the NZD fixed deposit is an excellent way to benefit from the higher interest rates. If you don't have any financial obligations in New Zealand and

---

[1] We've simplified the calculation, of course. You would be earning six months' of interest of half of 8 per cent, which is 4 per cent.

you want to exchange the NZD back to SGD eventually, you could consider rolling over the deposit by extending the duration of the deposit until such time when the NZD/SGD moves to a favourable level for you.

Currency is always volatile and unpredictable. This means that the chances of the rate reaching a favourable level are high. But you must be willing and able to wait it out while earning high interest rates. Many people are burnt financially because when they needed to liquidate to access funds, the exchange rate was against them.

Summarising:

- Currency rates are volatile. What you may earn in terms of higher interest rates can be eroded by currency movements.

- Investing in foreign currency makes sense when you have obligations in that foreign country. Whether you are planning to retire, buy a home or send your children to a school there, these are good reasons to have a foreign currency account.

- If you are investing plainly because of higher interest rates, make sure you have holding power to wait for the currency to reach a favourable level.

Predicting Exchange Rate Movements

Predicting currency movements is tricky, if not impossible, according to market experts. It is even more impossible if you are an individual trader. You may, however, believe you have the gift for accurately predicting exchange rates. Be careful.

The market is huge, and it is easy for global forces and players to influence prices without you having a clue as to what is happening or has happened. You are a sampan in an ocean with strong tidal tendencies.

The foreign exchange market is the largest and most liquid financial market in the world. It includes trading between large banks, central banks, currency speculators, corporations, governments and other institutions. The average daily volume in the global markets was last reported to be over US$4 trillion in April 2007 by the Bank for International Settlement.

In a financial sea moving US$4 trillion a day, what is your several thousands, tens of thousands or hundreds of thousands if you were an individual private trader? I shudder to think about it. I'm not sure if the market has any logic that you can understand in time to catch the wave. Even with an ear and eye glued to Bloomberg and Reuters, you will probably be too late to move, if you move after they have moved. Yet I know many 'investors' who enter the market believing they can beat it. I go cold in fear.

The Bottom Line on Investing in Currency
As a maturing and increasingly sophisticated investor, you must understand currency nevertheless. Owning an international portfolio of investments means that a major portion of your money is invested outside, not inside your country of domicile.

Earlier, I related how I bought an upper middle class one-bedroom apartment in Malaysia only to see it lose half its value over the Asian currency crisis in property price and in foreign exchange. I was exposed to two markets, but I did not fully comprehend this until I was hit. I lost about S$120,000.

INVESTING IN REAL ESTATE

If you have always wanted to own your favourite shopping centre, say Suntec City, but you don't have $1 billion in spare cash, you can own a small piece of it for as little as $1,000.

When you invest in a REIT (Real Estate Investment Trust), a team of real estate professionals buys and manages real estate on your behalf. REITs allow you to invest in real estate without buying property directly. The US REIT market is the largest in the world with over 50 per cent of total global market value. In Asia, the Singapore REIT market is the second largest after Japan.

REITs mostly specialise and do not mix and match the types of real estate they own. For example, some REITs may focus their investments geographically (such as by country or city), or in specific property types (such as shopping malls, industrial buildings and residential apartments). The first Singapore REIT is Capital Mall Trust, set up in July 2002. Six years on, there were about 20 REITs on the Singapore Stock Exchange (SGX). Table 12.3 shows a sample of REITs.

Table 12.3. Some REITs on the SGX

Name of REIT	Invests in ...
Capital Mall Trust	Shopping malls
Ascendas REIT	Industrial parks
Fortune REIT	Shopping malls in Hong Kong
Capital Commercial Trust	Commercial buildings
Suntec REIT	Shopping malls
Mapletree Logistics Trust	Logistics real estate

Benefits and Risks of REITs

REITs have several benefits that investors find attractive.

- REITs are traded on stock exchanges and are thus liquid when compared with buying real estate directly.

- REITs offer attractive dividend yields, typically 2 per cent above ten-year government bond yields. So if ten-year government bond yields are 3 per cent, REITs can be expected to give you 5 per cent.

But REITs have risks too.

- When interest rates rise, capital values are likely to be vulnerable. A higher interest rate means that the cost of borrowing goes up, and REITs will suffer from larger interest payments on their mortgages and bonds. REITs have all the risks associated with real estate. Their values will fall in an economic downturn when real estate prices are falling.

- REITs are exposed to depreciation which causes the capital value of REIT properties to decrease. This is especially true for REITs that invest in industrial property because the land that industrial buildings sit on is leasehold and not freehold. For example, JTC Corporation, the biggest industrial landlord in Singapore, usually leases industrial land for 30 years at a time. This is exactly what happens to your 99-year home lease when time runs out and the property is returned to the landlord.

In the end, remember that an investment in a REIT is first and foremost an investment in real estate. If you own a REIT, do a serious evaluation of the property sector as a whole every three to five years. Remember that even if dividend yields remain strong, the capital value of your investment can go down.

Investing In Structured Products

When two or more financial products are prepackaged into an investment product (which usually comes with some guarantee of returning the principal if held to maturity), the derived product is known as a structured product. The range of available structured products is wide.

Structured products can be very simple or very complex. The first structured products that turned up around the turn of the millennia were simple. If you put $1,000 (after upfront commissions) in such a guaranteed fund, the issuer (typically a bank) would use $900 to buy a quality bond that would mature to $1,000 after five years. By buying a bond, the fund is able to guarantee the return of the principal. Furthermore, as it is a guaranteed fund, the issuer would pay out of its own pockets if the bond defaulted, that is, if the borrower who took the $900 and promised to pay $1,000 cannot pay up after five years. With the leftover funds of $100, the issuer purchases a call option that is pegged to an underlying asset such as a stock index. When the stock index goes up, so does the value of the call option.

When the initial guaranteed products arrived in 2000 and 2001, the investment environment was poor and the US was in a recession.

Guaranteed funds were a hit. They guaranteed you wouldn't lose any money, and if the market recovers, you gain. But nothing is given for free. Low risk means lower returns, or if returns appear to be high, then some risk must be hidden somewhere.

"75-Year-Old Woman Lost $400,000 from Lehman's Minibond"

You must have seen this headline screaming in the Singapore newspapers. Many people besides her lost a lot of money when Lehman Brothers went bankrupt in September 2008. The phenomenon was not unique to Singapore and rippled throughout the world. As a result of the bankruptcy, the Lehman Minibond Series 5 and 6 structured products that were sold in 2006 became worthless.

The investment came with an 82-page prospectus that we struggled to understand despite having MBAs and backgrounds with numbers. People who buy structured products often do not understand what they have bought. Worse, we would wager that most of the salespersons promoting these products have no idea what they are selling.

There is one important point we want to make and it is this: Who would have thought a 150-year-old company such as Lehman Brothers could have gone belly up? No one did. Even when the company declared bankruptcy, the global finance powerhouse was continuing to win awards for its work that same year. For example, it was deemed "Best Credit Derivatives House" in Asia and "Best Structured Deal" (by *The Asset*). It was also named one of 50 best-performing companies in 2008 (by *BusinessWeek*). Who would have thought an award-winning company such as Lehman would sink like the Titanic?

The one piece of advice that we do want to give is this: NEVER PUT MORE THAN 20 PER CENT OF YOUR RETIREMENT MONEY INTO ANY ONE PRODUCT THAT IS NOT PART OF YOUR CORE PORTFOLIO. I will explain portfolios and our 3-basket strategy in the next chapter. This crisis has given me greater conviction that the 3-basket strategy is an important yet simple way to manage risk.

Investing In Commodities

Commodities are all around us every day. We eat them (rice and corn), feed them (cows), wear them (gold), and today more and more, speculate in them. A commodity is a basic, undifferentiated good. Let's take the example of sugar. A kilogram of sugar from anywhere in the world, whether it is India or Brazil, is pretty much the same product. Commodities are often used as inputs in the production of other goods. For example, wheat is used for cereal, animal feed, bread, cakes and biscuits.

Commodities can generally be classified into three main groups: Metals, Energy and Agriculure (see Figure 12.1 opposite).

- Metals (base and precious metals). Base metals are non-ferrous metals, that is, they do not contain iron and do not rust. Examples are copper, aluminium, lead, nickel, tin and zinc. Precious metals are rare and have high economic value. They include gold, silver, platinum and palladium.

- Energy. This group of commodities consists of products used to heat and power homes and businesses. The most common are petroleum and its byproducts such as crude oil, heating oil, propane, natural gas and coal.

- Agriculture (grains, softs and livestock). Grains are mostly grasses that provide edible grains or fruit seeds. Maize, wheat and rice account for 85 per cent of all grain production worldwide. Softs include cocoa, sugar, coffee and orange juice. Livestock refers to animals used for meat production such as cattle, sheep and pigs.

The Upside and Downside of Investing in Commodities

According to commodities guru, Jim Rogers, India and China will drive commodity prices even though global stock markets have been hit by the subprime and credit crunch crises. Even if the US economy does badly, another 3 billion people from China and India would drive demand. He, therefore, believes that commodities will be on a

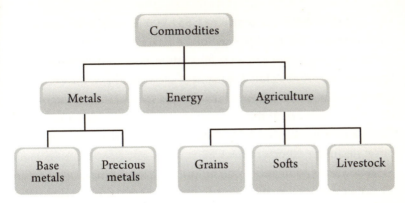

Figure 12.1. Classification of Commodities

bull run till around 2020. Why are China and India significant players in the global economy?

- There are 1.3 billion people in China to feed and clothe. China today has a literacy rate of over 90 per cent and a large middle class population of 100 million people who can afford all sorts of goods and services. McKinsey & Company expects 700 million Chinese to have joined the consumer class by 2020.

- The World Bank forecasts that India, with a population of 1.15 billion today, will become the third largest economy after China and the US by 2025.

Investing in the growth of India and China is exciting. With a large proportion of people yet to own mobile phones and microwave ovens, or to have their first bite of McDonald's or the equivalent fast food restaurant by then, the potential for growth in demand for commodities is clear. Investing in the right commodities can be viewed as investing in the future of India and China.

Commodity markets, however, are highly volatile. The 2008 global market crisis showed commodity prices fluctuating with every piece of news. Gold prices, for example, were going up and down, unlike in past market crises when gold prices went up when the market came down. In the ten years between 1998 and 2008, gold went up four times from US$250 per ounce to US$1,000 in early 2008, and then fell to around US$700 at the end of 2008.

In 2008, oil prices too were fluctuating as analysts were not able to predict where the global demand of oil would be in the event of a global economic slowdown. Take China's manufacturing exports to the US, for instance. If the US economy was depressed, where would China's new market be? Would its domestic market rise rapidly to offset declining exports to the US?

If you want to invest in commodities, there are many ways to do so. Some methods include spot trading (where delivery takes place within a few business days) and futures trading (where delivery takes place at a specified time in the future at a price specified today). Both methods require special expertise and dedicated time to track the markets. The list below are some examples of commodity funds that you can consider. Please do your homework and find out more before you jump in.

Some Commodity Funds

- The Diapason Rogers Commodity Index Fund — tracks the RICI, an index developed by Jim Rogers

- The Lyxor ETF Commodities CRB — tracks the RJ/CRB index, which is the world's oldest commodities index

- The UOB Gold and General fund and DWS Noor Precious Metals funds — invests in gold-related companies

- Singapore-listed Wilmar — the world's largest processor and merchandiser of palm oil

- For oil, you can explore ExxonMobil (US), PetroChina (China), Gazprom (Russia) and Petronas (Malaysia)

- For commodities trading, you can look at Noble, ADM and Glencore

You have many choices. There's no doubt in my mind that an investment in commodities makes sense for my bottom line for several reasons:

- It is a hedge against inflation.

- It is proven that commodities rise along with inflation. Consumer price indexes are used to track retail inflation. These indexes generally rise along with price increases in wheat, oil and iron ore.

- Participation in global growth. Demand for commodities will keep growing in industrialising and emerging markets as long as economies of large countries such as India and China continue to be successful.

- It is good for diversifying your portfolio. Commodities have a low correlation to stocks and bonds. In fact, commodities tend to do well when stocks and bonds are down. This means that commodities are a good addition to a portfolio as they reduce overall volatility.

INVESTING IN JEWELLERY AND WATCHES

For any woman who thinks that buying jewellery and watches is an investment alternative, I urge you to stop. Do your homework first before you consider it an investment. They are not. Not for the 99.999 per cent of the women reading this book. This is what the jewellers community in New York has to say:

> White diamonds that cost under $50,000 at a true wholesale price are not rare enough to be considered an investment except in a market that exhibits extreme inflation of the currency. Even then, these less expensive stones may drop dramatically in price when inflation is curbed. If you wish to possibly make a profit and have an easy time re-selling the stone, you have to buy a beautiful and rare enough stone so that there are more buyers than stones available at the time of resale.

Until you get into the league of owning the Hope Diamond, in all likelihood, all jewellery that you can afford to buy are expenditures. THEY ARE NOT INVESTMENTS. Please remember this the next time the jeweller tells you the $2,000 earrings you are eyeing is "an investment, it will go up in price". *Going up in price is not the same thing as going up in value.* When you try to sell the same item even when prices are up, you will not receive what you had paid for it. You will not see your jewellery give you a return. We covered this earlier on page 116. We need to stress it again.

Sapphires for US$100

Once I made a horrible mistake of buying a wrong gemstone. As I sat in a gemologist's office waiting for the valuation report, he told me stories of how he would go gem-hunting in Burma and Thailand, and how gems are traded. He said, "You can buy a bag of dark blue sapphires for US$100. Many of the stone fragments come from mining or cutting. They are bought to be made into beads and other industrial goods." He also said that most of the stones we find in mass market jewellery shops cost the jeweller a fraction of their retail prices.

From that day on, I stopped shopping for gemstones. I made myself a promise: If I were to invest in another gemstone, I must first invest in a gemology course and understand the gemstone market more. This way I will know what I am buying. If, however, I were to shop for fun and the beauty of a gemstone, I must not think 'investment'. It is NOT an investment until I can understand the gemstone market and I can evaluate the stone myself with some confidence.

So think carefully before you buy your next piece of jewellery. The item is only worth that amount because of one customer—YOU. If you walked away, it is uncertain if another will come along to appreciate it like you do. Any product with a market of one person, namely you, is not an investment product. Your last resort is the pawnbroker and you already know what price he would pay you for your 'used' jewellery.

By the way, I do walk into pawnshops as a customer looking at beautiful pieces of jewellery sold by people in despair. I usually do not buy. I have, however, once bought two beautiful watches from a second-hand shop. At the time, the market list prices for them were $50,000 and $8,000. I paid $8,000 and $2,000. I cannot imagine what the owner received. Both these watches are still in perfect condition and I got them for a song.

> Buying a diamond is easy. Selling it is another story. If you cannot sell it for at least the value you bought it at, it is *not* an investment.

INVESTING IN WORKS OF ART

Investing in art and collectibles, such as paintings, is rife with risks. They do not offer the more stable returns of traditional investments such as stocks and bonds. The variables that govern price can be very unpredictable. Events that can cause the price of an artist's works to soar include the artist's death, endorsement by celebrities and strong economic growth. Look for Damien Hirsch on Wikipedia and you will understand what I mean. If you are in the market for fine art, take note of the following:

- Low price transparency. Buying securities usually occur at fair market value in large market places. But when buying a piece of art, it is much more difficult to confirm that a fair price is being asked for and paid.

- Security. Investors are responsible for the safekeeping of the art pieces. If an antique gets damaged or lost, the value is lost. In October 2006, billionaire casino owner Steve Wynn accidentally poked a hole in the Picasso painting *La Rêve*, which he had just agreed to sell for US$139 million. The private sale would have made the painting the most expensive ever then.

- Liquidity. Securities can be sold much more easily than art and collectibles because securities are traded more readily on organised networks and exchanges.

For myself, I have so far never invested in art. I have never spent more than several thousand dollars for any piece of art. I don't call that investments. When I buy, I buy because I love the art piece, and not because I feel it would appreciate in value.

OVER TO YOU

What are some other things that you bought in the past thinking they were investments? Were they?

How much did you pay for that ...	How much is it worth today?
Patek Philippe watch	
Diamond ring / fur coat	
Christian Dior handbag	
Coins and stamps	
Donna Karan jacket that the magazine said is an 'investment' piece	
Red sports car	
Time-share resort	

> Market volatility is the fault of people who inflate stock prices beyond the value of the underlying company. When stock prices are rapidly flying through the roof and investors have a no-fear expectation that the market will rise and rise, it is usually a sign of a bubble.
> The possibility of getting rich is one of the main reasons people are burnt when markets crash.
>
> Therefore, watch yourself.
> Understand your underlying emotion before you invest. Remember, you are a small player in a very large market and that all said, you are a 'price-taker' without any ability to control how and when the market moves.

TULIPS AND OTHER FAMOUS BUBBLES

A bubble occurs when investors put so much demand on a stock that they drive the price beyond any rational reflection of its actual worth. Bubbles often appear to rise forever until they pop with the price crashing. And when they do, those who bought at the peak of the bubble's climb are left in financial ruin.

The Tulip Bubble
The tulip was brought to Europe in the middle of the sixteenth century from the Ottoman Empire. One of the most famous market bubbles occurred in Holland during the early 1600s when speculation drove the value of tulip bulbs to extremes.

At the height of the market, the rarest tulip bulbs traded for as much as six times the average person's annual salary. Tulips were exchanged for land, valuable livestock and houses. In February 1637, tulip traders could no longer bear the inflated prices for their bulbs. They began to sell. The bubble was bursting.

Suspecting that the demand for tulips would not last, selling began in earnest and a panic ensued. Some traders were left holding contracts to purchase tulips at prices ten times greater than those on the open market, while others found themselves in possession of worthless bulbs. Thousands of traders were financially ruined.

Unsuccessful attempts were made to resolve the situation to the satisfaction of all parties. Ultimately, individuals were stuck with the bulbs they bought. The aftermath of the tulip price deflation resulted in economic depression.

(Source: www.wikipedia.org/wiki/Tulip_mania)

The 1929 Depression
The 1929 depression occurred in the US when the market fell 90 per cent between September 1929 and July 1932. Just before that, Americans were bullish. World War I was won. Industrialisation

gave rise to previously unimaginable luxuries. It was a great time to be American.

Everyone believed that the stock market was a no-risk market where prices would just keep going up. People poured their savings into it without learning about the underlying companies. With the flood of uneducated investors, the market was ripe for some manipulation. Investment bankers, brokers, traders, and sometimes, owners, banded together to acquire large chunks of stock between them. They traded among themselves for slightly more each time. When the public noticed the progression of price on the ticker tape, they would buy the stock. The market manipulators would then sell off their overpriced shares for a healthy profit.

(Source: www.investopedia.com/features/crashes/crashes5.asp)

The Dot.com Crash

In the dot.com crash between March 2000 and October 2002, the NASDAQ Composite Index lost 78 per cent of its value. The NASDAQ is an American stock exchange. It is the largest electronic screen-based equity securities trading market in the US, with about 3,200 companies listed.

The Internet was created out of US military technologies and its popularity started to catch on commercially in 1995 with an estimated 18 million users. The rise in usage meant an untapped international market. Soon, speculators were barely able to control their excitement over the 'new economy'.

IPOs (Initial Public Offering) of Internet companies emerged with ferocity and frequency, sweeping the nation up in euphoria. Investors were blindly grabbing every new issue without even looking at a business plan to find out, for example, how long the company would take before making a profit ... if ever.

In 1999, there were 457 IPOs, most of which were Internet and technology related. Of those, 25 per cent doubled in price on the first day of trading. The dot.com boom and bust was a case of too much too fast. Companies were given millions of dollars by anxious investors and told to grow to Microsoft size by tomorrow. We all know that cannot happen. The CEOs of dot.com companies overpromised, the investors believed it and pushed it, the market followed until it could no more. Then it crashed, causing job losses, downsizing and closing of companies, and losses.

(Source: www.investopedia.com/features/crashes/crashes8.asp)

The 2008 US Property Bubble

Home valuations started to climb soon after the 2001–2002 recession. The property market resembled a money-making machine as profits and earnings kept increasing for property buyers, developers, the building industry and the mortgage market. A large component of consumer spending also came from the related refinancing boom, which allowed people to reduce their monthly mortgage payments from decreasing interest rates.

US housing prices peaked in early 2005, began declining in 2006, and may not yet have hit bottom today (at the time of this book's release in April 2009). Increased default and foreclosure rates in 2006 and 2007 by US homeowners started a financial crisis in August 2007 worldwide with bank, mortgage and insurance company collapses. In October 2007, US Treasury Secretary Henry Paulson called the bursting housing bubble "the most significant risk to our economy".

Bubbles may be definitively identified only in hindsight, after a market correction. Former US Federal Reserve Chairman Alan Greenspan said: "I really didn't get it until very late in 2005 and 2006." In 2008 alone, the US government allocated over $900 billion to special loans and rescues related to the housing bubble.

(Source: www.wikipedia.org/wiki/United_States_housing_bubble)

13 Diversification and The Three Baskets

What Is Diversification?

We discussed risk in Part Two. In investment, risk is reduced when we diversify. What is diversification?

The easiest way to understand diversification is to liken it to the dating game. Few of us would marry the first person we date. We date. We watch. We decide. Aside from the fun on a date, dating is about risk management. It is about finding the right person after meeting enough people.

In dating, we find out what works and what does not. Unlike investment, however, you cannot put the 40 excellent qualities of 30 men into a basket and get a composite man of your dreams. In some perverse way, the man we choose is probably the man least wrong for us as opposed to the man most right for us. We still have the 'yucky berries' in the man we finally settle for, oops, I mean marry.

In investment, we can choose the best characteristics of investment products and put them together in an investment portfolio. We can look for what we want and, assuming we can afford it, buy what we want. The sum effect of how the individual investment products perform becomes the performance of our portfolio.

The Law Of Large Numbers

The law of large numbers says that the exposure to any particular source of risk becomes smaller and smaller as we randomly add investment products (or securities) to a portfolio. How does it work? Simple. You add one investment product to another investment product, and if you have added them randomly enough, some of the up-down cycles of one product will cancel out the down-up cycles of the second product, giving you an averaged out evening effect.

To even out all the lumpiness of cycles, the experts say that you add about 20 securities to your portfolio basket. Selection should be random. Just keep adding securities till you reach about 20. With that number, most of the risk reduction benefits from this sort of random diversification would have already been maxed out. In other words, increasing the number of securities in the portfolio to 30 does not produce a significant reduction in risk.

> **DOES 'THE MORE THE MERRIER' WORK IN RISK DIVERSIFICATION?**
> A famous study that randomly picked New York Stock Exchange (NYSE) stocks for a portfolio found that risk goes down with each additional security put into the portfolio (Meir Statman, "How many stocks make a diversified portfolio?" Journal of Financial and Quantitative Analysis, September 1987). However, it was found that risk declines at a smaller and smaller rate as the number of stocks is increased. When the portfolio size reached 20 stocks, most of the diversification benefits are already realised, and very little additional benefit is achieved by adding more stocks.

How Do we Make it Random?

In Statistics 101 class when I was back in school, my lecturer said: "You type out the stock codes of all securities of a stock exchange on pieces of paper, throw those pieces into a hat, shake the hat and begin pulling out the papers one by one. That should be random enough."

This random selection process guarantees diversification and smoothening out of stock performance cycles. It does not, however, guarantee stock performance. To ensure that you have picked 20 stocks that are optimal, investment gurus recommend that you pluck these stocks from a hat of stocks represented by the stock market index. In other words, replicate the portfolio represented by the stock market index. This leads us to Asset Allocation which is a more precise way of diversification to manage risk.

Asset Allocation—The Wealth Management Way

A more effective, non-random way to diversify is to invest in specified proportions of stocks and bonds because their price movements tend to move in different directions.

For example, a person who is more risk-loving would have a larger proportion of her portfolio in stocks (say 80 per cent stocks, 20 per cent bonds) while a conservative investor would have more in bonds (perhaps 70 per cent bonds, 30 per cent stocks).

The proportion of your money that is allocated to each asset class is called asset allocation. So if anyone asks what your asset allocation is, your answer would go along these lines: "I have 60 per cent in stocks, 30 per cent in bonds and 10 per cent in cash." There is no right or wrong. There is only what you want to be exposed to against the return that you desire.

Asset allocation is the wealth management way. Warren Buffet is known to have said: "I was wired at birth for capital allocation." This wiring makes him the second richest man on earth after Bill Gates. In 2006, Warren Buffet was worth US$46 billion trailing Bill Gates' US$53 billion[1]. Mr Buffet's way of capital allocation, however, is not hands-off. He works with the company to drive performance and profits.

Asset allocation strategies or formulas differ from person to person and are based on the risk tolerance of the specific investor. A young executive typically has a higher risk tolerance than a retiree has. The young executive might, therefore, have an asset allocation of 80 per cent stocks and 20 per cent bonds (since stocks are riskier than bonds), while the retiree might have a less risky allocation of 20 per cent stocks and 80 per cent bonds. The idea is to mix and match stocks and bonds in the proportion that generates the highest return possible, based on the amount of risk you are able to tolerate. In

---

[1] Bernstein, Peter W. and Swan, Annalyn, *All the Money in the World: How the Forbes 400 Make —And Spend—Their Fortunes*. Knopf Publishing Group, 2007.

general, the higher the risk you can tolerate, the higher the proportion of stocks you would have in your portfolio relative to bonds.

The Warren Buffet Way Of Investing

No investment book is complete without at least some mention of Warren Buffet, the world's most successful investor. His approach is unique, focused, and it is important to understand what he is really saying as opposed to picking up bits and pieces from loose conversations.

The Focused Investment Approach

It is reported many times that Warren Buffet's focused investment approach does not support 'wide' diversification. He is of the view that if you have invested in the best company, any other investment *outside* of that investment is an investment that will lower your overall return. He says that a diversified portfolio merely means that the managers did not know what they were investing in, in the first place.

Once you know what you are investing in, and you should be able to gain control over it, the investment risks should be reduced and your potential return should be more assured. Recall Warren Buffet's famous words: "Never invest in anything you don't understand. For that reason, I don't have any technology stocks."

Of course, he is right. The incredible track record of Berkshire Hathaway proves it. However, the past focused approach is perhaps also why he is now saying that it is difficult for Berkshire Hathaway to continue its 'sterling' performance going forward. It would seem to imply that Berkshire Hathaway has already invested in as many as the great pickings that were available for investments, and that further investments today would only be investments in companies that were passed over before as being less optimal. The 2008 global market crisis offers Mr Buffet many opportunities, as stocks which are priced low vis-à-vis their expected future performance will show a revaluation in due course.

The Strategic Direct Investment Approach

The difference in views between someone such as Mr Buffet and others is, to a large extent, the war chest they command to complete their investment strategy. Berkshire Hathaway is recognised to be a premier strategic direct investor. A strategic direct investor is an investor who participates in the running of the company through intervention at the board level or, in some cases, at senior management levels.

Going by my past experience as a private equity fund manager, incumbent shareholders of unlisted entities who see your value as a strategic investor would price themselves fairly but gladly for your entry. As for listed entities, one can only guess the effect on stock price once a premier investor is known to hold a significant equity. A lot of research funding goes into finding out market responses to all sorts of events, so as to predict stock pricing. I am sure that somewhere in the world there is ongoing research by some graduate student on the effect Warren Buffet has on markets each time he makes an investment announcement.

While Warren Buffet does not, unlike most portfolio fund managers, invest through a diversified basket of investments, he is also known to have said that the best way to own common stocks is through an index fund. By common stocks, he means stocks listed on the stock exchange. The stock market index is the basket of stocks that best represents the performance of that market. The index is

Table 13.1. Summary of the Different Approaches to Investment

Investing in Unit Trusts	Owning a Diversified Portfolio	The Warren Buffet Focused Investment Way
Having some money but not a lot. Needing to make investments for the future.	Having enough money to invest in selected stocks or products for the longer term. Keeping a self-constructed portfolio that includes unit trusts and self-selected stocks and bonds.	Having enough money to invest significantly into companies to make a difference to the company. Having the ability to work with the management of a company if necessary for consistent and supernormal profits.

constructed by experts who use carefully determined methodologies (too technical to go into here) to work out what stocks and in what weight (amount) represent the overall market performance. The stock market index can be viewed as an indication of how the overall market is performing.

INDEX FUNDS AND ACTIVE FUNDS

When you buy a unit trust, its performance is always compared with some yardstick called a benchmark or index. For example, if you buy a Singapore equity fund, its performance is normally compared with the Straits Times Index (STI).

The STI tracks the performance of 30 of Singapore's largest and most established companies such as SingTel and Keppel. The index is generally representative of all the main sectors of the country from food and transport to hotels and financial services. In other words, when the STI on any one day goes up 2 per cent, we simply say that the market went up 2 per cent.

Index funds do not attempt to beat the market, rather they simply track it. The funds with the 'best' returns are still active funds that show that they can beat the index. When you pay good money for an active Singapore equity fund, you are hoping for two things. First, you hope that Asian stocks would go up because that would pull the performance of your fund up as well. Second, you expect that the fund manager does better than the index after expenses, whether or not the market is going up or down as shown in the graph below.

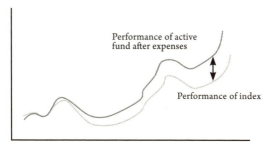

Figure 13.1. Performance of Active Fund and the Index

According to many studies and experts, however, most active funds do not beat their benchmark index as shown by the results of a 2007 S&P study of over 14,000 US funds. See Table 13.2 below.

Table 13.2. Results of S&P Study of US Funds

	% Active Funds That Underperformed Index (Year 2002–2006)
Large-Cap	72.2%
Mid-Cap	77.4%
Small-Cap	77.7%

(Source: Standard & Poor's Indexed vs Active, SPIVA®)

However, consider the fact that if only 30 per cent of US funds beat the index, that is still 4,200 funds that beat the index. That means there is still a very good opportunity to beat the index.

Studies of Asian funds show a different story where active funds have beaten their index quite consistently. One reason is that smaller Asian markets are less efficient and less followed by analysts. Some fund managers would, therefore, have an advantage in terms of analysis and information, thereby making more informed investments, than the overall market. The performance of their portfolios can outshine the Asian indexes.

In contrast, the US market is very large and monitored by thousands of analysts. The US stock market indices would, therefore, show the cumulative effect of thousands of decisions and analyses. Few fund managers can find information superior to what the market is already saying.

So, What Should You Invest In?

If the fund manager cannot beat the index, why are you paying him a professional fee in the first place someone might say. You might as well be constructing the portfolio yourself if you can afford to buy the stocks in proportions that comprise the index.

To construct a portfolio that follows the index, however, takes a large amount of investment dollars and time as you would need to buy in the right proportion. For example, if you have $100,000 to invest and stock A is 12 per cent of the index, then you will allocate $12,000 to stock A, and so on. And when stock A's price rises and becomes 15 per cent of the index, you will be expected to adjust your portfolio. Index funds take care of these details for us, and you can usually invest for as little as $1,000. Do check out the professional fees taken by the fund manager. Active fund managers who consistently outperform the market are paid higher than passive fund managers who buy stocks comprising the index.

The largest funds in the world are usually both active and index-linked investors. There is no need to be absolute about investing only in indexed-linked funds or only in active funds.

The 3-Basket System

Given that diversification is the way forward, we will now show you how to construct a portfolio of investments. Keon calls it his 3-Bucket System. I call it the 3-Basket System as I like to think of 'baskets of flowers' instead of buckets, which remind me of household chores.

The 3-Basket System can work for small investment sums and larger sums. It is a simple portfolio strategy. Depending on how you allocate your money into the three baskets and shift your risk to match your risk profile, this system will be a flexible risk management tool.

To illustrate this system, let's look at how Betty can invest her money for retirement. Betty is 45 and an engineer in a renewable energy company. She is divorced with two young children. She wants to retire in 15 years' time. She is a balanced investor, being comfortable with 60 per cent in equity (stocks) and 40 per cent in bonds.

The diagram overleaf shows what her three baskets look like (empty at this point). Basket 1 is for emergencies. Basket 2 is her main retirement basket. Basket 3 is her supplementary retirement basket where she can have risky investments for the purpose of learning, fun and even speculation.

Basket 2 (Retirement)

Basket 3 (Supplementary)

Basket 1 (Emergencies)

Betty has $130,000. As she earns $5,000 a month, she should first leave six months of her salary or $30,000 in her savings account for emergencies. This might be naggy to you, but it is critical for her financial health. Before she invests a single dollar, her emergency basket must be filled in case she loses her job or has an accident. These funds will mean she doesn't have to sell her investments in a hurry just in case the market might be down when an emergency occurs.

Betty now has $100,000 to invest. She parks $60,000 in a global equity fund and $40,000 in a global bond fund.

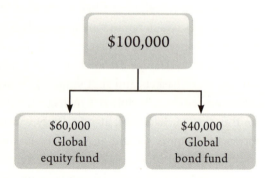

Of course, Betty could break her money up differently. For example, if she wants more control, she could choose funds representing the major economic regions of the world—the US, Europe and Asia. One suggested breakdown is shown in Table 13.3 opposite.

Table 13.3. Suggested Allocation of Betty's Funds

Region	Suggested Allocation	Amount
US	30%	$18,000
Europe	30%	$18,000
Asia	40%	$24,000
TOTAL	100%	$60,000

These three regions represent about 80 per cent of world economic output. You might ask, why bother, why not just invest in one fund? When you invest in a global equity fund, you have no control over how much the fund manager invests in a region. When you break things up and you have a view that Asia is going to outperform the other regions, you could have an allocation as shown in Table 13.4.

Table 13.4. Alternative Allocation of Betty's Funds

Region	Suggested Allocation	Amount
US	25%	$15,000
Europe	25%	$15,000
Asia	50%	$30,000
TOTAL	100%	$60,000

It is up to you and it is flexible. This is what Betty's baskets look like (Basket 3 is empty at this point).

Basket 1 (Emergencies) $30,000

Basket 2 (Retirement) $100,000

Basket 3 (Supplementary) $0

A few months later, Betty receives a $50,000 bonus from her job. She wants to take a spa holiday in Nepal and shop in Hong Kong. But first, she wants to invest $25,000. Just as she is about to put the money into more unit trusts, her friend, Daniel, calls her about an investment in a water treatment plant in the Middle East that uses new technology to desalinise sea water. Daniel is a speculator who loves buying securities all over the world and sometimes selling them within a month for quick profit.

This sounds risky, but Betty loves adventure and new technology. Can she invest without wrecking her retirement plan? Yes, she can so long as she *contains the risk* of doing so. There is a simple rule of thumb we can all follow—allocate no more than 20 per cent of your retirement money to riskier, non-diversified investments. We can put this investment into her Basket 3. Her investments now look like this:

To sum up, Basket 1 contains her emergency funds. Basket 2 contains her main retirement funds and Basket 3 contains her speculative investments, which equals 20 per cent of her total investments for retirement ($25,000 / [$100,000 + 25,000] = 20%).

Risk is controlled because if anything goes wrong with the water treatment investment, say it loses 30 per cent in value, while her main retirement portfolio generates 6 per cent, the net effect on her retirement portfolio is just -1.2 per cent (See Table 13.5)

Table 13.5 Betty's Portfolio After Loss Incurred in Investment

	Basket 2 (Main Basket)	Basket 3 (Supplementary)	Total (Retirement only)
Amount invested	$100,000	$25,000	$125,000
Current value	$106,000	$17,500	$123,500
RETURN	6%	-30%	-1.2%

The 3-Basket method of investing is simple and easy to implement.
The focus is on CONTROLLING RISK.
The baskets ensure that you have money set aside for emergencies, for retirement and for some positive investment risk that provides fun and adventure in investment.

14 Understanding Yourself As An Investor

You Are An Investment Risk

To invest means to take a risk with your money. How do you know whether you are a biscuit tin sort of investor or an adventurous risk taker? Beyond your risk appetite, do you really know yourself in investment terms? What would be relevant self-knowledge?

Your self-understanding must include:

- Knowing and setting your financial objectives.

- Knowing your needs and time horizons.

- Planning for your needs and the occasional wants (more about wants and needs later on).

- Understanding whether you have the willpower to go through with it.

Do you know that aside from market risk, you yourself are potentially a huge risk factor in how you manage your investments? Just as importantly, do you know how you will react when you see your investment going up or plummeting down? At the personal level, deciding upfront what you will do, rather than reacting when it happens, will help you execute an objective investment strategy and not react emotionally.

Fund managers exercise a great deal of discipline all the time, following an agreed game plan. (As to *whether* what they sometimes do is ethical is a debate for another setting.) They have 'stop gain' and 'stop loss' positions on all their investments in their portfolio. The extent to which they can or are able to execute this determines their success, along with market performance to projections.

You must get to know yourself before you pour all your hard earned money into an investment. Invest slowly. Take time to reflect on your investment decisions. This is why they say that women are better than men in the investment game. We women learn from our mistakes. That should be your encouragement to give it a go.

THE FINANCIAL RISK PROFILER

One fast way to understanding yourself as an investor is to recognise your personal risk profile. Your risk profile will give you an idea of how much of your available funds you should allocate into different types of investments, for example, riskier investments such as stocks, or less risky investments such as bonds.

Your investment time horizon is another parameter that is important. When do you need to start drawing out the money and how much at any one time?

A Financial Risk Profiler is a questionnaire that helps you understand yourself. It asks you a series a questions to determine your tolerance to risk. It is one of the first things a financial adviser might ask to run through with you. You can do it as a part of the beginner's investment kit to get a sense of yourself. Risk profiling is not a science. There are many risk profilers in the market, and you can use one or more to get a feel of yourself as an investor.

After risk profiling, your asset allocation strategy then tells you, for every $100, how much you should invest into stocks and bonds based on percentages that fit your risk profile. For example:

> What is your risk profile? What is your investment time horizon? You must know yourself before you pour your hard earned money into an investment.

- A risk-loving person might have an allocation of 100 per cent in stocks and nothing in bonds.

- A conservative investor might allocate 20 per cent to stocks and 80 per cent in bonds.

You will find that as you invest, you will begin to understand yourself a lot better, provided you take time to reflect on your investment decisions.

In general, a conservative allocation can be expected to bring less risk but lower, stable returns. Conversely, an aggressive and riskier allocation that emphasises riskier stocks can be expected to bring higher returns over the long term.

FIND OUT YOUR RISK PROFILE

Table 14.1 is a sample of a risk profiler. Answer all the questions by circling the choice that best represents your investment situation.

- Questions 1 and 2 ask about your age and investment time horizon, two objective factors that test your ability to take risk. They have each been given twice the number of points as the other questions because age and time horizon tend to weigh more heavily in considering one's tolerance for risk.

- The other four questions are more subjective in that they test your appetite for risk. Add up the points from the six questions to determine your risk tolerance score.

- The possible range of scores is 8 to 24. In general, the higher your score, the more comfortable you are with taking risk and the higher the proportion of stocks your portfolio should contain.

Calculate your TOTAL SCORE and record it here: _____

Next, check the Stock-Bond Allocation Table (Table 14.2 on page 206) for your risk profile. The Risk Profiler is usually used together with a recommended allocation for stocks and bonds. This sample risk profile has five allocations.

- If you are very comfortable with taking risk in exchange for the possibility of earning high long-term returns, you will probably have an AGGRESSIVE allocation where 100 per cent in stocks and 0 per cent in bonds is recommended.

Table 14.1. Financial Risk Profile

1.	**How old are you?** a. (6 points) Below 40 years. b. (4 points) 40 to 54 years. c. (2 points) 55 years or older.
2.	**When do you plan to use the money you've invested?** a. (2 points) Within 3 years. b. (4 points) 4 to 9 years. c. (6 points) 10 or more years.
3.	**Given two hypothetical unit trusts, how would you invest?** **Unit Trust A: Gives an average annual return of 5% with minimal downside in any one year.** **Unit Trust B: Gives an average annual return of over 10% but portfolio can fall 20% in any one year.** a. (1 point) 100% in unit trust A. b. (2 points) 50% in unit trust A and 50% in unit trust B. c. (3 points) 100% in unit trust B
4.	**How do you feel about losing money?** a. (1 point) I hate losing money and I am willing to accept lower returns. b. (2 points) I don't mind moderate risk. It's ok to see some fluctuation in my returns, but not too much. c. (3 points) I'm willing to take high risk because I believe returns will be higher over the longer term.
5.	**You accept that your portfolio will fluctuate in value over time. What is the maximum loss you could accept in any one-year period?** a. (1 point) 5%. b. (2 points) 15%. c. (3 points) 30%.
6	**Suppose the market lost over 25% in value in just one day today. How will that affect you?** a. (1 point) I will be so upset that I won't be able to sleep. b. (2 points) I'll find out what happened from the news or from my contacts. I might be tempted to sell. c. (3 points) I won't be overly bothered as it's probably a short-term fluctuation.

- On the other hand, if you are very uncomfortable about taking risk and you get ulcers watching the ups and downs of the stock market, a CONSERVATIVE portfolio is your best bet where the suggested allocation is 20 per cent in stocks and 80 per cent in bonds.
- For those who are somewhere in between, there is the BALANCED allocation.

Table 14.2. Stock-Bond Allocation Table

Total Score	Risk Profile	% Stocks	% Bonds
8–10	Conservative	20%	80%
11–13	Moderately conservative	40%	60%
14–16	Balanced	60%	40%
17–19	Moderately aggressive	80%	20%
20–24	Aggressive	100%	0%

Your Target Investment Allocation

Record your target investment allocation here. Check one.

_____ Aggressive

_____ Moderately aggressive

_____ Balanced   _____ % Stocks

_____ Moderately conservative   _____ % Bonds

_____ Conservative

Taking The Time To Invest

I have made more money from property investments than I have from other forms of investments. I know many others who have too. Yes, for sure, the property market rose and I was 'lucky'. But as someone said, luck favours those who are well prepared. Somehow, through the years, I was well prepared and lucky.

When I'm hunting down a property to purchase, for instance, I would spend months researching the market. I would have downloaded charts and information on past selling prices for the areas I am interested in. I would have computed the last done prices of properties by location and category. I would also have visited many properties.

I would also have telephoned so many agents that I use a fake name. Norma Sit is too difficult a name to use in such endeavours. Some days, I am Mrs Chee, other days, Mrs Tan or Mrs Wong. The Mrs works because these agents do not seem to bother with someone who is a Ms. They often think it is a 'Miss' when they hear Ms, and possibly, in their view, that single women do not have the money to invest in property. I get the impression that agents tend to dismiss such phone calls with monosyllabic answers. 'Mrs Young' will always get great attention as they think you are married to some expatriate and, therefore, loaded. So I switch around depending on what I need to know.

I go beyond that. To ascertain the type of neighbourhood, I would drive around observing the people who live there, the noise level and the traffic flow. I would do this on several days in the week to ensure that I really knew the property. What kind of people live there? What cars do they drive? Are the families young or old? Are they tenants or owners? I will ask myself: Am I willing to live there? If I am not, would others? How will the neighbourhood affect rentals? How will it affect the resale price? You can change your home on the inside and install a beautifully landscaped garden, but you cannot change a neighbourhood. If the neighbourhood sucks, your property sucks.

I became very good at understanding the property market as a small time investor. Good enough to make some money for myself. Big time investors have their charts and teams of people to do their analyses for them. As an individual investor, you need to do a lot of homework. Homework and some useful experiences to draw from as past benchmarks.

One of my benchmarks: Back in the 80s, I had the privilege of building my own home from scratch. Through that house building exercise, I learnt about government regulations, how much glazed and double glazed windows cost per square foot, the costs of designer doors, Grohe taps by design, and tiles, toilet and kitchen fittings by brands. I knew these costs at my fingertips. I have five very thick hardcopy data files of brochures and copied notes to show for that exercise.

Now when I go property hunting, I can identify renovation costs that went into most homes and what needs to be done to bring up the value of the house, if I purchased it. By the time I am ready to invest, I would have seen at least 40 to 50 homes at a rate of two to three a week, attended a few auctions and understood some of the dynamics supporting or negating the price for a specific property I intend to buy. I say 'some' of the dynamics as one can never know *everything*.

The point here is this: Whether we are buying property or investment products, WE NEED TO EDUCATE OURSELVES. Buying an investment product is not that much different from buying a gold Rolex halfway around the world. It just requires more homework, patience and dare.

Know yourself before you pour your hard earned cash into investment products.
Be patient.
Be knowledgeable.
Be daring when the time is right.

Part Five
Life's Passages

LIFE'S A JOURNEY

We have covered much ground in this book. We started with Self-Vision and Financial Vision, went through Personal Finance Management and as well basic information on Investment Management. This is no mean feat for any reader to cover in one book. If you have read till here, well done. We hope you have become clearer on what you have to do to achieve financial independence from ground zero.

The diagram below illustrates how important personal debt management and investment management are as building blocks to increasing net worth. Personal debt management particularly, however, underpins all investment strategies for building personal net worth. Only after you have managed personal debt well can you begin to talk about investment management.

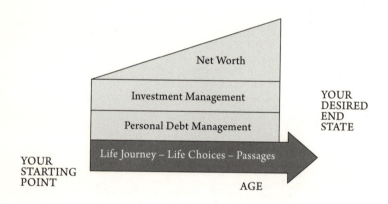

The two building blocks are fundamental in your Life Journey, if you are serious about becoming financially independent or rich. Our decisions through life may range from staying single to getting married and starting a family. They may also range from getting a divorce to remarrying and starting a family all over again. Each decision will impact you financially.

As we grow older and wiser, with our children leaving us with an empty nest or our becoming widowed along the way, our eventual state of happiness and well-being will depend on how we have managed our money and our net worth, as well as how we have managed our families.

Every third person will probably say to you, "Money can't buy everything" or "Money is not everything". That's true. Money cannot buy happiness, but without money, one's sense of well-being would be dampened and that underpins *sustainable* happiness.

This part of the book walks you through the different phases of life you may find yourself in and the choices you may have to make, and what the decisions are that you might want to look at to protect your financial well-being.

15 Single, Footloose and Fancy Free

Hey There, Georgie Girl ...

"... swinging down the street so fancy free ..."

I love this song! It reminds me of my twenties. I was footloose and fancy free. I danced and partied. I remember those glorious years by a gorgeous, metallic silver, slinky dress that I wore with 4-inch silver French stilletoes. I was a hot babe despite my imperfect BodyShop body shape. My father called me Petunia Pig because I would walk down the stairs every morning with a heavy 'dub-dub-dub' step.

But those were the days! Being young, flirty and beautiful, it was possibly the most fun time of my life. I party hopped with flair. And while I partied hard, I never got drunk or touched a cigarette or had one-night stands. I loved having a good time, but I never once crossed the line. On reflection now, there are a few things I wish I did better in my twenties. They are not regrets, but things I do wish I did better.

The Biggies in My Twenties

There were two things I cared about in those heady years: my career and meeting Mr Right. I wanted a job that paid enough so I did not have to listen to my overcaring dad anymore. I desperately wanted to find my Prince Charming. I suffered from the Cinderella Fantasy Syndrome, the one where the handsome prince appears and life is changed because of him.

Nowhere in my awareness then was the thought of buying my own home or investing in my own right. On hindsight, I was really not as smart as I could have been. In fact, I was really quite financially dumb. My saving grace was that I was achievement oriented and wanted to succeed in my career nearly above all else. That need to achieve 'protected' me from some really stupid decisions through the years.

Owning Property In Our Own Right As Singles

Owning our own homes as singles—what an empowering thought! Instead of growing up with the belief that one transited from our parents' home to our marital home, think of the empowerment that goes with this thought: "When I move out of my parents' home, I shall move into *my* own home."

I was in my early thirties when I learnt the importance of owning property in my own right. My son was already a few years old by then. My 40-year-old colleague, a single lady, enlightened me. From Monday to Friday, she lived with her mother in one part of Singapore, and on weekends, she returned to her own home. She said it was her private retreat to recharge, to read, to write and to paint. It was such a romantic, delicious idea—escaping from everyone to go home to one's quiet corner to write and paint. That was when I realised I should have bought my own home in my twenties.

> Singlehood is a great foundation for life before any other life choice.

Perhaps it is not unusual for single women to own their own homes. I just didn't realise then that single women owned or could own their own homes. And it had never struck me that I should do the same. There I was, liberated, fighting for women's equal rights, joining women's associations and working in very male dominated environments, but oh so *ignorant*.

It is a wise young woman who plans her finances to target owning her own home regardless of obstacles that may come her way, be they insufficient funds or restrictive government regulations. To marry young just to own an apartment, as is the case for many young Singaporean couples these days, is not something I would subscribe to. In Singapore, aside from the government subsidised HDB flats, you can, as a single, explore ways to own private property or resale flats. The prices of some smaller, private property homes are not so far above HDB prices. This is useful as it gives you a leg-up into owning property. If it was left to me, I would concentrate on home ownership, private or otherwise. Never mind the subsidy if you cannot see Mr Right in sight for some years to come.

Why Property?

Property is the one single largest investment you will make in your life. Property is also the one investment that has the tendency to appreciate with time, especially in prime cities. In Singapore, there is a strong relationship between property prices and the income of the nation. So as long as Singapore is doing well, property prices do go up over the long term. The sooner you are invested in a property at the right price, the better off you are. On top of that, you learn to track the market too. In ten years, the market can change drastically and if you were not already locked into a property when the price was lower, it is hard to play the catch-up game.

Imagine that you cannot find Mr Right, and when you hit your thirties, you decide to stay single. While your married contemporaries would have upgraded their homes several times by then, you would only be starting your journey into buying HDB property. If you had somehow found a way to own a small, private property in your twenties, that value would have risen with overall market rises. You would have begun bootstrapping upwards with each significant pay increase you get. Over five years of singlehood and ownership, your property could be worth quite a bit unless you were caught buying the property in a downward trend with prolonged price depression.

Whatever it is, you must watch your timing. There were two bubbles in the early 1980s and mid-1990s when property prices went on major bull runs before falling drastically back to the long-term trend line. The sharp run up in 1981 to 1984 was due to a severe shortage of private housing and also the Singapore government's decision to allow CPF money for the purchase of private housing. The property flurry in the mid-1990s was partly due to strong foreign buying interest and was made worse by a sharp increase in speculation activities. Anti-speculation measures introduced in May 1996 then brought prices down.

I have relatives who were caught up in the frenzy in a very big way in 1995. For a time, everything they bought went up, and they were sitting on a huge gold mine of five expensive, leveraged, private properties and a large plot of land. They borrowed heavily from the banks which were very willing to lend to them on the back of their family business. Then their business went south. And residential prices dropped severely. They suddenly found themselves in an overall negative equity position. One of the houses that they bought for $5 million, for example, was on a $4 million mortgage. When the price was revalued at $3.5 million by the bank, they had to top up balance of $500,000. The banks force sold some of their properties when they could not make the mortgage payments. The differentials between the loan amounts and the sale prices remain to be topped up.

All in all, my relatives who are now in their mid-fifties are still paying off $10 million in debt and have no way of retiring for possibly a long time. The family's entire fortune was wiped out by wrong timing and overexposure.

It would take us another book on property investment to discuss the subject comprehensively, so we will just run through the key points here. You should read up further on this to educate yourself and be well prepared to make your first purchase.

Some Advice
Three quick pointers here:
- Go for the best location you can afford.
- Ensure you enter the market at the right time.
- Stay invested in the property market.

Tracking the market is an important principle especially for city dwellers, and especially in Singapore. What do we mean? There is a story of a family who migrated from Singapore to Australia. They sold everything, including their apartment which they sold for about

Property Ownership For Single Women

In 2000, the average full-time female employee in the UK earned 82 per cent of the salary of her male counterpart, up from 74 per cent in 1986. Since 1992, in the UK, there has been a 52 per cent increase in single female home buyers. Single females are now snapping up one in seven properties, and account for 17 per cent of all new mortgage lending. Women are more likely than men to want to buy on their own. Eighty-five per cent of women quizzed said they would buy on their own, compared with just 78 per cent of men. More women than men agreed that they valued their independence. Below are some excerpts from blogs from www.bbc.co.uk.

I bought a place on my own last year. It gives you personal security and it's nice to have an investment when you're working hard. I've now bought a house with my boyfriend as well, so I have let the flat out. ≈ Lex, York

I first bought a property at 18. It was a terrible move, I didn't understand what I was doing and I was dragged into it. It was the end of the '80s and lenders were falling over themselves to get people up to their eyeballs in debt. Naively I took an interest-only mortgage which I paid into for eight years through some periods of extremely high and crippling interest rates. When I sold the property it went for less than what I had paid for it, and I had made no inroads into paying the lump sum of the mortgage. I was mortified. It must have cost me over £20,000.00. However, on the upside, it taught me financial discipline and confidence and, despite the rocky start, I now own my own house (albeit with a lodger helping out with my mortgage [my] having been made redundant). I have over £200,000.00 of equity in my property and that is a good feeling. Although sometimes I resent the constant worry of how to make my repayments, I know that in the long run it has been a good move. I also love the total financial independence. ≈ Isabel, London

$250,000. When they returned some ten years later, they wanted to buy another apartment in the same area but could not afford to as the prices there had gone up threefold. Their years away from Singapore impacted their ability to afford owning properties here.

In that sense, Singapore is a good *global* location for property investment, all things being equal. The current downturn will create global opportunities for property ownership in London, New York, Tokyo, Sydney and Singapore. Study the market well.

SINGLEHOOD AS THE WOMAN'S FOUNDATION IN LIFE

Many women, including myself when I was in my twenties, fail to see the beauty of singlehood. I used to think that marriage was the foundation that had to be set in place *before* I could build my future. My thinking was severely flawed.

If you are a single woman building a great life for yourself today, there is no need to press the marriage panic button. It serves women well to remember that unless they can build their lives as singles, their ability to succeed in a marriage may not be strong. In today's world especially, people need to find themselves first, know who they are, and then find the person to be with for the rest of their lives.

In the movie, *Runaway Bride*, the character played by Julia Roberts ate eggs cooked in different styles depending on the man she was with. Maggie Carpenter was confused as a person. She ate eggs half-boiled, fried, sunny side up, omelette, hard-boiled, raw. She was one moment a great explorer, another moment a good housewife, and another moment something else. She was whatever her beau was. IIke, the handsome journalist played by Richard Gere, realised that Maggie's confusion was the reason why she kept running away from the marriage altar. IIke set her thinking and off on a soul search of who Maggie Carpenter really was. I love this movie.

In singlehood, one of the greatest gifts is the ability and the freedom to discover oneself. Now I know there were some decisions I would have made differently if only I had the insight then.

GEORGIE GIRL'S PRIORITY LIST

If I could rewrite my life, my priority list in my twenties would be like this:

- Make a life plan for the next ten years of my life.
- Buy insurance for the major items in life.
- Put sufficient rainy day funds in my bank account and think of this fund as the 'Rainy Day' fund should I ever be left alone to fend for myself.
- Begin a *lifelong* love affair with financial products.
- Be brave enough to buy my own property without depending on marriage to make that happen, or at least begin planning towards buying my own home.
- Write a will.
- Find Prince Charming (last item, and not first or second item).

Apart from these, here are some other things that today's Georgie Girl ought to be thinking about.

Family commitments

I practised the principle of giving a portion of my salary to my mum when I started work. There were periods that I did not do it—like when I was out of a steady income. My parents really do not need my contribution on a day-to-day basis. But being committed and staying committed to one's family is important discipline. It's as important as the principle of 'paying yourself'.

Dating

WHO pays? Sharing payments on dates is an important principle. For one, if you have a mindset towards being financially independent, you should start by paying your own way through life or, at least, having the wherewithal to pay your own way even if you do allow others to pay on your behalf occasionally. Dating couples have four options when it comes to footing the bill: He pays all the time; she pays all the time; they split every bill exactly 50:50; they find a way to share.

I like it when people find a way to share. It may not be 50:50, depending on who earns more. The principle of income proportionality is a good way to look at how to share. It does not matter who pays more in dollar terms, as long as proportionately, it works out.

Wills

In many Asian families, talking about a will is often seen to herald bad luck and is to be avoided or even thought about. But even single people die. Why are wills important, you might ask? A will ensures that what you have goes to the person or persons you intend. Everyone knows that. Yet, people do not make wills for myriad reasons: They believe it is bad luck; they think it is expensive to get one done; they believe they are too young to die; they believe there is plenty of time; they are afraid of lawyers and they do not understand legalese; and they believe they have nothing to pass on.

It costs up to $2,000 to make a will with a top notch legal firm in Singapore. If you are like many of my 20-something-year-old friends, you might have bought watches, jewellery, a car, and perhaps have accumulated a tidy sum in your CPF. With some common sense, you might, it is hoped, have a net worth in the tens of thousands, if not in the early hundreds of thousands. So, if you are in your twenties, I would say making a will makes total economic and emotional sense.

Have you made a budget as a single, swinging young lady? Does the budget eliminate credit card debt? Have you set up your Freedom Account? When do you project reaching financial independence if you stayed single? When will you start investing? Have you started house hunting and planning to own property? Have you secured insurance? Have you made a will?

Interview With
Laughing, Dancing Jennifer

Jennifer Khoo is in her late twenties. She has long, shiny hair that changes colour every now and then since she works for one of the largest cosmetic houses in the world. Jenn works hard. She parties hard too. You can find her at crazy tea dances in town with her very hunky boyfriend. Both have terrific spirit to love and live life. She is Keon's best girl friend under 30. We love her!

Q How can you be so fancy free and yet so focused on what you want to achieve?
A I've put in place the major milestones I would want to achieve in my life, and that gives me the freedom to do other things and be fancy free. I like the story of placing stones in a container. First you put in the bigger stones (my 'must-haves' checkpoints of my life), then the medium stones (the 'can-haves'), and finally the smaller stones and sand (the 'good-to-haves'). Filling the container with just small stones means no space for the bigger achievements in my life. Of course, you can always add beer after the container is filled with stones and sand, because there's always space for a bit of fun in life!

Q What is your ten-year plan?
A In terms of career, I wish to embark on a regional business development role and earn more than $5,000 per month by the time I am 30 years old. Between 30 and 35 years, I would like to take a more strategic view of brand management and business with a high-achieving team under my care, and earn between $8,000 and $10,000 per month. At 35, it's to start my own business (either full or part-time), and dedicate sufficient time for my children. In terms of my personal life, it's to get married at 30 and move out into my own apartment. At 33, have my first child and at 35, my second.

Q What is your life plan?
A The perfect scenario goes like this. At 45, my business is on track and self running, leaving me time for other investments and personal pursuits. The children will be 13 and 11 years old then. By 50, I would have achieved sufficient passive income level of $10,000 to sustain a comfortable lifestyle. At 55, to finance my children at university and still have a great lifestyle.

Q What do you look for in a mate?
A Someone with an iron mind and a golden heart. He is driven and has a strong passion for life, yet is god-fearing and has a heart for humankind. Of course, he should earn more than me! He must be taller than I am, well-groomed and confident.

Q What if you are 42 and still unmarried?
A I will continue to date other single men (it's my right!); form my own joy luck club for single women above 40; go for regular botox; start adopting godchildren to shower my love on; go overseas to study; reserve a space for myself in a resort-style nursing home; and continue to date single men.

Q Is marriage necessary?
A For me, yes, because I want children. But if one day I should decide not to, I will not mind just having a mate to be with. It's important to have someone special in my life to share my joys and tears.

Q Who has taught you the most about living well?
A I would say my parents, and self-learning. Both my parents work. We belong to a high middle-income family. Although not millionaires, my parents live a good and balanced life. I'm fortunate to be born a very positive-minded person. I embrace life. And I treasure my books, which have shown me how to live successfully—physically, emotionally and financially!

Q What do you do for fun?
A Anything! I am curious and always like to learn new things. Sports: Blading, wakeboarding, dancing and my latest addition, golfing! Social: Emceeing, organising parties, helping with grassroots events, networking, chilling out with friends, catching the latest movies. Self-Improvement: Going for various seminars, classes, workshops to learn different skills and widen my knowledge.

Q What would your epitaph say?
A Jenn—Someone who knew the importance of loving a bit more, laughing a bit more, learning a bit more and is kind. Someone we love, laughed with, learnt from, and was touched by.

Q How important is money to you?
A On a scale of one to ten, money is probably eight. Health and relationships will come in tops on my list. Money is meant to be spent on people I love (including myself), and without health or meaningful relationships, there is no value in money. Then again, sufficient money is needed to maintain one's health, and to a certain extent, one's relationships!

16 Getting Married and Marrying Again

"Gerry, you are wrong! I hate to say this, but you are wrong."

I was having an early breakfast with my friend, Germaine. Everyone calls her Gerry for short. In her early fifties, Gerry is beautiful with wonderfully expressive eyes. She is terrifically smart, articulate and knowledgeable, and fascinating to talk to. Gerry was sharing her story with me about being married to a significantly older man. Her husband, Jonathan, came from an old European family where money is not an open subject; people just assume that the 'right' thing would be done in the name of honour.

This Thing Called 'Trust'

We started to discuss what-ifs. What if Jonathan passed away, what if she was left alone? Gerry had given up her best career years for him, accompanying him on all his assignments to far flung romantic corners of the world. She confided that she owned nothing in her own name and that she trusted her husband to do the right thing by her and his children. He had a son from his first marriage and a daughter with Gerry.

I told Gerry I was uneasy with the way she trusted her husband. I did not know Jonathan. Perhaps he really would be the perfect husband and gentleman, and do the right thing by her. But what if, I asked her, her trust was misplaced. In my mind, I saw loophole scenarios. I wondered if he might walk out as he got older. Also, what if he decided to will his assets to only his son? (Gerry had met Jonathan years after his divorce from the first wife; their own daughter was born after the son was independent.) From everything Gerry had said, he sounded like an honourable man with the old code of ethics. People like that never let others down, she said. If so, I thought, Gerry was lucky to be married to such a man. They are extremely rare.

Still, I felt Gerry was wrong. I felt strongly that she should talk to Jonathan and ask to see his will. She must know how much money he has and how much he intends to leave her. He may not live out the next five years, suffering as he does from low grade cancer. Going by mortality statistics for women, Gerry has another three to four decades to live.

Gerry also told me that she was not concerned about money as long as she was financially independent. I asked her what financial independence meant to her. She answered, "Working and receiving an income at the end of every month." I was shocked by her reply. Here she was, a super smart woman, but her definition of financial independence was receiving income with zero net worth at her age. I almost shouted, "Gerry, what is your work-life runway?" It was a very harsh question, but I did not want to see her as a helper in a fast-food restaurant, cleaning tables or toilets in her old age. Not her.

Between the time I first wrote the above paragraphs and the time this book went to print, several things happened. Jonathan moved out all of a sudden one day. Gerry came home to find the apartment empty. The next day, she discovered that he had closed down their joint bank accounts, moved their funds to his own accounts and moved in with his old-time gay friend.

I met Gerry the next day and learnt that Jonathan wanted her to go back to work in her fifties, even though he was fully retired and had close to $10 million to his name. She said he wanted her to earn her keep. She was not allowed to retire as the money was his, not hers, he said. It did not matter to him that she would find it extremely difficult to return to a corporate job at her age. He just wanted her to 'go to work'. Jonathan then went away to Europe for a few months and left her in Singapore with just enough funds to survive in a rented apartment. Then one day, out of the blue, he returned. Gerry was happy to see him. He was willing to discuss reconciliation but wanted her to abide by his terms. The last I know, they are still trying to work things out, in two separate households. As for Gerry, she is now working as a secretary in a small company in the construction industry.

We should never trust a man, even a very honourable man, so completely that we jeopardise our financial security. Yes, trust, but please trust with both eyes open.

THE MARRIAGE CONTRACT

Most of us grew up with the Hollywood model of marriage. Girl meets boy and they fall in love. They meet obstacles and overcome them together. They kiss each other and are married into eternal bliss.

Marriage in the historical context, however, was a lot more practical than the Hollywood starry-eyed kind. According to marriage educators, Sheri and Bob Stritof, "most ancient societies needed a secure environment for the perpetuation of the species, a system of rules to handle the granting of property rights and the protection of bloodlines. The institution of marriage handled these needs." The protection of property rights and bloodlines is also why ancient Hebrew law required a man to become the husband of a deceased brother's widow, for example.

Much is written and studied about the different forms of love, from the courtly to the romantic, from the platonic to the erotic. Today, it appears ugly to talk about money and marriage matters in the same breath. But throughout history, money and marriage were two things that went hand in hand. Here are two amazing facts about money and marriage that are hardly discussed today:

- Anthropology shows that early men went out to hunt, and early women stayed home to cook, breed and till the land. In tilling the land, the women owned the land and the fruit of the land. Since land, farming and agriculture produce recurring income, and hunting does not, women, in my view, owned the true wealth in those days of old.

- In many cultures, marriages were contracts entered into by two families, and sealed with signatures and financial exchange. There are many variations and forms of marriage in terms of financial and social obligations between the marrying couple. From here arose traditions such as arranged marriages,

marriages by proxy, engagements before marriages, dowries and dowers, bride prices and title transfers. It was not that daughters were not valued or prized; in some traditions, they were. Where families were rich, the daughter may be entitled to choose a bridegroom from among many possible suitors. In some wealthy families, the men were even asked to adopt the family names of the women they were marrying.

It was only in the recent last century or so that romantic love became a model for marriage. But who is to say whether romantic love is the better or right model for marriage when rising divorce rates is as high as 50 per cent in some societies today?

DE FACTO MARRIAGES

In Australia, long cohabiting couples have rights to the division of assets. This is known as a de facto marriage. Australian states, such as New South Wales, Victoria, the Northern Territory and South Australia, enacted specific legislation to provide de facto partners with some of the more important rights enjoyed by married couples, including the division of property that qualifies to be similar to 'marital assets'. My friend, Lynn, threw out her Aussie boyfriend who had been living with her for about a year. She realised that he was really not the kind of man to whom she wanted to give up half her home should he claim on her for cohabitation as a de facto couple.

MARRIAGE—A MERGER OF ASSETS

As seen, marriages in the past was a joining of wealth and power for those who had it. Today, we have forgotten this although some 'arranged' marriages among the wealthy still happen. Today, we remember the rituals of gifts and celebration but not the understanding of property mergers and ownership. In the context of human history, romantic love marriages are really a relatively new invention.

Do Your Sums Before Marriage

Many years ago, I was in Hong Kong to evaluate an investment deal with a company. Mid-way through the meeting, my counterpart requested that I send my company's balance sheet to him. He saw my surprised look and said, "In this deal, we are getting married together. Would you marry someone without knowing the balance sheet? I want to know your assets, your liabilities. I want to know the kind of partner I will have by doing this deal with you." In the end, the deal was too small for both our funds' appetite. But what my highly successful business associate said stuck with me for years.

Fathers might tell us to do our sums before marriage. Mothers often tell us to do our sums after marriage. Fathers want to know if the man can support their daughter. Mothers want to know that the man is not fooling around and that we control the 'wallet strings'. The best advice I received on marriage did not come from my parents. It was from that investment banker in Hong Kong.

So, before you take the plunge, find out the balance sheet of the person you intend to marry. Determine what the merger would look like. Decide if that is what you want.

You might want to ask these questions:

- What is my present balance sheet and income statement?

- What is our joined balance sheet and income statement?

- What is the projected future balance sheet and income statement? What is the probability of achieving this together?

- What might happen if there was a divorce?

- How do I protect my personal assets?

- How do I protect my rights to marital assets?

- Am I worse off or better off joining my assets to his, or better off separating the assets by structuring my ownership or clearly delineating ownership via prenuptials?

DOWRIES—A LADDER IN SOCIETY

In some societies today, the dowry system is recognised as a means for *men* to climb up socially in wealth, status and security! (While it is generally believed that a dowry is the money, goods or estate that a *wife* brings to her husband at marriage, there are also 'dowries' that go the other direction, from husbands to wives.) From fairy tales, we might want to believe in the magic of the poor peasant girl marrying the rich prince to become a princess. Too often, we forget that men are as entitled to looking for a rich princess to marry!

It is important to remember that people—both men and women—do marry to raise their status in society. We should be cognizant of this, whether it holds true or not in our specific case. And remember that while perhaps it does not hold true for you, would it hold true for your daughter one day when you have made your millions for her? Would she have a suitor who loves her or one who is eyeing your money? How will you protect her?

In my mid-twenties, I half-dated a very charming person, Frederic. He was tall, fair, funny and articulate. We graduated together and when we returned from Australia, he spent six months researching stock-broking as a career in Malaysia. One evening, when he took me home after dinner, he looked hard at my parents' semi-detached home which was in a good residential area. He said, "That's nice. Will your parents will this to you? How about your brothers and sister? My brother and I have already decided that we would take one each of our parents' semi-detached houses when they pass on."

I was stunned and did not go out with Frederic after that night. He must be crazy, I thought. Now on reflection, I think he was just being financially honest.

> Would you marry someone without knowing his balance sheet? More importantly, would you marry someone without knowing *your own* balance sheet?

Prenuptials And Postnuptials

I was at a lovely dinner party when the conversation shifted from the food in front of us to society gossip. Someone related how the matriarch of a well known family in Singapore demanded that her grandson entered a prenuptial with his fiancée to limit the division of any wealth to her to $3 million. (The net worth of the family runs into the hundreds of millions.) The demand for the prenuptial was made more than ten years ago. The fiancée was offended and refused to enter the prenuptial.

Today, they are living together but are not married. There is no third-generation heir to the family fortune. The matriarch remained unchanged in her view.

While some at the party agreed with the fiancée and that money should not be counted in love, I felt the matriarch was right in wanting to limit the exposure of the family's wealth to possible changes in marital status. When I expressed my thoughts, I felt a sudden change in the way my friends saw me that night. I had become a financially-driven woman in their eyes, and probably lost the 'femininity' of being a hapless female.

We discuss prenuptials in more detail in the next chapter. But I am highlighting it here because it is difficult to bring up an agreement for the division of assets at the point of divorce. No man would give up assets willingly if it disfavours him.

I want to make two points:

- If early women were wealthy as field owners, but lost their property because they did not know how to forge and wield steel for weaponry or raise an army to kill, there is merit in a woman today understanding and deploying a good defence strategy to protect her wealth. In fact, if she is smart, she must make this a priority. Do not assume that love is enough. When and should the love die, will you be able to stand financially?

- If the families of old understood and knew that they needed to protect wealth through marriage—and to grow wealth by combining the right balance sheets—and if approval from the King was necessary so that no family would become overly powerful through asset mergers, there is merit in seeing marriages in terms of balance sheets.

Please, therefore, work out your balance sheets before getting married and figure out what you must do to protect your money. Prenuptials and postnuptials are important legal instruments for women and men, but these are still new ideas in Asia. Most people seem surprised when they are mentioned. With the divorce rates high in developed countries, we ought to recognise that family wealth should not be negatively affected by unsuccessful marriages.

Should I Get a Prenuptial or a Postnuptial?

I would suggest that if you expect to earn more than your future husband or if you are the beneficiary to some family wealth, you should look into getting a pre or postnuptial agreement done.

A lawyer in Singapore told me the following story. A woman whose husband strayed in the marriage wanted a divorce. At that point, the husband repented his ways and asked for another chance. The woman then asked for a postnuptial agreement that would wipe him out financially if he strayed again. He agreed to it.

On the insistence of her lawyers, he had to get legal advice on the agreement and sign it in the presence of his lawyers. Her lawyer wanted to stress the point that he was aware of the consequences of default. He subsequently strayed, and knowing the extent to which he would be wiped out financially, he is protesting the postnuptial agreement, citing "agreement under undue duress". Her lawyers are confident that they have a strong chance of winning the case since the agreement was vetted by his lawyers and signed in their presence.

It is important to get a good lawyer when you are working out the pre or postnuptial agreement. It is equally important that the spouse has his own lawyers who will go through the agreement with him. This is so that in the event of divorce, the court knows that the agreement was well understood by both sides.

Law of the Land

Prenuptials and postnuptials, however, may not be legally binding, depending on which country you are from. In the UK, for instance, prenuptials are *not* legally binding and the courts can decide how assets should be divided. Agreements between couples cohabiting without marriage are, however, legally binding. It's no wonder people might be reluctant to become married in such a circumstance.

In Singapore, prenuptial agreements are not legally binding. Called "agreements in contemplation of divorce", they are not known as prenuptials per se. Chapter 353 (Section 112) of the Singapore Women's Charter states that the court "shall have power ... to order the division between the parties of any matrimonial asset ... in such proportions as the court thinks just and equitable" and "it shall be the duty of the court in deciding whether to exercise its powers and, if so, in what manner, to have regard to all the circumstances of the case, including ... any agreement between the parties with respect to the ownership and division of the matrimonial assets made in contemplation of divorce".

What does this mean? I am given to understand that in layman terms, this means that the court can consider prenuptial and postnuptial agreements in a matter of divorce, but the court is *not obliged* to order that the agreements be executed to the letter if it believes that the agreement is not "just and equitable". We will return to this in the chapter on Divorce.

Prenuptials in Second Marriages

Prenuptials are very important to protect pre-existing wealth positions for children of a first marriage. While we all want marriages to work, it would be a horrible blow to lose not only a life partner and a marriage but also one's family wealth. Seen from this perspective, not getting a prenuptial is irresponsible.

In Keon's words, a prenuptial frees the couple from second-guessing each other's intent, especially when it comes to second marriages and with so much at stake. Donald Trump in his book *Think Big and Kick*

Ass asked in the first chapter whether his readers have a prenuptial. He was of the view that if anyone was really serious about getting rich, they would get a prenuptial done. Keon and I cannot agree more.

What About Wills?

Just as there is a need to make a will when you are a single person, there is an even greater need to make a will upon marriage, or to remake your will as the case may be. Why am I stressing the importance of having a will when you get married? Because your marital status changes everything! Once married, the will you made when you were single is no longer applicable.

- If you are married, have no children and die before you made a will, the distribution of possessions will be shared between your parents and spouse.

- If you made a will before you were married, leaving your possessions to your parents, dog or favourite boyfriend, and you die after marrying without remaking a new will, the first will would be deemed void because of the marriage. You would be deemed to have died intestate.

- If you made a will when you were married and you got divorced because he strayed, your ex-husband may get the portion willed to him in that will—depending on how he was named. If your ex-husband was named in person in the will, the court may recognise him as being the rightful beneficiary. Would you want that? Oops! Sorry! You are already dead. To make sure this doesn't happen, you must make a new will upon divorce.

Since we are on the topic of wills, I would advise that you regularly review and change your will if one or more of the following situations occur:

- If you get married.

- If you change your name, or anyone mentioned in the will changes his/her name.

- If an executor or trustee dies or becomes incapable of carrying out his duties owing to ill health.

- If a beneficiary dies.

- If you subsequently sell or part with any property mentioned in the will.

- If there is any significant change in circumstances, for example, when you acquire property or assets which have not been mentioned in your will.

To Die Intestate

When making a will, it is important that you use a lawyer. If you don't formalise your wishes in a will, the law will apply its own rules to distribute your assets based on the Intestate Succession Act. Under the Intestate Succession Act, your spouse gets half of your possessions and your children get the other half divided equally among them.

Doris was a highly successful entrepreneur who passed away in a horrible accident while on a business trip. She was much loved by her staff and family. When she was alive, she took care of her sisters and their old, invalid father. She gave her sisters jobs in her company and found a top-notch home for her father to live in. Almost immediately after her death, her husband asked the sisters to leave the company and stopped paying the father's bills. Because Doris had died intestate, her husband got half of her possessions. It did not matter that she was not on good terms with him, or that he had many affairs which drove her to work relentlessly on her business, or that theirs was a marriage for the sake of appearances. It did not matter that it was her business with shares in her name and that her husband had absolutely nothing to do with it. Her death left the business to her husband and children. It also left her sisters jobless and her father homeless.

Make a will. Review it regularly with your lawyer. If you get married or remarry, review the will and change it.

The Gift Of Insurance

For married women, there are two areas of insurance that I would like to discuss: Insurance against death and insurance against divorce.

- Insurance against death. Statistics show that married people do become wealthier than single or divorced people. It goes beyond the pooling of assets to multiple factors, such as the positive synergy of being married. The corollary would then be that any person, on being widowed, would suffer a greater loss than they would have had to if they were single all those years. Loving couples often forget to insure themselves for each other in the event of death. For this reason, you should think of insuring yourself against death to provide for your spouse should you die.

- Insurance against divorce. Unfortunately, there is currently no insurance coverage available to compensate a person in the event of failure of a marriage. No prizes for knowing why. With divorce rates being so high and climbing, the insurer would be quite mad to insure a couple against financial loss in the event of a break-up. The closest insurance coverage against divorce that I have come across is an insurance that is linked to an investment product. The company provides 'coverage' against the financial impact caused by divorce, but promises an even higher payout for achieving such a milestone as a 25th (Silver) wedding anniversary. (See www.safeguardguaranty.com)

Insurable Interest

For many people, the thought of having an insurance tied up to a spouse's death, and benefiting from the death, is unthinkable. These people do not want to be perceived as gold diggers. But we should hardly have to worry about being seen as one. Why?

The law prevents people taking out an insurance contract on someone else's life (or someone else's property) unless they have a legal or financial insurable interest in that life. Insurable interest ensures that you cannot take out a policy on your spouse's life if he is worth more to you dead than alive. It also ensures that you would want the other person to continue living for as long as possible. Valid forms of insurable interest include being a spouse, being financially dependent on the person, or being in situations where there is joint ownership of real property or a business.

This concept of insurable interest was established to prevent gambling on the lives of others under the pretence of being insured. It was also to prevent the moral hazard of people taking out insurance on someone's life, and then 'arranging' for that person to die so that they can claim on the policy

What If I Marry A Bankrupt?

The proportion of bankrupt persons or those legally declared bankrupt in Singapore is low. While the numbers may be small, the devastating effects of bankruptcy are huge. The inconveniences imposed by the court and the emotional stress are very high.

Some important questions pop up with this issue. Will I be made a bankrupt if I marry a bankrupt? If I am already married and my husband is made a bankrupt, will I become a bankrupt as well? The answer is no. You are a separate legal entity from your husband or husband-to-be.

The True Cost Of Weddings

Weddings can kill marriages. Weddings are not marriages and marriages are not weddings. We all know that, but we get mixed up along the way. A wedding is a ceremony or a celebration of the marriage. Let's look at how weddings kill marriages.

In 2005, the average wedding in the US cost $15,000. In 2006, the figure increased by 73 per cent to $26,000. With 2.2 million weddings a year, the US market for weddings is worth $57 billion annually (Fairchild Bridal Group, 2005, Mc Murray 2005). Of these weddings, about half of the brides claim that they spent more than their budget.

Over in the UK, according to a 2004 report from London-based market research firm Mintel, the average cost of a wedding is around £16,000, an increase of 50 per cent from 1998. When you consider that the average salary in the UK was £25,170 before tax (for 2003), it means that the English couple spends close to a whole year's salary for that one special day.

Fifteen per cent of first marriages end up in divorce within the first five years, and over 25 per cent end up in divorce within the first ten years, with a remarriage rate of half within the first 3.5 years (US Census Bureau 2005). With these odds, I wonder why people 'invest' in lavish weddings. The 'industry' odds are against the 'investment'.

For many couples, the only way to fund their wedding is to make sacrifices, a recent survey by stockbrokers Brewin Dolphin found. About 15 per cent of couples had saved money by not going on holiday for a year, 9 per cent took on extra jobs and some 45 per cent had no financial plan in place to cover their wedding costs. The study also showed that for 10 per cent of the couples, the cost will ultimately be put on credit cards and that 2 per cent will even turn to re-mortgaging to fund the day.

So how much did I spend on my wedding? Keon and I had the most romantic wedding in a tiny fairyland chapel in Lake Tahoe. Only the minister and a witness were present. There was snow on the ground outside, and there was a small fire inside to keep us all warm. The ceremony cost us a total of S$300. Was our wedding less meaningful? I don't think so. You may not go the way we did with such a small wedding. For your own wedding, you should do what you feel is right. But remember that the same money can go a long, long way. Imagine spending $20,000 on a wedding banquet in a posh hotel. That money can go towards furnishing your new apartment or it can go towards the endowment fund for your firstborn when she comes!

If, however, you were to ask your friends, most might encourage you to spend as much as you want to because it is *your* day. If you ask the wedding planner, you will get a lot of gushing and compliments, soft music and persuasion to spend an even higher figure. Can you resist the spending? At the very minimum, THINK before you commit to a huge wedding budget that takes years to save for or repay.

LIFE OPTIONS IN A SINKING SHIP

Since marriages have, historically, been about the accumulation of assets and the protection of property rights, it is, therefore, not surprising to find that many wealthy couples stay together even when all semblance of married life has ceased.

Most of us know families who have stayed together despite straying husbands (less so straying wives). Most times, as long as the wife hung on to the marriage, the home was held together.

My friend Stephen once said to me, "Of course, the man would not leave the legally married wife for the other woman. It's too difficult. His financial assets are tied up with the wife, and in a divorce, he has to deal with the emotion of losing his financial assets and possibly the love of his children! The first wife has a strong hold on him that the other woman should understand. *It goes beyond love.*"

That was an interesting revelation from a man's perspective. It is a warning to women in affairs with married men, thinking that "one day he will leave his wife for me". My dear, the odds are against you.

For those of you in a marriage, when and if it is not working out, you have options. Divorce does not need to be the only way. The other options are to continue to live together as though married and to live apart under separate roofs. Whichever you decide, consider your financial status before you agree to it. This sounds cold, I know. I assume, of course, that you are not being mistreated or abused. If you are, for goodness sake, get out.

HAPPIER IN THAN OUT

Some couples I know meet each other more often in their companies' boardrooms than in the bedrooms. These couples are together because breaking up will mean a break-up in the family's wealth. For many, protecting assets for themselves and their children is more important than being 'forever' with their 'next fling'.

A good friend of mine, Suzanne, is in such a marriage. She knows her husband is in a long-term relationship with a woman. He is at the other woman's house four nights a week. She told me, "At this point, Norma, I have stopped caring. I have my house and my children. The two of them think they will last and be together forever. I laugh. It's a matter of time. Of course, it hurts to think he would do this to me. But I am not going to walk out. If I did, she will get him plus everything else I have built. I do not want to lose this house. She says she does not want him to leave the children so he gets to stay here at home. Maybe she is just playing a game. I don't know. But I do know that if I walk away, she will walk in. I would have given almost everything to her after all these years of struggling with Keat. That would be very stupid of me."

I call this kind of thinking 'she is happier in the broken marriage than outside it'. I know many women who choose to live this way. Not all are financially dependent on their spouse, but they choose not to give up their married lifestyle for a lesser lifestyle once divorced. So long as the home equilibrium is not shifted, they are fine with the status quo. Perhaps my friends who carry on living this way are wise. Whatever it is, they are certainly most tolerant. After all, marriage was established to protect property and these women are doing exactly just that. This, however, is not me.

> Do you need a pre or postnuptial agreement to safeguard yourself should your marriage end through no fault of either party?
> Have you made a will after marriage?
> Are you insured for each other?

Interview With
Guy Baker, International Author
And Speaker On Wealth Management

Guy Baker is the managing director of BTA Advisory Group, California, US. Guy helps families typically with net worth in excess of US$25 million to plan their financial roadmaps. He is frequently in Asia to give talks and visit his good friends. He is scheduled to be president of MDRT in 2010, an organisation comprising the top 5 per cent producers around the world in sales of insurance and investment-linked products.

Q How did you know Colleen was the right one for you?
A Colleen and I met in college. When I met her, I felt there was something very special about her. She was honest, a good thinker and open to communicating on a deeper level than anyone I had met before. One thing led to another as our friendship deepened. Then she called and said she needed to talk to me. It turned out it was confession time and she told me she had a boyfriend she had been seeing for nearly two years, and he was not happy that she and I had become close friends. He wanted her to stop seeing me.

What could I say? This was a huge surprise, but I took it in my stride. We had a final date and said goodbye. But afterwards, I was hurting. I was not mad at her, just very sad. So I sent her a flower and a note saying I hoped we could still be friends. We spoke on the phone that evening and every evening that week. By the end of the week, she told me she had broken up with him and was free to see me. That scared me to death. What had I done? All of a sudden I was facing a real, permanent relationship and was not sure I was ready for it. But because I had dated many women and was uncomfortable with all of them, I did not want to lose touch with Colleen just because I was scared. So I stayed connected with her, despite my fear.

School finished for the term and we had the summer ahead of us. I had a holiday job in Los Angeles and that was close to her home. So we saw each other regularly. When school started up again, we were still seeing each other. I was beginning to think our relationship was deeper than just friends. She did too. At Christmas, I decided to ask her to marry me and she accepted. I graduated the following June and we married in July.

Q You are the main earner. How do you split the money to spend?
A Colleen has never been employed during our marriage. I have always earned all the money. It took a long time to figure out how to handle our differences. She has always been very good with money but spends differently than I do. I buy big things for cash. She buys little things. It seems like a lot more to me because it costs a lot to run a household with four kids. They are all grown now, but during the years, every time she spent money it was like a dagger to my heart. I saw it as one less dollar I could save and invest for our future.

We solved the problem finally by establishing a budget and my giving her a paycheck every month—regardless of our finances. My income was always commissions, so it was feast or famine. But I could always make certain she got her paycheck. That way, I never had to audit her and the way she spent was none of my business so long as she didn't come back for more. She never did. It worked great and we still do it today. It was just unfortunate it took us over ten years to figure it out.

Q You've been married over 40 years. What are your top three secrets to a great marriage?
A Being married for 40 years is a true blessing that can only happen if you are truly committed to each other. There can be no second thoughts or desires for it to be any other way. When you walk through life together, it is more than a stroll, it is a power walk. Are there any secrets? I doubt if they are any secrets, but let me share my thoughts.

Live unselfishly. That does not mean you never get your needs met, but it does mean that you are looking for ways to serve your spouse. My needs are not more important than hers. Treat the other person with honour and respect in all circumstances. This means no swearing, name calling or saying things you should not have said. It also means being willing to apologise if you are out of line or have offended the other person.

Live within your means. Money is one of the fundamental battles in every marriage. Each spends money in different ways. But in the end, there has to be an agreement as to what you are trying to accomplish. Without this agreement, you sow the seeds of discontent. Set goals and adhere to them. Have a way to measure your success. Most importantly, make big decisions together and never have secrets. A successful marriage is an open marriage—there are no secrets.

Enjoy each other sexually. The other big problem in marriage is sex—when, frequency, intimacy and communication are all big problems that can make or break a marriage. It is important to communicate honestly on these issues. If you are committed, honesty will increase your love and respect.

Most importantly, remember that men and women are different in many ways—not just physically. They think differently. They act differently and they feel differently. So learn to appreciate the differences and enjoy them. Marriage is not a competition. There is no winner or loser. It is a team sport and there is no I in the team.

Q Have you ever considered divorce?
A Absolutely not. Divorce was never an option. In fact, through the marriage counselling I have done, I see that the single biggest cause of marital friction (besides money and sex) is the fear of divorce. And until each spouse can look the other in the eye and say, divorce is not an option, it will always be an option. And if it is an option, what do you do? You plan your escape route. What type of commitment is that?

Colleen and I had to do that. However, it didn't happen until we had been married over 25 years. Our family had gotten out of whack. Our two oldest had become really dysfunctional. They both had to go through a rehab programme. Colleen started therapy and through the process reached the conclusion she did not like me very much. I was not her only target, however. At that point, I was not too fond of her either. But divorce was not an option for me.

She had told me many years earlier that she did not want me to stay married to her because of some hyper loyal commitment to God. But at that moment, my commitment to my vow was all that was holding us together. I did not know if she was thinking divorce. But I knew I was not on her popular list. We finally decided to confront the issue. We sat on the couch and stared each other down. Finally, the D word emerged and I told her it was not an option as far as I was concerned. She told me the same thing. Then she told me that she did not like me very much right now, but that we need to be nicer to each other and treat each other with respect.

I thought that was a great idea. So I affirmed her commitment and we rekindled our love for each other. It took some time. But knowing that she did not want to leave the marriage made a big difference to me. I did not have to wonder what she was thinking or whether she was going to drop the bomb today. All we had to do was to be kind to each other and allow each other space. The result was we healed our marriage and have grown closer together as the years have passed.

Q What other advice do you have for a newly-wed couple just starting out?
A There is a wonderful book written by Dr Emerson Eggerich called *Love and Respect*. He was a pastor who did marital counselling. His total failure with many couples led him to study the Bible and see what he was doing that was so wrong.

He soon discovered the secret to a long marriage. The Bible tells husbands to love their wives and wives to respect their husbands. He had read this many times but had failed to realise why the Bible stressed love and respect.

It was then that he realised how differently men and women are wired. A survey of men, asking them which they would rather have—the love of a woman or her respect—yielded some interesting results. Almost all of the men said they would rather be respected than loved.

In other words, their need for adoration, honour and esteem far outweighed their need to be loved.

The women, on the other hand, valued love far above any other emotion. To them, love covered a multitude of sins. Her need for love was measured by how she was treated—flowers, gifts, time, dates. The man, on the other hand, only needs a word of encouragement and a pat on the back to feel on top of the world.

Here's the rub. The woman tries to get love by being disrespectful of the man and the man tries to get respect from the woman by being unloving. This crazy cycle drives both crazy and to the point of divorce. So if you want to have a happy marriage, it is important for the woman to communicate to the man her admiration and respect for his talent, his ability to earn a living and his desire to protect her. The man, on the other hand, to get the respect he craves and deserves, needs to love his wife. To protect her, provide for her and treat her with love. This means doing little things for her, taking her on a date and caring for her even when he doesn't want to do it.

This simple formula works and will separate the children from the adults. Try it and you will find miracles happening in your marriage.

Q Do you believe in prenuptials?
A I don't believe in it personally because I think it sends the absolute wrong message to your spouse. It says: "I love you honey and want to be married to you, but in case this doesn't work out, everything I have is mine and you don't get any of it." A marriage is a partnership for life. There can be no compromise. If it is not, then why are you getting married?

17 Money And Your New Family

As roles change, life responsibilities change. I remember when my daughter Elizabeth arrived into my life. Whether it was post-natal depression I will never know, but I was suddenly obsessed with the need to plan for old age. I felt the urgency to buy insurance and to put aside money for retirement. I had this sudden shift from being footloose and fancy-free to being 'responsible'. I became completely paranoid about not having enough in my old age, and launched in five different directions at the same time to save and invest. It was sheer craziness. No one needs to panic like that.

Children Change Everything

A married couple's budget changes overnight when the baby arrives. The monthly budget suddenly features a huge chunk of expenses related to BABY and later on CHILDREN.

We spend a fortune raising our children. Look at what US data says:

- In a 2004 study, the US Department of Agriculture found that families earning $41,700 to $70,200 per annum would spend about $184,320 raising their children to age 17.

- Families making $70,200 a year or more spent $269,520. Higher income families in urban areas in the West spent the most—$284,460.

- Costs do not drop proportionately for lower income families. Such families spent $134,370.

The study did not take into account certain expenses, such as heavy medical bills or pricey private schools. The study did not take into account the millions of students who are supported in part or in full by their parents. To cover that, add another $20,000 to $150,000 for a four-year education, depending on the school.

We do not have equivalent research numbers for Singapore households. The numbers may even be higher dollar-for-dollar since Singapore families have live-in helpers. Furthermore, car and property ownership in Singapore costs significantly more than in many cities in the US. Sending our children to good institutions overseas would incur a hefty bundle.

Higher Costs for Single-Parent Families

We expect, and statistics show, that it costs about the same to raise a child whether on a single- or a dual-income family home, i.e., US$124,000 versus US$130,000 from age 0 to 17 (information by the US Department of Agriculture, 2003). This sum, however, forms a significantly larger portion of the single parent's income. At the same time, single-parent homes suffer from higher costs in housing, transportation, childcare and meals.

RAISING A FAMLY: WHAT IT MEANS FOR THE FAMILY BUDGET

Perhaps people start families because they want to be complete. My two children are probably the reason I do most of the things I do in life. They changed everything from the day they were born. They defined me as a person and stretched my capacity to comprehend the world and to love. Yet, if one sat down to do the sums before one started a family, one would never do it. The numbers are intimidating. Consider the following.

The Rainy Day Fund

This is the fund you set aside for emergencies. Singapore residents are luckier than most as we have fallbacks for medical emergencies via Medisave, a compulsory health insurance scheme. Nonetheless, you can still set aside a Rainy Day fund for other situations, for example, for loss of your job, or when you cannot work for a period because you have to cope with your husband's emotional problems, or you have to stay at home to look after a relative involved in a bad accident. Such emergency funds also come in very useful should your bathroom ceiling suddenly leak because the apartment above yours has a plumbing problem.

A Bigger Home

Having children requires a bigger home. Once the baby arrives, you will need space to accommodate the child and the new live-in helper. If you have two children and they are of different genders, you will eventually need two rooms for the both of them as they grow older.

The Cost of Education

It costs S$250,000 to S$500,000 to put a child through university if she attends a top overseas institution. Living expenses will then be no longer incremental to your own household's. You are setting up almost half a household overseas. If it was a local university, the expenses would be lower to put your child through university over a period of three to four years, assuming she lives at home.

According to the Association of American Universities, the cost for 2007–2008 undergraduate tuition fees plus room and board for the ten highest-priced universities came up to between US$44,556 and US$47,147 per annum. These universities include Columbia (top of the list), University of Chicago, Brown University, Harvard University, Massachusetts Institute of Technology and Yale.

In a study done at the Centre for Research in Financial Services in Singapore's Nanyang Technological University, a three-year business degree in Singapore which costs $35,000 today will cost $80,000 in 18 years' time. Which means that while it may cost me $35,000 to support my son through university now, I would need to pay at least 50 per cent more by the time my daughter is old enough in about seven years' time.

Comparatively, the study showed that it would cost $190,000, $300,000 and $390,000 compared with $80,000, $130,000 and $165,000 today for studies in Australia, the UK and the US respectively.

For any parent, these numbers are serious considerations whether one has one child or a brood of three!

Knowing how much education costs, you would be smart to set aside money for your children for their education from the moment they are conceived. There are many products available. Not to do it thinking you will have the cash ready when they need it would not be wise. Would you also be able to say to them, "No, I can't afford it" when they show every promise of being able to make it in life?

Pocket Money

When my son Brian turned 17, I asked my colleagues how much pocket money they gave their children. I had no idea how much a 17-year-old should get and I wanted to be fair to my son. My colleagues said they gave their children between $500 and $800 per month, which was spent on transport, entertainment, lunches, and meals out with their friends. I was shocked. My colleagues were upper middle class professionals with pay packets ranging from $8,000 to $14,000 per month. The sum they gave to their children excluded tuition fees, clothing and holidays, they said.

I thought giving my son $600 a month is extravagant. How would families earning less than $5,000 a month cope, I wonder? Honestly, I don't know how families with lower incomes deal with children's pocket money today. Children today seem to need so much.

To teach my son the value of money, I encourage him to work at McDonald's which pays $3.50 to $4.00 an hour. At the same time, I hire youths who work at my company for about $6 to $8 per hour, earning about $50 to $80 per day.

Children's Needs and Wants

I was at a neighbourhood barber shop with Brian two years ago when my neighbour walked in with her son. As we chatted about gifts for our children, she mentioned that she had just bought her son the newest electronic gizmo that cost $1,000. That was his reward for doing well in school. I was not sure about rewarding a child with that much for doing something he should be doing. The point here is that our children's own needs grow from year to year, and so too their wants.

Is a mobile phone a need or a want? Is the latest phone model a need or a want? When all her classmates own an iPod, is my daughter's request for an iPod a need or a want? I have maintained that those are wants and not needs. For wants, my children need to work for them. For needs, I will provide.

Planning Inheritance

A good friend of mine, Dr Lilian, told me at our second meeting that she has made a lot of money in her lifetime. She is in her sixties. She said that she has parked her money in a trust for her son. Her view was that even though he was happily married, she did not want him to give away what she had earned to his wife should they ever divorce. This is despite the fact that she adores her grandchildren. I salute Dr Lilian for her financial wisdom.

On a recent trip to Kuala Lumpur by bus, I struck up a conversation with a fellow traveller. My new friend was in a quandary. His two daughters were "great girls, all grown-up", and still caring about their parents; one was a doctor and the other an engineer with Microsoft. His two sons, on the other hand, were giving him a hard time. They dated girls who were out of control and sported the wildest tattoos and the craziest hairdos. He and his wife had nothing against the tattoos or the multicoloured hair, but they felt that their sons should not be marrying women picked up from some hot bar. In their view, these women were not marriage material. My fellow companion was at wits' end wondering how to structure his will. A civil servant, he saved heavily to educate his children in the UK and for his own nest egg.

I told him about Dr Lilian's trust for her son. Her money will never be released to her son in one lump sum but will pay an annuity for the rest of his life, giving him the means to live reasonably well. But it will never pay an ex-wife if such an unfortunate event should happen to him. My travel companion was delighted to hear this.

Family Trusts

A trust is an effective legal device to protect and preserve your assets and resources whether you are alive or dead. The settlor, usually a person, gives money and assets to a legal entity called the trust. The money or assets are administered by an individual or a financial institution, the trustee, for the benefit of the designated beneficiaries. Trusts are useful vehicles because they help in the following ways:

- A trust allows you to maintain privacy if you do not want the public to know how your assets will be distributed.

- A trust can help you minimise estate duty, which is a death tax on your assets before they are distributed to your beneficiaries. Estate duty, however, would not be applicable to Singapore tax residents as it has been abolished.

- A trust can help protect your assets from creditors.

- A trust can outlive generations.

Trusts are simple in concept, but they can be highly complex because of the ways they work in different jurisdictions. If you wish to explore setting up a trust, speak to a professional such as a lawyer or a trust company.

Family Investment Holding Companies

With effect from April 2008, Singapore introduced a new investment holding vehicle for families to group their assets for ease of management. This vehicle enjoys tax protection for dividends and certain types of investments. If you have assets you want to preserve as a family, it is useful for you to find out more about this new structure.

The Family Budget And Your Financial Independence Account

Many books talk about budgets and the importance of not overspending. We have earlier given a simple budget outline that you can use for any phase of your life. We include here, on the opposite page, a detailed budget template for young families. Understanding budgets is easy. Staying the course with your budget takes discipline.

Once again, the most important line in the budget—whether you are married or single—is still the line where you auto-deduct funds into your personal savings/investments account for your retirement or your financial independence. Whether married or single, you MUST maintain this account.

YOUR SAVINGS FOR INVESTMENT SHOULD STILL HAPPEN BEFORE THE REST. PAY YOURSELF FIRST!

Over To You

What are the actions you have taken to protect your new family? Have you:

- Rewritten your will?

- Bought your children education endowment policies, health insurance and insurance policies at low premiums?

- Considered setting up a trust one day when you want to pass on inheritance to your children and to ensure that it is not squandered?

- Set up a Rainy Day Account on top of your personal Freedom Account?

Be more determined to become financially independent so that you are not a burden to your children in your old age. Guide them from an early age to understand finance but not with a poverty mindset.

Money And Your New Family 251

Figure 17.1. Structure of a Family Budget

Total Monthly Gross Income			$ —
Taxes	$ —		
Savings for Investments	$ —		
= Total Monthly Spendable Income			$ —
Fixed Expenses			
Housing Expenses:			
Rental or housing loan	$ —		
Utility bills	$ —		
House insurance	$ —		
Maintenance & repairs	$ —		
Property tax	$ —	$ —	
Car Expenses:			
Loan payments	$ —		
Petrol	$ —		
Road tax & car insurance	$ —		
Maintenance & repairs	$ —	$ —	
Debts			
Creditor name Amount outstanding before payment			
1._____ _____	$ —		
2._____ _____	$ —	$ —	
Others			
1._____	$ —		
2._____	$ —	$ —	
Expenses: Children			
Childcare	$ —		
School fees & supplies	$ —		
Tuition fees	$ —		
Medical bills & prescriptions	$ —		
Enrichment classes	$ —		
Pocket money	$ —	$ —	
Expenses: Others			
Family			
Groceries	$ —		
Dining out & entertainment	$ —		
Medical bills & prescriptions	$ —		
Phone & internet bills	$ —		
Clothes	$ —		
Pet supplies	$ —		
Newspapers & magazines	$ —		
Holidays	$ —		
Others	$ —	$ —	
Personal			
Donations & tithing	$ —		
Club membership	$ —		
Clothes & personal grooming	$ —		
Gifts	$ —		
Treats with friends	$ —		
Self-education	$ —	$ —	$ —
Monthly Surpluses or Shortage			$ —

18 Divorce

I was in Johor Bahru, having driven across the Singapore-Malaysia causeway to attend a wedding dinner. The bride was stunningly beautiful and the groom was drop-dead handsome. When it was time for the bride to give her speech, she said something that still resounds in my mind: "It's the happiest day in my life. We hope this works." It was the strangest thing for a blushing bride to say—on her wedding night, she hopes it works?

I never had a Plan B when I got married. Marriage was for forever. When I got divorced in 1998, it was after 13 years of trying in a marriage that just would not work. All that time, I wanted a fairy-tale ending. It has taken me ten years to say this publicly. It is called 'growing up'. Today, depending on your circle of friends, divorce can either be an acceptable state or one that is frowned upon.

The No-Fault Divorce

No-fault divorce is divorce in which the dissolution of a marriage does not require fault on the part of either party to be shown. Either party could request and receive the dissolution of the marriage despite the objections of the other party.

A team of researchers at the University of Oklahoma examined the effect the adoption of the no-fault divorce law had on the divorce rate across the 50 American states. The researchers found that the divorce rate increased across those states which implemented no-fault divorce laws[1]. Perhaps when divorce is linked to specific reasons, it is just too difficult for people to bare their emotions and shortcomings in public,

---

[1] Paul A. Nakonezny, Robert D. Shull, Joseph Lee Rodgers. "The Effect of No-Fault Divorce Law on the Divorce Rate Across the 50 States and Its Relation to Income, Education, and Religiosity.". Journal of Marriage and the Family (May 1995): 477-488.

and to pinpoint what or who went wrong. People want to say that the marriage failed, that it was this *thing* called 'marriage' that failed and not they who failed.

But failure is failure. We need to admit it to grow. It doesn't matter whether the failure occurred at the beginning of the journey by having married the wrong person, or along the way because of inability to adapt or find an amicable solution, extra-marital affairs, or failure to protect and nurture each other. Admitting failure gives us the freedom to change for the better and to move forward.

WOMEN ARE WORSE OFF IN A DIVORCE

Newspapers sensationalise women who take away millions in divorce settlements. The statistics, however, show that women are worse off financially than men in a divorce. In a study reported by *The Telegraph* (UK), sociologists who tracked the income of divorcees over seven years concluded that divorced women would be better off finding a new husband than trying to return to work! The UK study of more than 4,000 people found that while a man's income increases by 11 per cent on average after he parts from his wife, a woman loses around 17 per cent of her income.

CHILDREN ARE NOT BETTER OFF

If there are no children involved in the divorce, there is little to be said as two persons should be free to live as they need to, to find contentment and their measure of happiness on earth. But if there are children involved, it is a different story.

Despite the numerous encouraging words you will receive from friends that "divorce is okay", "children are resilient" and "children will bounce back", studies show differently. Paul Amato of the University of Nebraska and Alan Booth of Pennsylvania State University concluded: "For children's sake, some (high conflict) marriages should not be salvaged. But in marriages that are not fraught with severe conflict and abuse, *future generations would be well served if parents remained together until children are grown.*"

Perhaps this is why some of my friends remain married despite being very unhappy. The conflict at home is kept at a manageable level for the sake of the children.

The Best Strategy: Get A Prenuptial

Divorce rates in Australia, the UK, the US and Singapore range between 20 to 50 per cent. One of your best defence strategies against the problems associated with divorce is to get a prenuptial done. I have already said this earlier.

If you KNEW that you had the probability of being hit one in five times by a falling meteorite just standing out in an open field on a bright sunny day, are you going to stand in that open field? If you did, I think you are mad.

If you KNEW that going up to Kuala Lumpur from Singapore with the luxury buses had a 30 per cent probability of your being involved in an accident (whatever kind), are you going to make the journey? I think you will cancel the trip immediately.

People believe in fairy tales even when presented with statistics that say otherwise. They spend a fortune on wedding celebrations, buy a terrific wedding gown and Cinderella designer shoes that cannot used for anything else, and put themselves in debt as a result. They then pat themselves on their backs and say, "We made the right decision. We had a great day."

If you KNEW that the odds are high that your marriage may end in a divorce, if I were you, I would get a prenuptial done to secure my future. Just treat it like insurance. You don't want to die and you will not die, but you take out an insurance just in case you do. You don't want a divorce and you will not divorce, but you make out a prenuptial agreement just in case something disastrous happens.

If you are already in a marriage without a prenuptial, you should do your sums and ask the right questions before jumping into the divorce. Only one thing is worse than getting married without doing your sums. IT IS GETTING A DIVORCE WITHOUT DOING YOUR SUMS.

When it comes to divorce, whether you have an agreement in place (before or after the marriage), to determine how property should be divided has become of importance. As discussed earlier on pages 229–232, Section 112 of the Singapore Women's Charter enables the court to consider any such agreement.

Indeed, in recent cases, the Singapore court has shown to give consideration to such agreements almost as though a pre or postnuptial was in effect[2]. On 10 February 2009, the Singapore Court of Appeal made a landmark decision showing that while prenuptials may not be enforced automatically, they will also not be rejected outright. In other words, the court will give such agreements due consideration in case of divorce, depending on the circumstances and the reasonableness of the terms.

So while there may be no such thing as a pre or postnuptial agreement in Singapore, but given that Singapore courts have moved forward to *consider* such agreements, do you not feel that some protection is better than no protection? Shouldn't you then consider a prenuptial or a postnuptial as the case may be if the situation at hand merits having such an agreement?

Make such agreements in happy times, so that when things go wrong, you have done whatever you could have done to manage your downside risk in a potential divorce. Remember that making agreements during unhappy times are a near impossibility for both men and women. Always engage a local lawyer with specialised expertise to handle such matters. (For information on pre/postnuptials around the world, please see www.international-divorce.com.)

NEGOTIATING A DIVORCE

My good friend Benny was married for many years to beautiful Maria. Their marriage broke down when she learnt that Benny had cheated

---

[2] Ref TQ v. TR, [2007] SGHC 106; decision date 11 July 2007. The Singapore High Court has enforced a prenuptial agreement entered into in the Netherlands between a Swedish wife and a Dutch husband.

on her. In his heart, he knew he really loved another woman, Sophia, more passionately than he loved his wife. He left Sophia only because he could not bear to part with his two daughters. Sophia had given him an ultimatum to leave his wife. Benny chose to choose his daughters over Sophia and stayed in his marriage.

Three years later, Benny and Maria were hardly speaking to each other. Both had lawyers at war negotiating the divorce. Benny was so fed up with the process and the climbing legal fees that he decided to spend his past savings so that she would have little to claim from him.

Another good friend from Australia, Daniel, decided not to work after his divorce. The ruled settlement to his wife was based on a large percentage of his earnings. If he earned nothing, she got nothing. He said that he did not want to pay alimony to "that money crazy woman" (his words). So Daniel became a beach bum. He said to me, "Norma, for goodness sake, why should I slave away like a dog to decorate her in designer clothes? Forget it. I would rather just hang out with my mates on Bondi." Daniel was a qualified dental surgeon.

Both Benny and Daniel failed to negotiate their divorces.

Choose the Right Divorce Lawyer

Spend time choosing a lawyer. Remember that lawyers are paid by the hour and if you get a trigger-happy one, your lawyer can have more to gain than you at settlement. When I wanted a divorce, my lawyer friends advised: "You should use someone who cares and wants to help you save the relationship even if the marriage is gone. And use someone who cares what happens to your children along the way."

Although you might really hate the horrible person you once loved and married, and although you want to stick a knife into him and use a bazooka to shoot his brains out, the worst thing you can do is to get a 'mean-fighter' lawyer for your divorce. Unless your future ex-husband is paying for your high legal fees, prolonged negotiations and fights will kill you both.

Good lawyers are peacemakers. They know that more is at stake than the property to be divided, especially if there are children. As to who are the good lawyers, meet at least a few and hear what they have to say. And listen to how they say it. If they say things like, "We are really going to stick it into that horrible son-of-a-b***h", I suggest you get out. Root for the one who says, "Let's stick to the facts and get the facts straight."

You do not want a divorce lawyer to sympathise with you and your state. You want one who gets the job done in the cheapest possible way, with the best outcome.

But before we go there, let me tell you that divorce is not a good option if you can reconcile with your husband. Divorce tends to make people poorer and less equipped for life, not more. Are you really sure you cannot reconcile with your husband? How have you tried?

Cordiality is a Good Strategy

I know many women who stay on in a marriage even when their husbands are unfaithful. For these women, if they have done all their sums (money, emotions, children, life, support, future, opportunities and states of happiness), I applaud their choice just as I would applaud the choice of a woman who did all her sums and decided to divorce her husband.

I also know wealthy Asian men and women who are still married to each other despite affairs and relationships, whether discreetly or openly, outside their marriages. They know that divorces are messy. To many of these men and women, the husband-wife relationship is only one part of the total equation of being legally bound together. So preferably, they have their cake and eat it too. In the words of a friend of mine: "You can still have a good home without a good marriage."

Whatever you decide, make a decision and stay in control. Do not lose control by letting your emotions go haywire. What do I mean? You shout. He shouts back. You scream and cry. He screams and walks out. You cry. He sleeps out. The next day at the lawyers, no one talks to anyone. Things drag on. Both want everything, which is not possible. The lawyers get richer, you get poorer.

Your Financial Rights In A Divorce—Alimony

In the past, women were, more often than not, entitled to alimony or maintenance from their husbands in the event of divorce. This is not necessarily true anymore. This issue of maintenance is governed by Section 114 of the Singapore Women's Charter. The court in deciding on maintenance matters for the wife will review if she is working or capable of working, and if the husband is unemployed or incapable of working due to reasons such as disability. Women, therefore, may not always get maintenance from their husbands. Fathers, however, are required by law to provide maintenance for their children, even if the man is unemployed.

Fairness in the court is seen in Section 114(2) which outlines that the court shall endeavour to place the parties, so far as it is practicable and just, in the financial position in which they would have been if the marriage had not broken down and each had properly discharged his or her financial obligations and responsibilities towards the other.

In other words, you will never quite be able to sue his pants off without your designer wardrobe being cleaned out at the same time. To me, that's fair. Furthermore, under the new provisions of the Act, husbands are entitled to ask for maintenance, but knowing how proud most Asian men are, this is unthinkable for most men.

Some Food For Thought

I once read an article that gave an important clue to how the rich and poor deal with emotional issues. I cannot remember the author, but I remember the message. It is that the world is divided into two classes of people: the thinking class and the emotional class. The poor tend to be the emotional class whereas the rich tend to be the thinking class.

It is not that the rich do not have emotions. They do, but they do not allow their emotions to dictate the way they act. Likewise, it is not that the poor do not think. Of course they do. But when it comes to decisions, the article said that the poor allow their emotions to run their lives. Meaning, if the poor did not feel like going to work, they will call in sick. But if the rich feel lousy about going to a function, they get dressed, grit their teeth, get out the door, network hard and make opportunities work for them.

What the article taught me was that the rich tend to have cooler heads and are able to think themselves out of situations, rather than reacting with their emotions. Someone said: "If you want to be rich, emulate the rich." Follow how they think, how they behave, and yes, even how they dress to some extent.

Here's a short test for you. How would you react if you find your husband in bed with a woman when you got home one evening? What would you do if you found out from a good friend that your husband was in an affair for the last eight years? What would you do if you found the condom pack he keeps, you counted it and found ten condoms missing?

My friend Lynette accidentally found a condom pack in her partner's computer bag while they were both on holiday in Bali. On questioning him, he said it belonged to his friend who travelled to Bangkok frequently on work. Lynette waited to the end of the holiday to break up with him but not before she made him buy her an expensive piece of jewellery and witheld sex for the rest of the holiday. Lynette kept her cool throughout the entire period.

A study done by Forbes showed that while almost 50 per cent of US marriages end in divorce, only 20 to 30 per cent of the Forbes 400 (rich and wealthy) actually divorce. Of this, those who do divorce are on average richer than those who don't. According to Judith Stern Peck, a therapist and director at New York's Ackerman Institute for the Family who counsels families on the brink of divorce, people get divorced if their lifestyles on average do not suffer[3].

So what do the rich do? The really rich find ways to manage family wealth as a unit. They know that if *monies were divided, it does less.*

---

[3] *All the Money in the World,* Peter W. Bernstein and Annalyn Swan

Each person might become wealthy in his or her own right, but it is so much harder to drive less money to work for them. So they stick together. Case study after case study shows it.

Professional services in the US exist to help families manage family feuds to ensure civility and cordial transactions. This is for the overall good of the 'clan' and the assets it controls. Death, marriages, divorces and births are all clan related. This is one way wealth generates wealth and is kept from one generation to the next. This is also one reason why the really rich stay rich.

Over To You

If your marriage has stopped working for you, or for the both of you, what will you do? Check the list below for all that applies to you.

- I'll sue him for every cent he has because he cheated on me and I need the money for my new life.

- I'll give him everything because without him I am nothing anyway. I don't want money. I want him!

- I don't know and I don't care anymore.

- I'll run away as soon as I can and start afresh. I don't care about the money.

- We must sit down to work things through. If he cannot do it now, we will do it when things have cooled down.

- I have my children. I want to make sure he gives me money for them (How much? Everything of course). I won't let the horrible man see them at all. He is such an a*****e!

Ivana Trump is reported to have said: "Don't get angry, get even!" That's because she was married to Donald Trump. For us, the better bet is:
"DON'T GET TOO ANGRY. WORK IT OUT!"
Remember, the cooler you are, the more you gain. You have to care as it affects the rest of your financial life and possibly your children's.

Divorce In Singapore:
Some Questions And Answers

Please find out what the law says about divorce, matrimonial assets and division of property in your own country. Always be updated as laws can change from time to time. Please do not assume. Pay for sound advice before you rush into divorce, and please be aware that some divorce lawyers are after dragging out cases for self-interest.

Q What is a matrimonial asset?
A Most couples will have acquired a home during the course of their marriage. Some will have other assets, such as a family car, businesses, bank accounts or insurance polices. If the property or asset is a matrimonial asset, then it is part of a pool of assets that the court will divide when the couple goes to court to get a divorce. If the asset was acquired after the marriage, it is a matrimonial asset.

But if the asset was acquired by you *before* the marriage, it is a matrimonial asset if:
- It has been used by your spouse, or the children, while you were living together.
- It has been substantially improved during the marriage by your spouse, or by both of you.

If the asset was a gift, or was inherited by you, it is not a matrimonial asset except if it is the matrimonial home or it has been substantially improved during the marriage by your spouse, or by both of you.

Q How does the court decide on our share of the matrimonial assets?
A The court's decision will be based on Section 112 of the Women's Charter. The fact that you or your spouse did not pay for a particular matrimonial asset is not conclusive. There is no particular formula used to divide the property. The court's decision is made after it has

heard all the evidence. The court will decide what share is just and equitable in the circumstances of your case. The court will look at:

- Each spouse's direct financial contributions, such as salary earnings.

- Each spouse's non-financial contributions to the welfare of the family, including looking after the home and caring for the family.

- The children's needs.

- Any agreement that both of you may have made regarding the division of the matrimonial assets in case of a divorce.

If you and your spouse are unable to agree on how to divide the matrimonial assets, the court will ask each of you to file an Affidavit of Assets and Means in the ancillary matters stage of your divorce proceedings. Alternatively, you may request a Resolution Conference at the Family Relations Centre to help you and your spouse reach an agreement.

Q Is there any way for my spouse and I to ask the court to decide who owns a particular piece of property? We are still married.
A Yes. An application to the court may be made under Section 59 of the Women's Charter.

Q How will the court decide who owns the property, and in what shares?
A The court will apply general principles of property law to your dispute. In other words, the court will decide your dispute according to the same principles that apply in property disputes between people who are not married to each other. You should seek legal advice to ensure you do the right thing.

(Source: http://app.subcourts.gov.sg/family/faq.aspx?pageid=3704.)

Q What if one or both of us is bankrupt?
A When a person is made bankrupt, the Official Assignee will step in to manage all his assets except for the HDB flat and CPF money. The court will still divide the matrimonial assets in the same way as in a case where neither spouse is bankrupt. But the Official Assignee may attend the ancillary matters hearing to make representations on behalf of the bankrupt spouse. If you and your spouse have reached an agreement on the division of the matrimonial assets, you will need to obtain the Official Assignee's approval before the court will endorse your agreement. For more information on bankruptcy and the role of the Official Assignee, you may wish to refer to the website of the Insolvency and Public Trustee's Office

Q Can I keep our HDB flat after the divorce?
A That depends. If the HDB flat is a matrimonial asset, the court can make an order for your spouse to transfer his share of the flat to you. But it is very important that you check with HDB that you are eligible to retain the flat. You must do this before the ancillary matters hearing because the court will not be able to give you an answer to this question. Only HDB can provide you with the information that you need.

It is also very important that you check on your own financial status to see if you can reimburse the CPF money that your spouse used to buy the flat, and to pay any cash amount that your spouse may ask for in return for the transfer. You may need to make some enquiries with your bank. Again, you must do this before the ancillary matters hearing, because the court will not be able to help you with financing the transfer. You should refer to the HDB and CPF Board websites for current information on HDB and CPF regulations and policies.

19 Widowed But Not Unhappy

Women Live Longer
Most women should expect to outlive the men in their lives. The worldwide life expectancy for all people is 64.3 years. Men can expect to live to 62.7 years old and women to 66 years, a difference of more than three years. This difference in life expectancy varies by geographical region. In North America and Europe, this difference is four to six years. In Russia, it is more than 13 years.

This difference drops as a person gets older. For example, a 50-year-old woman's life expectancy is 82 and a man's 78. This four-year gender-biased difference drops when both the man and woman are 85 years old. They can expect to live to 91 if female and 90 if male[1].

The Yucky Berries On Being Widowed
Several years after my first husband and I were divorced, he passed away in an accident. While technically I was divorced and, therefore, could not be deemed his widow, his death hit me no less than if we had still been married. I was his only living relative in Singapore and, therefore, had to administer all matters related to his passing on. It was extremely painful. In that one week, I lost 9 kg.

My friend, Jannie Tay, uses the words 'yucky berry' for things that are unpleasant. The yucky berries in this case were very yucky and memories of those weeks still impact me today. What did I know about coffins, flowers, cremation, probates or anything? I remember buying the mid-priced coffin because $1,000 was too cheap and $15,000 was too much to burn. It is strange how even in moments of grief, one had to think of money. I wanted my son to comprehend the process with me and to reconcile his father's death, so I brought him along to help

---

[1] Social Security Administration Actuarial Tables at www.ssa.gov

me make decisions. Which coffin should we buy for Daddy? We chose the $3,500 one.

The week he died, 9/11 happened. Watching the grief on TV and seeing how it impacted people around the world, I somehow became removed from my own grief. I could feel no more inside me. Only the numbness and the distant knowledge of a reality that someone I loved had died, even though we were already divorced and we had both moved on from that first marriage.

Within the first week, long lost relatives came along and started to claim things that were his. In fact, on the very next day after his death, one of my former in-laws wanted to know where the will was. The relatives wanted items such as his Mont Blanc pen but not his Manchester United tee-shirts. Yet, it was the Manchester United icons that defined my late ex-husband and not the Mont Blanc pen that I gave him.

So be prepared. People will come out of the woodwork, claiming their right to things of value. It is painful. They have their reasons, including how they want to remember the deceased. And you? You might be too numbed to know how to react. I was.

We will grieve. We don't want to be left behind or alone. We might even feel guilty that our spouse had passed on ahead of us. Sometimes, we get angry that they left us to deal with the pressures of life and living. Whatever our emotions, they need to be managed. As we grieve, we need to focus and plan ahead.

The Importance Of Wills

In the case of my former husband, what was most important was his will. We both made wills when we were still married. His will remained in force even when we were divorced. He had not remarried and he did not die intestate. That will looked after our two children.

Dealing With The Estate

Always hire a good probate lawyer to work on your deceased husband's estate. Understanding estate duties, probate law, executors, trustees and the rest of it was beyond me in that state. I was lost and numb.

I had to trust my lawyer. I was fraught with worry as to whether my children would have anything if the will was contested since we were already divorced. In the end, the will held together, and I can proudly say that my ex-husband cared for his children all the way through with his last act of having kept his will intact. Divorce and death may not change the tie between two persons once married. This, I believe.

The Rich Widow

Husbands and wives who spend time working together to build their matrimonial wealth are the ones kindest to each other. Therefore, if you were involved in managing money with your husband through the years, you are one of the 'lucky' ones. If one party did it all, and the other party did not know what went on, sudden death deals many blows. Not only is the person gone, but the knowledge, thinking and decision making are all gone too!

Lock it Away Fast
If your husband passed away, and if you were never involved in understanding money matters up to the point he passed away, my first recommendation to you is to lock away the money he left you until you have taken some time to understand how to manage money. DO NOT MAKE ANY INVESTMENT OR GIFT, NO MATTER WHAT THE PRESSURES.

Relatives, friends and financial advisers will all seem to know what to do with your money. Relatives may not be good friends even if they suddenly appear to be best pals when they realise you have money. A good friend or a caring relative does not equate to a good financial adviser. As for financial advisers, they may even promise you great returns. Beware! Widows are easy prey for them to earn fat commissions fast.

Please put the money into a fixed deposit in the bank until you have time to think and are able to make sound decisions. It takes time to get over the pain. And please be careful of people who appear from nowhere to care for you. Money makes good friends overnight. Suitors might even appear overnight.

The problem is that when you are in a state of grief and loss, and receive a large sum of money, you might make a rash decision to pass the responsibility away. Let someone else look after me again, you might say. "This person ... this wonderful new person in my life ... he is a widower too ... he cares. I can ask him for help." Keep money out of the equation, and by all means, explore the relationship and friendship without letting money enter the conversation.

Take time to recover and take time to find out whom you can trust. For the time being, if you are left with money, trust no one, perhaps, except yourself. Remember that there are conmen who make a career of cheating widows. No one can help you if you lose common sense when most needed.

Take Time to Educate Yourself

Your husband left the money to you for your well-being. You need to sort out how to manage it. It begins by reading and finding out. Give yourself a small income from month to month while you take your time to find out. Money does not disappear when sitting in a bank account or an asset such as property.

The Poor Widow

If, however, your husband left you with little, you have a lot of work to do ahead of you. Everything in this book still applies, only you now need to do it with a cool determined head and a steely heart.

- If you have children, you need to focus on them as the reason to keep going and becoming financially independent.

- If you don't have children, you may have more leeway and time to grieve, pull yourself together and keep going.

- You should get support from a widows' network if you can. If you are too sad to meet people, meet other widows online. Friends help you recover.

- If you have a job, keep it. Ask for lighter duties if need be, but keep your job while you recover.

- If you don't have a job, you need to get one fast. Like my friend Mei, whose husband died and left her penniless. She pulled herself up and got going after two years.

Don't give up. Get help. You might also want to talk to your member of parliament or visit the social service centre and see how the social workers can help you. There are some relief grants that the government hands out to special cases.

> Widows are divided into two classes: the bereaved and the relieved.
> ~Victor Robinson

If You've Been Left A Maze

What if your husband left you a maze of assets and liabilities? What if the paperwork ahead completely freezes you dead in your tracks and you wonder how you are going to sort it all out?

- If probate matters are already settled and you have come to own shares in a small business or a company with a maze of difficulties, you should seek professional help with what you need to do.

- If the assets and liabilities come in the form of his personal assets or loans, you would receive the net assets via probate.

- Note that net liabilities stay with the deceased's estate and are not claimable on you.

Time Heals

Most importantly, remember that time heals. Just take the time to find yourself again. Anything from six months to a year is necessary to heal.

Make decisions to CONSERVE cash and not grow cash in those few months after the death. It's less risky that way. Your judgment can be clouded by the death and your own emotions. Decisions made immediately on being widowed may be emotion-based, rather than logic-based. Please watch out for this. No one else can for you. If someone comes along and tries to rush you, walk away.

The law will not be kinder to you if you enter a contract in a distressed state, unless you can prove that a state of duress was caused by the party benefiting from the contract. And that takes time and money to do.

Over To You

Has your husband made a will? Do you know what is in it? Do you know where it is kept? If he died tomorrow, would you have enough? If not, what do you intend to do financially?

Remember, your life goes on and you have an obligation to yourself to live well for the rest of your days. How will you do it?

> Put up your financial guard should you be widowed. With money in the bank, you can find it in you to have a full and great life still.

Interview With Perlita Tiro, Super Dynamic Grandmother

Perlita Tiro is managing director of Tiro Consulting Services, which she founded with her late husband in January 1989. Tiro Consulting is a shareholder firm of EMA Partners International, a worldwide group of executive search consultants of which she was chairman in 1992 and Asia Pacific coordinator from 1998 to 2005.

Perlita made history at the Rotary Club of Singapore by being the first woman to be elected to the board in 2002. In 2004, she also became the first woman in the club's 75 years of existence to be awarded Rotarian of the Year. She served as vice-president of Rotary for 2005–06 and 2007–08. She is also the vice-president of Women's Business Connection in Singapore.

Q Your daughter was in university when your husband passed away. What were your first thoughts regarding money?
A My first concern was who was going to look after me, as I was suddenly alone in Singapore with no family support. Also, how could I handle my daughter who listened more to her father than to me? The next was who was going to help me manage the company we set up —especially its finances. Then, how about our personal investments, which my husband looked after while I ran the company?

Q What were you working as at that point of your life? How did you cope with work and being left as the sole breadwinner?
A Let me answer the last one first. I coped with great difficulty and determination to move on, and the biggest help was trust in the Almighty God. A handful of close friends were there to help. They not only provided moral support but also provided avenues for financial support, like giving me assignments which they could have done themselves or asked other firms to do. They will always be in my heart.

I was into the seventh year of running the executive search and recruitment firm that my husband and I founded. I was not a salaried employee. I had to pay salary to my staff and rent to the landlord. Even though my husband was only working part-time before he passed on, he provided me with a lot of strength in terms of moral and emotional support and ideas. He was also the one keeping track of our investments in the shares market.

The Asian financial crisis took a toll on the company and that was when I missed my husband the most. Revenues and cash flows thinned out and I was thankful that we had adequate reserves to draw on to stay afloat. It always pays to be conservative when it comes to managing cash flows.

I also have my ageing father to support and that commitment becomes tougher as he gets older, especially after he suffered a stroke. My father was my greatest motivator for further education. He even paid for my MBA course fees although I was already working by then. I will never turn away from my commitment to look after him.

Q What are the things regarding your personal finance that you wish you did differently before your husband passed away?
A What helped was that our family home was already in my name and fully paid for, and it did not need to be declared as a part of his estate. My husband had thought that he was likely to pass on earlier as he was much older. So he put the property in my name, in case anything happened to him. I had no mortgage payments to worry about.

What I could have asked him to do after we got married was to get life insurance coverage. When we were both salaried employees, we both enjoyed term life coverage under our respective employers. We did not see the necessity to have separate personal life coverage outside those companies. When we later set up our own consulting company, I was the only one who took coverage, being the key person running the organisation. If only he too had life coverage then, it could have been easier for me.

Q What are the things regarding money issues that you wish you did differently in the first few years after your husband died?
A I could have declared more dividends from the company to put into my personal account and to accumulate my personal investments in more conservative funds.

Whereas my husband would have been conservative or had the time to watch over the riskier investments, I invested both company and personal funds into high risk-return investments. I ended up incurring substantial losses as I did not have the time to personally watch over the market developments. I was too busy with work. Those were the times of the Enron and dot.com busts. I could have cut losses had I been able to monitor the market better or engaged more reliable financial advisers.

Q What does financial independence mean to you? How would you define that for your own life?
A In general, financial independence means being able to sustain a comfortable lifestyle on my own. At this stage of my life, it means sustaining my current lifestyle with minor adjustments for as long as possible, with enough investments to provide me with adequate returns for sustaining myself and my father, while having some leeway to help the needy and to ride over emergencies.

Q What are three things you would advise young women in terms of their personal finance management?
A Learn to budget expenditures early. By nature, young women in Asia tend to be happy-go-lucky where personal financial management is concerned. Unlike in the West where children start moving out of their family homes when they get to be financially independent, in Asia, the children enjoy the safety net of living in their family homes until they get married. Some remain living in the family homes even during the initial years of their marriage. Hence, the pressure of budgeting comes much later.

Keep an account separate from your husband, whether you contribute to the family income or not. It is not a matter of whether you trust your husband or not. It is simply preparing yourself to be financially independent, for any event. This should not be mixed up with your allowance for home and children's expenditures. Put the money into safe investments. Capital-protected investments would be my bet, although some advisers say these could be pricey.

Finally, separate and build up funds or investments purely for the rainy day. These should not be touched otherwise.

Q What are three things you would advise young women in terms of planning their lives?
A I was asked the same question by Female magazine some time ago. The advice is the same. Women should aim for the highest possible level of education first, then start to establish their careers before settling down. Of course, they should not stop dating, just because they have launched their careers. Those who concentrate too much on their career might find that by the time they wish to get married, the possible partners they may have been eyeing are already hitched with other women.

After three to five years into their careers, they would already have established themselves and proved their worth to their respective employers. This would be the best time for marriage. Then plan to have children after two to three years. Building a family too soon after marriage might be a recipe for difficulties. It is good for a young woman to strengthen the bond with her husband before a third person comes in. The baby is a third person! The time for discovering each other and further strengthening the couple's respective careers can happen at the same time. Delaying having children until too much later, in favour of career-building, is not advisable either.

Finally, work hard and play hard while you can, and plan for your twilight years. It is never too early to plan for the long term.

20 The Other Woman

The Other Side

This chapter is not about how bad or how good the *other* woman is. I have seen families broken by infidelities and I have heard my friends cry broken-hearted, not knowing why their husbands rejected them for another. I have witnessed pain and I have felt the deep pain in me as I empathised with them.

This chapter is for The Other Woman because The Other Woman needs to protect herself financially. After all, she is a woman—real, alive and with her own life challenges—just like the rest of us.

The 'Other' Relationship

It is well documented that female birds and fish prefer 'mated' male birds and fish to those 'single'. According to Donald Pfaff, who is head of the Laboratory of Neurobiology and Behavior at Rockefeller University, a series of experiments showed that female mice consistently preferred the scent of 'mated' male mice to that of 'single' male mice. (www.sciencedaily.com)

To quote Pfaff: "Our data suggest that female mice may use, or even copy, the interests of other females based on olfactory cues. It could also be seen as a female trusting the mate choice of another female." Pfaff says that the female mice's preference was so strong for the mated male scent, to the solitary male scent alone, that they preferred the mated male scent even when it was tainted with the scent of infectious parasites.

In the world of humans, this preference is possibly reflected in the lament of many single women: "All the good ones are taken." My recently divorced friend, May Lin, complain that she now has to wait for some of the good men she knows to become divorced or to be 'recycled', as she calls it. May Lin is in her early forties. Living in

Australia with its high divorce rates, she knows that 'good men' will be 'recycled' eventually. She just needs to wait!

Are the 'good ones' really all taken, or is it a preference in our minds as we subconsciously calculate the probability that if someone was not taken by the time they are in their late thirties, they must probably be awful husband/partner material?

There appears to be roughly two types of 'Other' relationships. The Other in the form of a young woman, possibly a social climber, clinging on to an older married man for the comforts he brings. And The Other in the form of two older persons who fall in love after having been unhappily married to others for years.

Money For The Other?

In reality, The Other has a raw financial deal:

- There is no protection for The Other by way of financial support or legal claim of any type in most countries. The registered legal wife maintains all financial rights and claims in the event of the man's death.

- There is no 'divorce' for The Other. When the relationship ends, it ends.

- Promises made can be unmade, and any assignments too. The Other as beneficiary can be changed or the policy terminated. Do we marvel then why The Other would claw at whatever she can while he is alive, be it property, presents or gifts of money?

What's Good For The Gander

I know a special lady who was the CEO of a large company. In her late forties, Marianne fell in love with Joseph who promised to love her. She was already married with three children. Her husband was a known philanderer. Marianne had an affair with Joseph for three years. But the relationship could not stay a secret for long as both were high flyers in the corporate world. Rumours flew. People talked.

Unable to take the whisperings and knowing looks, Marianne and Joseph agreed to separate from their spouses and be married.

Marianne commenced divorce proceedings and told her family of her infidelity. Her husband walked out. Her children followed their father. Joseph also told his family, but his family worked hard to change his mind. In the end, he did not go through with the pact he made with Marianne, apologising that he was returning to his family.

What can anyone say in a situation like that? That he was wrong? That he was a low life form to have defaulted on Marianne? Or that he should have never defaulted from his family in the first place? Marianne could only wish him well. She lost her family and Joseph. In her heart of hearts, she knew he did not love his wife. But she knew that he loved his *family* and could not break the family up.

As a married woman, I find it only too easy to judge and to say, "Serves Marianne right!" But hold on! Marianne is a wonderful person. She has a great heart; she serves in local communities and donates time and money to charities. She loves deeply and sincerely. She was a romantic who wanted to believe that she could have that one special love in her life. Her marriage to her husband was difficult. He was constantly unfaithful, but when told of her unfaithfulness, he divorced her without a second thought. What was good for the gander was not good for the goose.

The shame that came with the unravelling of Marianne's life impacted her badly. Her job suffered. She was asked to leave. She struggled at her new place of work, unable to cope with the fall from leadership to a job several rungs down the ladder. Joseph, meanwhile, continued to rise in the corporate world. Her former husband started a new life with a young woman. Fighting depression, she decided to migrate for a new life in a place where no one knew her.

Winter Betrayal

My Aunt Jessie was The Other Woman. She is my mother's best friend. Aunt Jessie was in her late forties when she met 'her man'. He was in his early fifties. He bought her a small terrace house in Penang, and she moved in with her son from her second marriage.

Aunt Jessie's first marriage had ended with another woman claiming her husband and she lost custody of her young daughter. Her second marriage ended when her husband walked out to be with a much younger woman after he became successful in his business. She had given up hope of marital happiness when Harold came into her life.

Harold was caring and loving towards her, but he had a family of his own. He was well known in the Penang community. Everyone knew that Harold and his wife lived separate lives in the same household. That notwithstanding, Aunt Jessie did not want to break up the family further. She had felt the pain of her own families being broken up by third parties twice. She just wanted to care for Harold and be cared for in return. She did not mind being at the fringe. The community soon knew my Aunt Jessie to be Harold's 'second wife' or the 'small wife'. It was a status that used to be acceptable in Penang society.

The terrace house was in Harold's name. Aunt Jessie had no legal relationship with Harold, even though the community accepted her. Some 20 years later, when she was in her sixties, Harold broke up with her. He asked her to leave the small terrace house that she had come to call home, giving her one month to move out. No money, no 'alimony', no title ... nothing. All the past promises he made suddenly went dead.

Aunt Jessie then finally understood why Harold saw her so infrequently in the past year, saying that he had business to deal with and his will to sort out. In the break-up, no explanation was given to my aunt other than he was getting old and it was time to move on with his life.

Poor Aunt Jessie rang me late one night to tell me she was moving to the UK to live with her sister. She said she had no idea what she would do there at her age, but at least she would have a roof over her head. She did not know what else to do. Her savings were insufficient for a new home. She had trusted Harold by becoming his 'second wife'. For her 20 years of love, she was left with nothing overnight.

Speaking As A Wife

Often enough, we blame the broken home on The Other. At a recent dinner party, I heard how all the partners and associates of a well known professional firm sent to work in Shanghai have set up second homes there. It was the inside story of the firm. The wives of these partners and associates did not know it. But the entire firm did.

How shocking, we women cry out! How dishonest of those men and their colleagues not to tell the wives, we feel. Among the men, a silent code exists. No one speaks of such relationships although they might know about it. You might think that getting to know your husband's friends well enough means they will be 'fair' to you and tell you about his flings. But it doesn't work that way. A man who breaks the unspoken code of silence is seen to be one who has a knife to wield, or has self-interest at heart.

I believe women behave differently. Women who care would pull their friends aside and have heart-to-heart talks to help their friends protect themselves. Men and women play by different rules. Women should meet my sophisticated friend, Catherine, who is known in Malaysian socialite circles by her title and nickname, Datin Kitty. Catherine understands these rules.

Catherine is married to a wealthy chief financial officer of a listed company in Malaysia. She accompanies him wherever he goes. When I asked her why she was always with her husband, she said, "It's as much my responsibility to ensure he does not stray as it is his responsibility not to stray. So I will go with him everywhere, no matter what time and distance. I will make sure I am there even if it is hours and hours of boring business talk which I have no interest in. As his wife, there are millions at stake for me. What if he meets some bimbo at one of these business meetings? Don't you think I should be there?"

Catherine made me realise that wives often do not know that they need to look after their relationships with their husbands and to protect that relationship. Catherine was not the possessive type. She was just very clever with how she went about doing things. Her husband valued her beautiful presence and was proud to have her by his side. Staying beautiful always and tracking her wealthy husband was Catherine's choice in life. I don't agree totally with that choice but I respect her unique wisdom.

Brain Power

I was having dinner with an old friend, Quincy. He said to me, "You know, Norma, you're attractive but not beautiful." I was about to throw beer over him. He laughed at how peeved I was.

"Don't get angry with me. Men can have beautiful women any time and all the time. But for a man to stay in love and interested in a woman, it has to be more than skin-deep beauty."

I put down the jug of beer and listened.

"You are interesting and that will keep a man engaged with you for a long time. After a while, men do get tired of beautiful women. But to have good conversations and good companionships, that is meaningful."

Quincy was, of course, making a calculated pass at me, appealing to my intellectual vanity. I did not go for it. But there was truth to what he said.

Three months ago, over two margaritas and dressed in a sexy blouse, my friend Pat was crying her heart out to me. She asked me what to do with her husband. He had lost interest in her. They had not made love for eight years. She said, "Look at me. I'm still beautiful. Look at my body. It's perfect with all the toning and exercises that I do." Pat has the Perfect 10 body. She is tall, has amazing features and long silky hair. When I walk next to her, I look like something the cat dragged home on a rainy day.

I know Pat's husband. I think he lost interest in conversing with her. He was a money market professional with a first-tier bank, handling millions every day in a fast-paced environment. Pat had not progressed all those years that they were married. Mentally and emotionally, she had stayed the same. While both started with basic education, her husband broke through and progressed up the social and corporate ladder to a position where he commanded and held high earning power.

I can only imagine what his female colleagues and business associates looked like in comparison to my dear friend Pat. They would be sophisticated where she is sexy. They would sound cultured where she sounds like the girl-next-door. I wondered what Pat could have done to keep her husband's interest. I concluded that she should have spent time educating her mind.

To keep conversations alive (and keep the husband interested in her!) I believe that a wife should develop a range of interests and become interesting as a person in her own right, and not become his shadow intellectually. There are many things a wife can do.

- Go for courses and attend classes.

- Get involved in charity work. This is a great way to meet people and broaden one's outlook in life.

- Interest him in the work you are doing and embark on some common projects together.

- Get interested in something that matters to him, whether it is football, music, writing, reading or attending concerts. Spend time on it with him. Just having meals together do not count. It is not an interest that you both share unless he writes for a gastronomy magazine.

Advice For The Other

Get Out if You Can

If you are The Other, my first advice to you is to get out if you can. Elsewhere in this book, I related what my friend Stephen once said to me: "Few men will ever leave their wives. They have children and assets with their wives. They have very few, if any, assets with their lovers. The lovers will always lose out."

To the women who then think that having an illegitimate child with the man is the way to secure his heart, think again. Stephen also said: "Most men can segment the way they feel. This is why men can go to war and come home to their families. This is why even murderers may have loving wives and children. Most women can't. Women tend to love with all of themselves. Men are different."

What Stephen says is worrying. While there may be cases of men loving their mistresses or lovers for a lifetime, situations of men leaving their families for mistresses may not be all that common.

If You Can't Get Out, Get Financial Security

As The Other Woman, if you cannot get out because you truly do love him, you need to find financial security so that should anything happen, you would not have given away years of your life for nothing. Here are some things you should know and some tips if you wish to stay the course:

- Having your name inserted into his will is not fail safe. He can change the will anytime without informing you.

- Naming you as a beneficiary into an insurance policy only works if he names you in person by name and if he does not change the policy before he dies.

- If you have property with him, you should have sole ownership with him as the buyer and mortgagee. Get a one-time premium mortgage insurance on his life to ensure that the home is paid for should he die.

- Get a regular 'income' from him and save it away for rainy days and emergencies. Get supporting documents that these are monetary gifts to you, not loans.

- Never depend on him for your financial security. Always be financially independent in your own right!

Last Words

As a wife, I do not like the idea of there being the possibility of The Other Woman. As a wife, I would wish for women to find their own men without disturbing the domestic peace of another household. However, there are realities and circumstances that vary from case to case.

We live in a complex world. People are complex creatures and sometimes the best person with the best intention can find themselves in difficult, compromised situations. If you are The Other Woman, please get out if you can. If you can't because you believe you have found your soulmate in another woman's husband, please do protect yourself. Do it without hurting the children and the wife if possible. The hurt inflicted on children is often irreparable and no love is worth the kind of pain caused.

Are you The Other Woman?
Are you in a situation where you are considering becoming The Other Woman?
If yes, please do think about your financial situation and whether this journey is worth it in the long run, both emotionally and financially.

21 Becoming The Matriach

Matriach And Leader

Since women live longer than men statistically, they are likely to outlive their husbands, and for some, their sons. The Chinese say there is no greater sorrow than for a mother to bury a son. Nearly all of us know of an elderly woman or two who have outlived her sons and is the oldest living person in the family. So, tell me, you are a woman, the odds are that you will outlive most male members in your family, what would you like to be when you are 70, 80 or 90?

My Self-Vision

My great-grandmother died when she was 90 years old. My maternal grandmother, who was widowed after the birth of her last daughter, died when she was in her late eighties. My paternal grandfather passed away when he was 104; his wife is still alive and well today, more than 15 years later. I have longevity genes.

I look forward to the day when I am the matriarch of the family. My question is what sort of a matriarch will I be? Will I be someone my grandchildren love, or someone my own children are afraid to hear from just in case I decide to visit? I am determined to be one whom they love, respect and want to be with. I want to be someone they will fly half-way around the world to visit once a year with their children so that our times together can be light-filled and love-centred. I have a self-vision that I will be the wise woman of the family.

I am determined to be pursuing life with a passion in my seventies. I have a picture of myself where I am still active and contributing to society. I would have started an orphanage or two, created a foundation fund for my orphanages, done something significant for Thalassaemic children by then, and I would live a quiet life in an art commune in a country with a temperate climate.

I hope to live till 89. After that, I hope to have a good death. So morbid, you say. Well, when you plan for life, you must plan for death. You cannot live well until you understand what it means to die well.

I remember the older women who have served in volunteer committees and programmes with me. Some of them served in the background, unnoticed by most but doing important tasks such as ensuring that things were in place, lights were switched on or papers were where they should be. They inspire me. I would want to be still of service to society when I am older.

Role Models

My Aunt Susie is a good role model. In her early seventies, she walks to her church every morning to open the doors for members seeking solace and lights the candles for prayers. How unseen, yet how meaningful a service she gives to humanity in her own way.

At the other extreme of success, women in their seventies can be running companies and organisations, or be leading a global cause. In April 2002, Secretary-General Kofi Annan named Dr Jane Goodall a United Nations "Messenger of Peace". Messengers serve as advocates in a variety of areas, such as poverty eradication, human rights, peace and conflict resolution, HIV/AIDS prevention, disarmament and environmentalism. In 2003, Dr Goodall became a Dame of the British Empire, the equivalent of a knighthood. She is in her seventies and continues to work tirelessly, talking to youths about the need to preserve the environment.

What a vision to aspire to. To bring good to this planet. To be like my Aunt Susie who serves quietly in her church or to be a global influence like Dr Jane Goodall. Both are great women serving humanity in ways they know best.

The Criticality Of Financial Independence

To pursue one's dream, to live as one chooses, and to have a good end to one's life... these are good things to do. BUT, we cannot live with that freedom and clarity unless we are also financially independent to do so. It is no fun to be poor when one is in the sixties. It is no fun to have to eke out a living, working the grind daily. Yes, it is good for us to stay engaged and be gainfully employed if we can be. That is great for our spirit and our mental health, but I would not like to be in the situation where I *have to be* employed in my sixties, or I starve and lose the roof over my head.

The Secret To Happiness

In my research for this book, I was combing the Internet to find 'the secret of happiness'. Someone wrote that the secret to happiness is to repeat a specific mantra every morning. The mantra is this: "I am always truthful, positive, and helping others." The secret is in the word 'always', not sometimes, not depending on how you feel, not depending on how your boss feels, just always. (www.howtobehappy.com) Try it. It works. Being happy and staying happy as we grow older must surely be what it is all about.

Look Good, Feel Good, Help Others

My wonderful friends in their early sixties will never speak with me again if I name those who have gone under the plastic surgeon's knife. Amongst us, we have removed lines, tucked flesh, pulled wrinkles, and lipo-sucked until we have bodies that fit into fashionable outfits and we look great. Yes, we all know we are older now, but we still want to look great, and even more importantly, FEEL great! Keon reminds me that when I need even more drastic plastic surgery, I should go for it. He is right. So there it is, another kitty for you to save towards—your major appearance overhaul when you are older!

Finally, It's About People

I was at a dinner party with a group of wonderful people who give time, money and energy to social causes. Sitting next to me was Peter Ong, the regional managing director of Gallup Organisation. He asked me, "Is money important?" Was it a test question?

I responded, "Money is not the most important thing in life. But having money is critical as a foundation to a sense of well-being. Without a sense of well-being, we cannot be happy."

What an inspired answer! It came to me in a flash!

Peter looked surprised at my answer. He then confirmed that a recent Gallup poll showed that money is important to most people for a sense of well-being or satisfaction with life. Happiness, which came after the sense of well-being, however, was closely related to the kinds of relationships that we have in our lives.

Researching further into the Gallup Public Opinion Poll 2004, I found that while only 45 per cent of unmarried people say they are happy, 62 per cent of the married people say they are happy. The unmarried people included those who were never married, divorcees, the widowed and those living with their partners.

So there you have it. To finish well, it is what our parents told us from the beginning. Relationships matter. People matter. Things and money, yes, they are important, but at the end of the day, it is *people* who count.

> At the end, having achieved financial independence, it is about people ... the ones who love us, the ones we love and the people we can make a difference to in our lifetime.

> What is the vision of yourself when you are in your sixties? Seventies? Eighties?
> How much money will you have then?
> Will you be happy and in love with life? If not, please start walking towards a new vision of Self today.
> Gorgeous, Sexy and Rich is yours to claim. Do it now!

Note From Norma

The *Gorgeous, Sexy and Rich* Response To The 2008 Economic Crisis

The 2008 economic crisis holds many lessons for men and women around the world—how we managed, invested and grew our money, and also how we should *now* manage, invest and grow our money going forward. While the crisis is fraught with many threats, it holds many opportunities. This might sound like a motherhood statement, but it is nonetheless true. To know which are threats and which are opportunities, women need to be educated to see which is which.

I started writing this book before the crisis imploded on the world. But as Keon and I reflect on its devastating effects on millions of lives all over the planet, we believe the lessons in this book continue to be valid. I am glad *Money for Women in Good and Tough Times* is being released at this juncture. It carries lessons through the crisis as it carries lessons for women before and after the crisis.

In specific, we urge you to look into alignment of self-vision and financial vision, and balance. And on financial matters, to look into budgeting and investing, bearing in mind risk management and diversification in your invesment approach.

We hope you enjoyed reading this book. Please share your thoughts with me at norma@gorgeoussexyrich.com.

Thank you for purchasing *Money for Women in Good and Tough Times*. The proceeds of this book shall be donated to The Children Of ASEAN (TCOA) initiative, jointly founded by leading businessman and social activist, David Ong, and myself. To read more about this cause which supports orphanages in the ASEAN and works against child prostitution and abuse, please see www.childrenasean.org.

A Man's Point Of View

"Becoming financially independent is not easy for a woman. There is something about the thought of dependence that seduces us all. But few of us have the luxury of being taken care of. We either make it on our own or we don't. We either can support ourselves or we can't. We either figure out how to take the skills and talents we have to make a living, even thrive, in a period of economic downturn or we have a meltdown of our own.

But here is what I know for sure after reading this well written book. *Money for Women in Good and Tough Times* gives you a clear insight that a woman doesn't become a full self until she figures out a way to take care of her personal growth and her own finances—even, or especially, in financially difficult times. As long as a woman has yet to know that she is capable of sustaining herself, as long as she is economically dependent on others, as long as she is psychologically dependent on someone else for her thinking, her income and her survival, she does not yet belong to herself.

What comes across very clearly is that out of a healthy sense of independence comes self-esteem, self-discipline, self-worth and self-awareness. And a recognition of the God-self in the self. A very insightful book which brings great comfort during difficult days."

David T. L. Ong
Former senior executive at Merrill Lynch Pierce Fenner and Smith, Deutsche Bank, Credit Lyonnais, Svecia Securities and Asset Management

---

Mr DAVID ONG also sits on the advisory boards of private companies, family foundations and NGOs. These positions include: Member of the Advisory Board of the Rai Family Holding and Rai Foundation; Chairman of the Global Advisory Council of the Development Alternatives Group, India; Member of the Advisory Board of Jane Goodall Institute; President of ChildCare Foundation; Founder of the World Diaspora Bank, World Diaspora Forum and World Diaspora Foundation.